SWINGMAN: What a Difference a Decade Makes
by Alexandra Allred
with
Marshall Allen

©2010, by **Alex Allred**

Copyright notice: All work contained within is the sole copyright of its author, 2010, and may not be reproduced without consent.

Dedication

To the ultimate swingman! May you continue to shine and inspire those around you. You were …. Heaven-sent!

Acknowledgements

'Be fearless but be kind' is a guide my parents offered me and for this, I am forever grateful! Marc and Karen Powe, along with my sister, Michelle, have always supported me in my adventures – no questions asked, and I can't ever thank them enough.

You will always hear mother-in-law jokes or horror stories about how intrusive they can be but … I've got a keeper! During times of tremendous strain and frustration, Bonnie Allred has been my rock. Alongside my father-in-law, John Allred, they held my hand when times were tough. Thanks, Ms. Bunnie. Thanks, Pa.

And while my college buddy-turned- husband, Robb, agonizes over my tree-hugging ways, he continues to stand by me. (Robb, I don't think you understand the power in your words when you tell me you are proud of me.) ☺

But it was the support of my three beautiful, nay, gorgeous children (inside and out) and tremendous heart of the Downwinders at Risk organization and all the people of Midlothian who made this book possible. There are simply too many names to list!

Thank you Earthjustice (Jared, I still smile at the image of you spitting up coffee all over your keyboards as the Big Rick picture scrolled across your screen) for your continued support and to the Cedar Hill Sunday Starbucks gang for the laughter, the debates and the stories. Thank you, Dan, for your encouraging words – you will never know …

Finally, to those who lost a family member during the writing process of this book, I am deeply sorry for your loss. Women like Marcia Walker, a fighter to the end, exhibited a kind of grace and strength we all can only wish we could have.

To all, I hope this book offers guidance, hope, laughter and the determination to always strive toward greatness. Be fearless but be kind!

Table of Contents

Preface	
Chapter One	Christmas 1999
Chapter Two	Christmas 2000
Chapter Three	Christmas 2001: Here We Go Again
Chapter Four	Christmas 2002
Chapter Five	Marshall's Family
Chapter Six	Christmas 2003
Chapter Seven	Christmas 2004
Chapter Eight	Christmas 2005
Chapter Nine	Coincidence and Faith Collide: What a Difference One Woman Can Make
Chapter Ten	Marshall's Law
Chapter Eleven	Town Hall Meeting & The Fall Out
Chapter Twelve	Christmas 2006
Chapter Thirteen	On God's Green Earth
Chapter Fourteen	All God's Children
Chapter Fifteen	Christmas 2007
Chapter Sixteen	Swingman
Chapter Seventeen	Christmas 2008
Chapter Eighteen	Hell Freezes Over
Chapter Nineteen	Christmas 2009
Chapter Twenty	The Revolution: What a Difference a Decade Makes
Postscript	
Bonus Chapters	Christmas 2010
	Christmas 2011
	Christmas 2012

Prelude

Dear Reader –

As a former editor for a magazine I was trained to write short, concise, feel good stories that steer clear of politics or anything that may be perceived as controversial. But for this particular series of events, I must prepare you for a rather unorthodox style of writing. I don't know how else to present this wild ride to you.

In my everyday life, I am anything but afraid to take on controversial topics. Or, so I thought. As a kid living in Moscow, Russia, I managed to slip past Secret Service and into the same elevator with Sen. Ted Kennedy, sat on a curb with singer Elton John while he had a smoke, and ate lunch with boxing legend Mohammed Ali. Actually, on that last one, I confess I really didn't know who he was at the time. In later years, I managed to finagle a phone call with Queen Noor for help with a homework assignment. In recent years, my flatbed trailer hosted a gigantic bust of Gov. Rick Perry's head, with perfectly coifed hair, kissing a cement stack, during his 2008 Gubernatorial bid for Texas governor. While Gov. Perry toured the state of Texas for his re-election bid, his giant head followed. Interestingly, he didn't appear to like this very much and often sent state troopers out to question the legalities of towing a giant head. We – the environmental group I was aligned with - weren't trying to make trouble, but we had to speak out against the local industry we believed to be polluting the environment.

I've never been afraid of much, but then I was raised that way. Be fearless, but be kind. Those were the instructions handed to me by my parents. And so, I have lived my life fearlessly. I have two black belts and was named *Athlete of the Year* by United States Olympic Committee after being named to the first US women's bobsled team (coincidentally, I was four and half months pregnant at the time). On my wedding day, my sister, Michelle, and I chased down and caught a shoplifter, and I briefly played professional women's football. During a test drive on the Volvo gravity car – only two in existence – the brakes failed as I was headed down a mountain, head first, into a busy intersection. Only the power of pure adrenaline and my cool Harley Davidson steel-toe boots prevented me from being crushed (I still have and love those boots!).

As a kid, I took dares to run through the Afghani Embassy compound, knowing there was a guard dog. It had been vacated after the Afghans pulled out during the Soviet invasion, but the dog was a looming presence. My friend, Karin Stanton, and I did balance beam acts on our

8th floor balcony, skateboarded down "death hill," tap danced for cab fare in the middle of Red Square, and as a daily routine, outran KGB agents hell bent on following us.

I believe my willful behavior may be hereditary. My mom was the first person successfully to take a picture of the underbelly of a Soviet tank in the late 1970s for the Pentagon and tells a frightening – though highly entertaining – story about being chased through an old cemetery by KGB agents on the outskirts of Moscow. She also verbally dressed down a would-be attacker and has the scariest mom don't-mess-with-me stare-down ever to be witnessed by small children. My dad, besides serving two tours in Vietnam and being awarded numerous medals of bravery over the years, has guarded top secret files from suspected insurgents, refusing to leave as a fire swelled around him when the US Embassy in Moscow was on fire; he was assigned to "watch" certain dignitaries in the late 1980s and often did things and went places where Michelle and I were not privy. *He could tell us but then he'd have to kill us.*

In fact, Daddy's obligation has been the going joke in our family for years. Psst. Daddy is trying to kill us.

Daddy's promise nearly came to fruition during the late 1980s while he had been assigned to work in Tunis, Tunisia. During that time, my mom wanted my sister and me to visit during our Christmas break from college. Daddy made the arrangements, and we were to fly from Dallas, Texas, with a layover in Frankfurt, Germany (my place of birth), then fly on to Tunis. It was when we were in Frankfurt that Michelle and I came to two startling revelations. We would not be flying Luftunsa or British Airways, the two more reasonable choices. Rather, we would be flying …wait for it … Air Tunisia where no one spoke English, they served not colas and refreshments but entire cases of duty-free cigarettes, and everyone was smoking unfiltered cigarettes. I think even the babies were smoking. Luggage was piled on the tarmac, surrounded by heavily armed soldiers while we were to identify what luggage was ours. Mine was nowhere. And I had no seat. Instead, I was given a drop-down steward seat. Thus, the second revelation. Daddy was trying to kill us.

Truly, our father's intentions should not have been so shocking to us because, you see, he'd really been trying to kill us for years. We just hadn't realized it.

When I had my appendix removed, Daddy thought that was a great time to "kill two birds with one stone" and wheeled me up to the fourth floor to get 14 shots in my arms for allergy testing. Was he hoping for an anaphylactic reaction? He never once thought to warn Michelle and me that taunting the KGB agents in Moscow, Russia, was a bad idea or that after our car hit a rabbit in France we would be eating it for dinner. When the driver stopped to retrieve the half-flattened bunny, we girls were certain that our kindness was so that we could plan a proper burial for it – not eat it!

While in Africa, after being explicitly warned not to leave any window open, he did not open the window to his own room open but that of his daughters in known lion territory in a wildlife preserve in Kenya. Though we were not mauled by lions, we were then forced to sleep on hundreds, if not thousands, of giant Kenyan moths that had been drawn to the light and opened window. As we rolled around in the dark, dead moth bodies crunching beneath us, we should have known: *Daddy is trying to kill us*. Instead, I only heard Michelle's faint whispered voice, "I hate Daddy."

His proclivity for torture would also explain why he would never stop during long car trips. He was trying to cause kidney failure. But we didn't know. He tricked us by giving us great college educations and making us *believe* in ourselves. Oh, what treachery.

Our blissful ignorance came to an abrupt halt, however, at the Frankfurt airport as we rounded the corner to find dozens of Arabic-speaking Muslims complete with women dressed in burkas. Michelle and I were speechless. No, this can't be right. So, we stood in line. And stood and stood. We were actively overlooked and ignored but, at last, made our way to the counter to ask – we'd hoped in English – for some assistance when a man literally shoved Michelle to the side. He actually shouldered her. She was but a mere woman.

At first, we were too shocked to speak. I looked to the attendant behind the counter, also a woman, for help, but her cultural ties would not allow her even to look at us. So I did what any good woman would do. I called him a jackass and a pig man. The last one seemed to stir a reaction, ever so subtle, because Muslims find pigs repugnant and filthy, so Michelle and I continued to berate Pig Man.

On the plane, its interior construction dictated that the door to the bathroom was exactly one inch longer than the actual width of the isle so that every person who exited the bathroom – located directly across from the drop seat that no sane person is ever actually supposed to sit upon - could slam the bathroom door into the drop seat. And I do not know if Arabs have super tiny bladders or if this particular batch of passengers just all really had to go a lot, but in all my years of extensive traveling, I have never seen more people use one single bathroom more often than what occurred on this flight.

It's a much longer story that involves probably years of lung damage due to all the excessive smoking but it ends like this: when we lost power and began to nose dive (fortunately, no one wet themselves because they had all already gone multiple times to the bathroom), it was none other than Pig Man who burst from the bathroom and fell across my lap. But I never prayed. The thought never occurred to me. Nor did it for Michelle. Later, she would tell me that she said 'goodbye' to me in her thoughts, and then she continued to listen to her music. Michelle was listening to Barbara Streisand while I was blaring Def Leppards' *Hysteria*.

If I did call to any higher power, it might only have been when I said, "God, please get Pig Man off of me!"

Don't get me wrong. It's not just Pig Man who turned me off of religion.

There are plenty of living, walking, talking examples of the Christian, Jewish, and Muslim faiths that turn my stomach. That raging bigots, murderers, rapists, scam artists, and pedophiles, not to mention litter bugs, regularly and religiously (no pun intended), attend service, declaring that we're "not all perfect" and believe that their God will receive them, is revolting to me. Even more so are all the people who will tell otherwise decent, kind people that they will go to hell if they do not attend church. There is something really, really wrong in such blatant hypocrisy and narcissism.

Not once, in the midst of all our adventures, did we pray. That's my point. I don't resort to something that I thought was futile and pointless.

No surprise, my sister and I were not raised in the church, though both of my parents were. But between two tours in Vietnam and the constant moves between Louisiana, Texas, Maryland, back to Texas, on to Hawaii, Arizona and then to Maryland again (before moving to Arkansas, Kansas, Virginia, and overseas tours), my parents drifted from the church. During his tours, my father saw horrendous things while fighting a war. He was not killed or otherwise punished for no longer attending church. Instead, he survived, came home to us, and had an amazing career in the military.

My good friend, Curtis Reece, was once stabbed in the heart when he was trying to break up a fight. He was kind hearted – an irony not lost on those who loved him – and he couldn't stand to see people fight. While the blade was not meant to strike him, it pierced his heart and was nearly fatal. His momma, super religious, had prayed and prayed for him to recover fully, and he did. He lived just long enough for him to become my really good friend and to have me tease him one day about not exercising enough. Later, all alone, he would decide to go jogging. His heart burst from the previous injury as his heart pounded, and he died in the arms of strangers on a sidewalk some two miles from his home. God was not there, no matter how hard his momma prayed. If I could have prayed, I might have asked God why he'd let me tease Curtis. It's not my nature to tease people like that. So why did I? And why did he listen to me?

Strange things happen. My father was detained and held *incommunicado* for several days by the Kuwaiti government in 1986 by men in a region who fight in the name of their God, Allah, or his prophet, Mohammed. Neither was there for my dad, who had simply pulled over to the side of the road to look at some Soviet military equipment being transported from Kuwait to neighboring Iraq. Moscow had invaded Afghanistan a few years earlier, and now the Soviet Army was elbow-deep in Iraq. For that reason, my father, a military intelligence officer, who spoke both Arabic and Russian, was curious about what exactly the convoy was transporting. As the convoy sped by, two cars stopped, and my father was "arrested." The circumstances, like much of my father's career, were classified. I know few details. But I know they weren't nice to him. And I know he didn't pray. Why would he?

God evidently hasn't been there when hundreds of thousands of innocents around the world have been slaughtered in the last two decades simply because they were from the wrong village, the wrong religion, the wrong ethnicity, or the wrong tribe. God has not been there when women and children have been beaten, raped, and tortured. Women in the Darfur region of Sudan are routinely captured by militias that belong to the various combatants and raped for hours.

Where was God? Where is God?

Why has God simply let such horrors and injustices happen?

And so I believed that life is a series of coincidences that link us, sometimes good, sometimes bad, to each other and throughout history. It really appeared to be that easy.

I did not believe that God sent the KGB agents to flood our apartment or set fire to the embassy. Nor did God empower us to get out of the apartment or away from the fire. God didn't help me get on the women's bobsled team, either. It was straight up hard work. Trust me.

There have been no big consequences for me or my family for NOT believing in God. We've done pretty well for ourselves. People always flock to the God thing when they're dying. The most horrible, sinister, deplorable dictators throughout history would rape, pillage, destroy almost everything in their path, but always, on their deathbeds, they always called for a priest of some sort. Yeah, sure ... *now* you want to make peace with God. And don't even get me started on the hows and whys so many people would be willing to blow up entire bus loads of innocent children in the name of their God or Allah.

The absurd way religion is used to justify brutality is just another absurd rationalization that kept me from religion. Yet, by 2008, I was actually wondering if God sleeps.

What?! It's insanity. Not about God sleeping, but that I would even entertain that there was a God. Ludicrous! I never, ever, never, ever, never thought about such things because I knew the answer…there is no God. The bible is a beautifully written book of random stories. That's it. Jesus, while presumably a real person, was just a man who may have possibly been delusional. God and religion is an ideal.

Now, however, I become emotional about the subject of God. It's crazy! As of this writing, it is the closing of the year 2009, and I – the ever-convinced agnostic/sometimes atheist am wondering if God sleeps. I'm talking to a preacher who also likes to sing and dance, have a horse that is possibly Mormon, and began believing in the idea that God sent me to a Rottweiler and a large black man in a wheelchair. Crap, if I didn't know me, *I* would think I was crazy.

But to understand how this came into play, to understand what a huge leap of faith this is for me to even being talking about God or wondering if He sleeps, you must understand my background, my family, and the wildness of our lives and that of Captain Marshall Allen.

When I went to sleep on the evening of October 7, 2007, I had a strong sense of myself and how I fit into the world. Because I was raised to look at things at face value, because I wasn't duped into the religious game of "believe or you'll go to hell," and because I believe that for that reason alone my motives are more pure, I wasn't worried about the afterlife. I wasn't worried about judgment, Heaven, Hell, and certainly not if God somehow intermingles in our lives. He doesn't. I would have told you that was pretty clear based on events I previously described.

I was not looking for answers. I was not looking for help or to be whole or for some divine intervention. I was content. I was happy. Complete. Then, again, Marshall Allen was not looking for any answers, either. For that matter, the people of Midlothian, as a whole, were not questioning what was happening. It was just business as usual.

Then, Marshall went for a bike ride that would change his life forever and send him on a path that would affect and influence more people than he could ever imagine. Five years later, I went for a bike ride – same day with the same 30 mile route - that would change my life forever and send me on a path that would affect and influence an equally diverse and large number of people.

Chapter One

Christmas 1999

Dear Friends and Family –

Our third baby, Tommy, was born this past summer, and I sent out a letter to all sharing news of our new addition and how well things were going. I – regretfully – did not show this letter to Robb. Despite his ongoing delusion that wives should always consult husbands, I mailed out the letter without his review. Days later, he called me from work. He asked about "this letter" I sent out. It seems that some friends and coworkers commented on the letter. Probably, foolishly, they thought they were being polite. So, I read the letter to Robb, and he groaned. Everything, he said, was entirely too happy. People don't want to hear happy things, he said. People don't want to know about how great things are going for other people, he said. "Why do you think people always put out holiday letters," I asked. "People want to know how you're doing."

Not so, said he. He said people want to hear something like, "We're headed for a divorce, and our children are going to juvenile court." So, in that fine spirit, I thought I would write a letter that Robb would approve of:

We're not headed for divorce, but I am married to an idiot.

Our children are not headed for juvie (yet), but Kerri was put in time-out for pushing her beloved guinea pig, Penny, down the slide. Penny's little life flashed before her eyes. Actually, it is pretty amazing how much speed a little rodent can pick up going down an eight-foot twisty slide! At four, Katie has reached a stage where she does this terrible screeching noise when she is having difficulty doing something like putting on her shoes. She seems to be easily frustrated lately. Maybe she is coming down with the middle child syndrome, which will surely result in years of therapy and counseling. No doubt, it will all come back to the fact that she was raised in a household where people aren't supposed to be happy. Maybe her unfortunate happiness is why she is constantly pretending to be a kitty cat, down on all fours, meowing and (dangerously) rubbing against unsuspecting legs. During the summer, she was being a kitty cat in the pool near a group of women who played along with her. Katie became so engrossed in her role that she forgot herself and licked a woman's knee.

We have some real trauma in the household. Sosi, our pound-puppy of nine years, has a growth on her shoulder. Our other dog, Nala, has incontinence. My sister, Michelle, visited, and her dog, Kinder, who cannot be stopped from eating people's underwear, broke loose into the backyard while Penny the pig was grazing and nearly killed her. This may also lead to years of therapy for Kerri, who was screaming helplessly as Penny's little pig legs tried to outrun an ambitious Doberman Pincher. While Penny did escape, making it under the fence just in the knick of time – or click of teeth – all our neighbors were drawn outside because the screaming – a vague recollection indicates the loudest screams were coming from me (how embarrassing).

We got a brand new minivan this year, but it's hard to keep clean with three kids, two dogs and two guinea pigs. Robb doesn't understand how cheerios can be mashed so permanently into all the fixtures of the backseat, but, then, he rides alone in his own precious truck, listens to his own music, and doesn't have the theme song of Snow White and the Seven Dwarves constantly drumming through his brain. He's crabby because he joined a new group at work where everyone got huge bonuses except Robb. He came in too late and gets nothing.

I've gotten a few more book contracts but nothing big, and my dreams of writing the great American novel seem to be too far to reach. Kerri believes that it is good luck for me to write with Penny perched on my shoulder. While she is a sweet pig and does love to snuggle against my neck under my hair, it is just a tad distracting to write with a pig on my shoulder. The fear of pig urine down my back looms mightily.

We almost hit a duck the other day. The slamming of brakes to save momma and ducklings, which resulted in being rear-ended, was complicated by the fact that Michelle had recently had neck surgery, was still in a brace, and now believes that I am trying to kill her. Kerri has a planter's wart on her little foot. Katie's teeth are too far apart, and she might have to wear a retainer later in life. It is always raining here in Ohio, so when the sun does make a rare appearance, the natives appear to be confused by the blinding ball in the sky.

I have a dentist appointment next month that I'm not looking forward to, but Robb flat out refuses to go. He's probably going to lose all his teeth, but Robb says this is a non-issue because he believes he'll be dead before he reaches the age of 50. There is no known reason for this belief; this is just what he thinks.

And so, as we muddle through our daily, dreary little lives, I wonder and think about our friends and family. We can only hope their lives are better than ours. Perhaps it is your love that will keep us strong, allow us to forge ahead, and gives me the strength to deal with the fact that I'm married to an idiot.

P.S. There is every possibility that this letter won't even get to you because of the terrible weather or the impending Y2K and all the problems that will surely surround it!

Love,

Alex

The Unconquerable Marshall Allen
...and his rise to the top

"I know what it says, but. . . " Al Jones suddenly wanted to know. "What does that *mean*?"

Al and Marshall Allen were on a return trip from Ogden, Utah, after moving Marshall's mother to DeSoto, Texas, when Al pointed to a deer crossing sign. It was 1999, and it had been a long trip, particularly for Al. Born and raised within the Dallas-Fort Worth city limits, Al was a bonafide city boy. Ironically, he was a city boy who had lived in the section of Fort Worth that had no paved roads, but he was a city boy all the same. The nearly 1,200 mile jag into Utah had left two impressions on Al: Utah had an abundance of deer crossing signs with nary a deer in sight and only white folks. It was puzzling. Or distressing. Or both.

That he would care enough to inquire about the signs is just his way. He needs to know. He needs to understand the purpose of the sign in the middle of the desert.

Marshall deadpanned that the signs had been strategically placed along the highway so that the deer, when so choosing to cross, would know exactly *where* to cross.

"They cross at the signs," Marshall deadpanned to his friend. "That's where the animals cross. Whenever they see one of those signs, they know it's safe to cross there."

Marshall would argue that the bluest of skies was actually green just for the opportunity to mess with someone, but because of his tone and mannerisms, few people would argue with him.

Marshall Allen, a captain with the Fort Worth Fire Department, was teaching a number of courses at the Fire Academy in addition to his full-time workload at Station 17. He was a rising star within the Fort

Worth Fire Department, and many had pegged him to be a future fire chief. But it was 1999, and Marshall was happily doing what he did best: instructing others. Among some of the courses, he had become deeply invested in counterterrorist classes, teaching recruits how to assess and work possible terrorist sites. It was two years before the U.S. would be hit with the worst terrorist attack on American soil, but "terror was on rise," Marshall had concluded.

He used an incident from 1984 when a cult in Oregon, in an effort to rig an upcoming election, placed bacteria in salad bars in local restaurants to justify his suspicions. Although no one died, some 750 people became sick from salmonella.

That had been an unusual incident in the U.S.; most forms of terrorism had been exclusively overseas. But the 1993 garage bombing under the Twin Towers by Muslim fundamentalists, the incident at Ruby Ridge, and the shootout between the Branch Davidians and federal agents in Waco that unfolded on live television sent a loud message. Indeed, terrorism was on the rise.

The April 19, 1995 Oklahoma City bombing served as a teaching tool for Marshall. When Timothy McVeigh and Terry Nichols used 12 bags of ammonium nitrate fertilizer and a rental truck to blow up the Alfred P. Murrah Federal Building in downtown Oklahoma City, valuable Intel was later gathered, allowing progressive cities like Fort Worth to teach emergency responders how to react appropriately. Responders were also taught the importance of weather, standing up or downwind from chemical agents, noting secondary devices, and safely moving people away from the scene, among other things. But no one could have foreseen what would happen on September 11th, 2001, and no one could have imagined what would happen to Marshall just two months prior to that attack.

By 1999, Marshall was "small" at 280 pounds. Years prior, he'd set the Fort Worth fire fighters record for powerlifting when he was an impressive 340 pounds of rock solid muscle. He and his best friend, Al Jones, another fire fighter, had long ago given up pick-up basketball games. Also hovering at 340 pounds, Al had agreed with Marshall that "we were just too big." Someone, they concluded, was going to get hurt. Instead, Marshall had picked up the recreational sport of cycling. More than five years into his marriage with Mary and now helping to raise her four children from previous marriages, Marshall was finally settling down.

At that time, he and Mary were beginning to have problems in their marriage, but Marshall will still say 1999 was one of the best years of his life. He was an adjunct instructor at the fire academy, was working seven days a week, and was stationed in one of the busiest fire houses in

Fort Worth. He was the most sought after instructor at the academy and was widely viewed as the "been there, done that like no one else" kind of a guy.

Of his stature, the on-going joke in the firehouse was that Marshall had better hope he never went down because "there's no way we're dragging your big ass out." With his gear on, Marshall weighed over 400 pounds. Of his personality, the on-going belief was "there's no stopping Marshall Allen." He was a monster of a man with demons no one knew about. To the outside world, he appeared to be in command at all times, but the inner turmoil was slowly killing him. Some of his most peaceful times were when he was alone with Al. Over time, they had become more like brothers than friends. And teasing each other was just another aspect of their relationship. Convincing Al that deer do, in fact, cross the street only at the properly appointed deer crossing destinations was a mission.

"The entire time I grew up in Utah," Marshall later remarked about that road trip, "I don't think I ever saw any animals near one of those signs. Hell, I never saw a falling rock at one of those falling rock signs!" But just moments after Marshall had remarked on how deer crossed only at the signs, four or five deer suddenly appeared.

Both Marshall and Al watched in stunned silence as the small herd sauntered into view down a hill and across a clearing on the right side of the highway. They approached a fence bordering the road and never slowed down. They all cleared the wire fence as gracefully as Edwin Moses routinely clearing hurdles. And they did so at a point directly in front of a deer crossing sign. The deer galloped across the highway, and without breaking stride, they cleared the second fence as easily as the first and went on about their business.

Like his new furry friends, Marshall didn't miss a beat. He made a small, reassuring gesture toward the road and the sign and said, "You see there."

Al's response was the only one he could possibly offer.

"Okay," he said.

Protecting God's Green Earth

Also in 1999, Tom and Julie Boyle decided to move to Midlothian, Texas. It is a small town just 25 miles south of Dallas. They purchased a three-acre lot, built a house, and settled into real country living. "We bought a baby John Deere tractor. We got a black lab and somehow acquired a goat," Tom wrote. Like every family that moves to Midlothian, the Boyles were aware of the three cement plants surrounding the town. "Midlothian was called, after all, the cement capital of Texas. With three major cement plants – Ash Grove, Holcim, and Texas Industries or TXI – some, in fact, call Midlothian the cement capital of the world.

"I hardly noticed the cement stacks. Red oaks and bluebonnets were growing on me. I bought an Audubon book to identify birds. As a Republican, I believed in free enterprise and figured regulators probably kept the plants on a short leash. The whining environmentalists were wackos. I was more concerned with the grammatical error on the downtown neon sign that read, 'the Cement Capitol of Texas.' Besides, everyone said the cement plants dumped truckloads of money into the community and schools, which we loved. The teachers and staff were terrific. Life in Midlothian was good." (1)

By the time I met the Boyles, this sentiment was long gone. They were angry and, in some ways, paranoid about the world around them.

Chapter Two

Christmas 2000
Season's Greetings!

  Well, it's that time of year again, and as many of you know, we have our very own Grinch. For those of you who are new to the Allred holiday letter, husband Robb has set a precedent for us: No cheery news. No one, he says, likes to read how happy other people are or how swell things are going. So, it has become our tradition to bring our own doom and gloom into your homes, making all your lives seem just a bit better.

  What Robb could not have foreseen was how wildly popular this letter would be. Last year, I sent it to a number of his co-workers. As it turned out, just before a big meeting, Robb's boss opened the event by reading aloud the Allred holiday letter. And for those of you who know the freakishly private Robb Allred – which makes many stop to ponder the union between said freak and myself – this was a painful meeting for Robb. The glances of amused coworkers seared into Robb's flesh as he was sure they were taking a part of his soul or now know that he will actually stand over a freshly baked cake and eat the entire middle of it without thought or remorse. Or that if he goes to lunch with coworkers, and if one of them orders the same menu item Robb wanted, he believes he can no longer order that item because it violates some weirdo man law he has established. So, on with the news …

  Indeed, this was a year of major disappointment! I continue to write but actually ***almost*** had something rather exciting come along. I'm the almost-girl. Truly, this is hard for me to write because, by all counts, I shouldn't even be here. I should be in Australia. I entered – for fun – as a contestant for the television show ***Survivor***. I never even heard about the first calling, so when the show began looking for contestants for their ***Survivor II*** show, a woman from my kickboxing class downloaded the application and brought it to class for me to fill out! I did, made a two-minute video of the family, me, some bobsled stuff, and sent it off. Two weeks later, I got a phone call. If Robb hadn't been standing right there, I would have thought he was playing a prank on me – as he is apt to do. They wanted pictures. Oh, boy! Two weeks later, I got another call. I made the cuts from over 56,000 applicants to 800. Oh, boy: oh, boy! I was to meet with two of the show's producers in Detroit, Michigan. I did. I made the next series of cuts and was sent a plethora of materials and waivers (Robb also had to sign that should I fall off a cliff, be eaten by a saltwater croc, or bitten by a python, he would not sue—he signed) and oaths that I would not inform the media of my final cut. It was pretty cool, and I was down to the last 50!

Then I got a phone call. Apparently, in the first show, they didn't have any baby-boomer moms. No one represented the 40-something category, and because they are charging $1 million each from their major sponsors, they had to reach and satisfy a certain target audience. One of the producers personally called to say that she had really wanted me, but my age had worked against me. "You're too young of a mom." Imagine that. Here I've been worrying about premature aging for nothing. I was told that should I try for ***Survivor III*** this would not happen again, but that they had to make certain people happy this time around. I don't mind saying I was pretty bummed. When you have L.A. hot shots telling you, your husband and your sister that "She's perfect for the show!" it kind of sets you up for disappointment. Secretly, I think Robb was relieved. With Tommy in diapers, Robb is not emotionally equipped for the job of full-time dad.

If I was going to consider another go at ***Survivor III***, I lost the desire when ***Sports Illustrated*** expressed an interest in my trying out for a women's professional football team and writing about the experience. To be continued …

Apparently in last year's letter, Robb felt that while the theme was gloomy – what with me confusing medication with Nala's incontinence pill and all – that I shared too much information … like accidentally swallowing the dog's pee-pee pill. I can still hear the howls of laughter from the vet's receptionist when I called to make sure I would be okay. So I promised this year I would not share too much. I'll condense sentences. Here goes:

Robb decided to save money by cutting his own hair and bought his own kit, declaring, "This thing'll pay for itself!!" He is bald. We took a road trip with a baby, a five- and seven-year-old. We should not have done that. Robb is now working from home. We still live in our little shack of a home, so it feels as though he and I are working on top of each other. Robb apparently has some peculiar form of Tourettes Syndrome that causes him to randomly blurt out lyrics from songs or movies that have no relevance to whatever is happening at the moment.

He tries to help with the girls and will sometimes sit with Katie to watch "Dora the Explorer," but it is not helpful when he tells her that Dora's dad is in a Mexican prison doing 10 to 15. Nor is it helpful when he sings them their bedtime song, "Baby's Boat's a Silver Dream." It is a beautiful classic that he has butchered with, "Baby's born without a spleen." He's not allowed to sing anymore. He says he just didn't know the words, but we know better. He's got issues.

With Tommy now entering toddler phase, nothing is safe. He is Robb, Jr. The dogs run when they see him coming, and he's broken more lamps, clocks, picture frames, stereo speakers, and dishes than I can count. Virtually all the furniture in the living room has been removed. There are baby gates up on almost every doorway in the house, and he makes me cry a lot because that boy's not right. Baby-proof materials don't work because he breaks them. Now, we have motorcycle bungee cords over everything. Nothing is safe. Nothing is free from harm, and we tell ourselves this every night when we go to bed and every morning when we wake.

Robb took a business trip to Fort Lauderdale and managed to go deep-sea fishing and catch a five-foot-long barracuda that put up such a fight that all the skin was torn from Robb's hands. Tough guys don't wear gloves. We spent much of our savings to send the disgusting thing to a taxidermist. What we got back is even uglier, and it looks plastic! Robb has declared that it is "beautiful," but it looks like a hideous big plastic fish from a flea market.

Kerri and Katie dressed up as Powerpuff Girls for Halloween. Everyone thought Katie was a little princess but kept asking Kerri, "Oh, and are you a bumble bee?"

Perhaps this is my fault. Because Kerri has grown up training with members of the U.S. women's bobsled team, she thinks throwing up from exercise-induced exhaustion is normal and believes Powerbars (my sponsor) are candy bars; she doesn't understand that girls are made up of sugar and spice. We got hooked up with a pretty snooty Brownie troop – very prissy girls. All the other families were members of the country club while we live in a small rental home. But never were the differences made so clear to me than when I pulled up early to a Brownie meeting to find all the girls outside playing freeze tag. Fast, powerful, competitive, and full of boundless energy, Kerri was "it" and was happily screaming, "Tag! You're frozen!" as she, using a stiff-arm tactic, happily and cluelessly sent designer-wearing Brownies flailing and crashing to the ground. Wearing her hand-me-downs and ready to rumble, Kerri had no idea she was actually hurting people. She was "it!"

Who cares, anyway? I was actually kicked out of my Brownie troop. Stupid Brownies!

Kerri dared Katie to drive Tommy's musical ice cream truck down the twisty slide. Katie was pretty banged up. She is definitely going to need braces with the spacing in her teeth – which isn't helped by the fact that she keeps placing pretzel sticks between her teeth and walking around like Dracula. Our guinea pig, Star, died. Robb has athlete's foot but denies it and rubs it on everything. Sosi, the lab mix, brought us a dead animal, which is pretty amazing because she is pretty much blind and deaf. We had a mouse in our garage and tried to catch it humanely, but the darned thing kept eating the peanut butter and escaping so Robb finally bought the killing-kind of trap. Whap!

Now when we play, "What Am I?" – a favorite pastime in the car - Katie likes to say, "Well, I'm little and soft and brown and Daddy broke my neck. What am I?"

Here's to a calmer year next year …

Love,

Alex

The Unconquerable Marshall Allen
…and his rise to the top

Marshall Allen is a wonder. But to properly describe this man, who defies gravity, overrides obstacles, and breaks down barriers, is a vast chore. He is the perfect example of perseverance, dignity, and grace.

At the writing of this book, Marshall's best friend, Al, is unable to see how amazing his friend really is. Like Marshall, Al has run in and out of burning buildings. He has saved lives, wrestled death, and, many times, lost the match. Despite his best efforts to save the lives of accident and burn victims, he can't always win. But from time to time, both Marshall and Al have themselves cheated death. Marshall is a living example of that. Still, because of, or despite, it all, Al's perspective is skewed when compared to others who know Marshall. For fire fighters, dealing heroically with death is simply a way of life.

Since their rookie fireman days, Al and Marshall have been together. Who, but an incredible person, could have beaten death and conquered life? And who, but an incredible person, could have supported and encouraged, pushed and demanded, and been a true friend, the epitome of the word "brother"?

Together, they talk about the pain a mother feels as she weeps for a dead child or the hopeless feeling as the jaws of life retract the lifeless body of a teenager who might have accomplished great things in life. They were there, unable to stop those terrible happenings. For them, having witnessed such disasters, Marshall's achievements seem somehow less magnificent. In truth, this is the account of one man's extraordinary adventure. His story is more of a social commentary about who we all are and our collective purposes in life.

Marshall Allen was born to a white mother and black father in the 1950s in Holbrook, Arizona. He was quickly given up for adoption. Twice he was given back to the adoption agency when unrelated white families realized that the beautiful, fair skinned, curly-headed boy they had adopted was black. As time passed, he was abused by a foster family, rescued by a local sheriff's department, and eventually adopted into a black family. His was a life filled with turmoil, abuse, and frustration. But he went on to become a Golden Gloves boxer, the first black fireman in Salt Lake County, Utah, and one of the first few black firefighters to battle the good ol' boy network in Fort Worth, Texas, in the 1970s.

Faced with his incredibly quick mind and, probably, a photographic memory, few people have successfully matched wits with Marshall. When a car he wanted to give to his stepson needed a new engine and he knew having it done professionally would cost more than the car was worth, he bought a manual, read the chapter on engine swapping, and did it in about four days. He still beams when he recalls the day the Mercedes -- the car he'd been told by mechanics was too complicated to work on -- whose engine he'd exchanged in his driveway - started on the first attempt. He had become interested in building his own airplane with the idea of flying it. He'd built several model airplanes for the sole purpose of allowing his children to take the controls and fly the plane until it crashed. His thinking was that he could always build another. There was no obstacle he could not overcome.

Once standing over 6'4" with the physique of a Greek God, his record as a power lifter with the Fort Worth Fire Fighter Olympics still holds today. Ironically, it was a Lt. Brian Harris who informed Marshall that such a record even existed as Harris had been trying to break it for years. Today, he remains handsome, funny, and warm.

Also very handsome and incredibly powerful, Al commanded much attention. But unlike his friend and despite many of the battles they shared over the years, Marshall holds no animosity against whites. Politically, Marshall is open to all ideas. He craves healthy debates on all subjects and greets all people with equal enthusiasm.

By all accounts, he appeared to be on top of the world. Few knew, however, that he battled severe depression. He'd contemplated suicide, and his rages were so severe and violent that he feared he might one day kill someone. While he was rising to the top in the Fort Worth

Fire Department, wildly popular among his peers and supervisors, he battled demons.

Today, Marshall is a quadriplegic. His hands are inoperable as a result of the damage suffered to his spinal cord. Today, he requires metal hand braces to aid in mechanically articulating his fingers in and out of a pinching motion. When he laughs or sneezes, there is no noise. The thoracic, intercostals, and abdominal muscles are now inactive because there is no electrical impulse from the nervous system, thereby making it impossible for him to project any sound. Yet, he drives his own van, holds down a full-time job as a captain with the Fort Worth fire department, and is greatly admired not only for his tenacity but also for his strong work ethic and leadership.

In 2000, when he was standing tall, he was miserable. The energy he had to muster to put on his "game face" was exhausting. Every morning, he would look into the mirror, talking back to his own reflection with the daily chant, "It's show time."

The show time, the challenge, was to make it through the day without saying what he was actually thinking. Depression, Marshall later said, "is like gang life. When you're that depressed, you don't give a damn about yourself or anyone else.

"When I was a kid, the only reason I didn't kill someone who was mean to me was because I knew it was wrong. At least, my parents had instilled that inside of me." But as he got older and the rage did not dissipate, his objectives changed. "Then, the only reason I didn't kill people was because I didn't think I could get away with it and I thought I had too much to lose." His career. His dogs. His house. In that order.

In the early 80s when Marshall was studying for his engineer's test and still working as a swingman (usually a rookie who goes from station to station, filling in where he may be needed), he picked up a part-time job at the Tinder Box, a specialty cigar store in a shopping mall on the west side of Fort Worth. The owner, Nicholas Poulos, was a crotchety old man who rarely shared stories of his time as a WWII pilot. But with Marshall, there was an instant connection. He would be the only man to ever fire Marshall from a job but not because he was not satisfied with Marshall's work. In fact, quite the opposite. Concerned that Marshall was not studying for his engineer's test, he banned Marshall from his store and was first in line with congratulatory hugs when Marshall passed the test.

Nick Poulos, the first generation of Greek immigrants to be born in the U.S., grew up in Hell's Kitchen, New York. He understood poverty, discrimination, and the need to succeed. And he understood that

Marshall was not the average, young American male. For no other explanation than that, "He let me stand around and listen while he talked to other WWII war vets," Marshall said.

"I remember one time I asked him, 'What keeps you going back up there,' referring to the fighter planes." Statistically, he had a 50/50 chance of being shot down each time he took to the air. "He said it was 'the other guy' syndrome. He said, 'You always think it's the other guy who's going to be shot down, not you.'"

Amidst his own depression, Marshall also had a bit of "the other guy" syndrome. He did not pray he would not be shot out of the sky. Rather, he merely tried to uphold the standards of his father; there was nothing that Morris Allen found more loathsome than an able-bodied, young male out of work. So even while Marshall contemplated suicide, he pushed on at work, outperforming nearly everyone. He excelled at his tasks, tests, physical conditioning, and leadership. Still, he knew he needed professional help with his depression. He was ready to accept death as a way out of his own torment. But in one more year, as he was rising through the ranks at the department, he would permanently be in his custom fit wheelchair, and he would be stronger and wiser than ever. How he got there – to that place, to the chair where he is now confined – is but a fraction of the story.

Protecting God's Green Earth

By the year 2000, business was booming in Midlothian. More and more families were moving into the small town. There were only a handful of traffic lights in town, but its reputation for having a good school system drew more people to rural living.

Local politics seemed to mandate that every mayor in the last few decades was somehow related to someone who worked at one of the three cement plants, and no one in this "company town" asked questions as high levels of curious emissions came from the various cement stacks.

On the other side of the country, however, a little known woman named Erin Brokovich had been seriously injured in a car accident and had hired Jim Vititoe of Masry & Vititoe to handle her case. As the story goes, she was quickly hired on with the law firm as a file clerk after the case ended, and it was then that she noticed a number of questionable medical records involved with a real estate case. What she found was that the residents of Hinkley, California, had been exposed to toxic chemicals throughout the 1960s, '70s, and '80s. Specifically, Chromium 6 had leaked into the groundwater from the nearby Pacific Gas and Electric Company's Compressor Station.

By the time she and Ed Masry were done, the largest tort injury settlement in U.S. history was settled, ending in a total of $333 million in damages for more than 600 Hinkley residents. Under the direction of screenwriter Susannah Grant, director Steven Soderberg, and actress Julia Roberts, the movie **Erin Brokovich** made its debut in 2000.

Fourteen years prior to Erin's movie, the North Texas Cement Company (then called Gifford-Hill and most recently renamed Ash Grove) in Midlothian began burning hazardous waste. It was the first plant in Texas to do so, and because of a loophole in the law, it did not have to apply for a full federal permit. Briefly, before the people of Midlothian came to look at hazardous waste as "normal," there was an outcry. But these good people were denied a hearing because they were one day late in submitting petitions. Why? So as not to arouse further public outcry, North Texas had labeled their activity as "resource recovery" rather than what it actually was – the burning of hazardous waste.

This "resource recovery" allowed the 1965 cement plant to be paid to burn the same kinds of wastes as a commercial hazardous waste incinerator without having to apply the health and safety standards required of an incinerator. A second Midlothian cement plant, TXI, had complained to the Texas Air Control Board that this was a very dangerous process as toxic metals such as lead were emitted – unregulated – into the air. Yet, when TXI saw the profits, they also began burning hazardous waste in 1987. And like North Texas Cement, TXI made sure their permit request to burn hazardous waste was quietly passed before a public hearing could be held.

The history of Midlothian has two parts. First and foremost, the town was born from its natural resources. Natural spring water that rose from deposits of Balcones Escarpment limestone, prevalent in the area, attracted early settlers. The area proved to have excellent soil for farming cotton, corn, and wheat. When the Atchinson, Santa Fe, and Topeka Railroad came through Midlothian, the town was officially put on the map. Farmers built homes alongside the tracks for easier transport, and families prospered.

Today, the chalk and shale of the limestone serves as an excellent resource for cement production. So excellent, in fact, that three cement plants were built all within a close proximity of each other, almost encircling the small town.

With a growing population, however, came problems. In the past, citizens were typically kept in the dark as to the inner workings, health issues, and political stance of the cement plants. Through the history of both the cement plants and local politics, permits to burn some very dangerous materials have been passed with nary a public notice, a hearing, or a vote from everyday citizens.

For many residents of Midlothian, this was the first time they had heard anything about hazardous waste burning. But because Midlothian's three cement plants and steel mill accounted for anywhere between 55 to 65 percent of tax revenues for the city, few concerned citizens had a voice. It had become common practice to build and operate similar cement plants in rural towns, mostly in the south and mid-west as the less populated, less educated residents were unlikely to ask questions, and small towns accepted the economic boost. But as more communities began to speak out, the federal government passed a new set of regulations to govern boilers and industrial furnaces burning hazardous waste.

By 1989, North Texas Cement and TXI were burning tens of thousands of tons of hazardous waste at the Midlothian plants. Still, they wanted to burn more. To do so, they needed on-site tank farms to receive and mix in-coming wastes, and for this, they had to apply for their first federal permits. Finally, there was no getting around the local and state handouts, and this time, they couldn't call it "resource recovery." Because of the excessive amount of emissions, the gig was up, and they had to call it what it was – hazardous waste burning.

Although these were new regulations, they were still not the same stringent regulations required of commercial incinerators, and they did not require a full federal permit. Instead, they created something called "interim status," which meant the cement plants could operate indefinitely without a full permit. "There were no regulations. They could have burned a dead cow if they wanted to," Sue Pope said, matriarch of the Downwinders at Risk organization. (See www.downwindersatrisk.org)

BIF rules (boilers and industrialized furnaces), as they were termed, were put in place, but they merely institutionalized the inequities in the status quo. An EPA whistle-blower released a memo showing EPA and industry collusion in writing the new regulations.

Newly-elected governor Ann Richards was listening and appointed Air Control Board Chair, Kirk Watson, to create a task force with the specific goal of reporting back to him on the issue. Representatives from the industry as well as private citizens were chosen – one of them being a local activist named Cynthia Fava. While it had been recommended that the cement industry should adhere to the same standards, those recommendations were never enforced.

It was one roadblock after another before the American Lung Association, local PTA groups, physicians, and environmentalists pushed politicians to respond. In September 1994, new guidelines were being drafted regarding hazardous waste burning and emissions, but it all came to a grinding halt with the election of Governor George Bush in November of that year. Not only were previous draft proposals ignored, but metal emissions were increased by 800 percent and dioxin emissions increased by 500 percent.

By 1997, Gov. Bush had promised concerned citizens he would create a program that would reduce air pollution from the state's oldest and dirtiest industrial facilities "without resorting to government-mandated regulations" by giving immunity for past violations to the biggest polluters. Then, he set up an easy permitting process "that excluded most public participation. To receive these benefits, companies simply had to voluntarily obtain permits and abide by the program's modest pollution requirements" (2).

What most Midlothian residents, let alone Texans, understood was that the state's biggest polluters were allowed to self-regulate and self-report.

By the year 2000, as the Allred family unknowingly prepared to move to Midlothian, health issues were on the rise in that very town.

The town's population was just over 6,000, and the three cement plants and steel mill were emitting 1,502,123 pounds of Chromium, lead, manganese, mercury, and sulfuric acid--to name a few. Dioxin, the worst of the cancer-causing agents, was the cherry on top of the toxic sundae.

But, of course, none of this would mean anything to us at the time. We were living in sprawling suburbia USA in Westerville, Ohio, just outside Columbus. If asked, I would have believed that strict policies were in place to protect American citizens. But, honestly, who even thinks about such a thing? This is America, right? We take care of our own. Besides, I had bigger worries. Tommy seemed to be getting stronger, more agile, and daring every day, and while we couldn't prove this definitively, we feared that he was actually trying to destroy us.

He constantly placed toys – seemingly innocent toys – in the threshold of every doorway in the house. Suddenly, little army tanks, building blocks, and rubber toys turned into weapons of mass destruction: at 2 a.m. responding to Tommy's cry in the night, we risked mortal injury.

Neighbors knew to keep an eye out for Tommy as he began escaping from the house. Even Ms. Pat Caston, a retired elementary school principal, commented that Tommy surpassed the activity level of the typical boy. He was Tsunami Tommy.

We (briefly) considered purchasing a home in Westerville but simply could not afford it. I was a stay-at-home, starving-artist mom, and Robb was only beginning to climb the corporate ladder. Therefore, Texas had two very positive aspects. Robb's family lived there, and housing was more affordable. So, as the year drew to an end, we began seriously to consider a move to Texas. We knew we wanted land, a safe place where Tommy could run wild and be free and have the time of his life catching lizards, climbing trees, and, I hoped, riding horses.

It was luck, you know? Pure chance. Coincidence. A random string of events that linked things together and allowed us to find our home. Nothing divine. Nothing holy. Just pure chance. And we took it!

Chapter Three

Christmas 2001

Here we go again.

For those of you who are unfamiliar with the annual Allred holiday letter, its purpose is this: People want to know about unpleasant things. So, in that holiday spirit:

The new year started with a bang when I got food poisoning from Jenny Craig's beef stew. My fault, not Jenny's. My clue of more than a year's past due expiration date should have let me know what horrible things would happen to me if I chose to eat expired beef. But some of us always have to learn the hard way. I was so desperately ill I thought I would die. I wanted to die. As I slipped in and out of consciousness, Robb whispered to me, "Is there any stew left?" He wanted to test his long-running streak of not throwing up (not since January of 1991). Do you know how rude it is to ask a dying person such a question? But because he's so stupid, I had to ask Michelle (my sister), through ragged whispers, to get rid of the toxic stew so he wouldn't do himself in.

We moved to Midlothian, Texas (1 ½ hour drive from Robb's parents), in July. Leaving Ohio was rough. Saying bye to friends really stunk, but even worse was the driving. Picture this: me, Kerri, 8, Katie, 6, Tommy, 2, Nala & Sosi (two 70- and 80-pound dogs), and Penny & Sparkles (two three-pound guinea pigs) trapped together in a mini van for 22 hours. While Robb happily and peacefully drove his truck to the tunes of his heavy metal music, I listened to Blues Clues and Rappin' With Elmo. He would tell you he's suffered enough, though. It has been a tough year for him: I was asked to do a story for **Sports Illustrated**, trying out for a women's professional football team. I tried out for and made the roster as a defensive end, #31, for the Austin Rage. As I was doing my try-outs, little Tommy landed a gig modeling for a catalogue, leaving Robb to utter these words: "My wife is a professional football player and my son is a model!" I think it was around that time he developed some kind of facial tick.

As we settled in Texas, we had to contend with grossly oversized crickets and mosquitoes and vile little creatures known as fire ants. There should be a sign posted at the Texas border declaring, "We're proud to have ya, but don't move here in July." It's so hot in July, cats pant. Hair can actually melt on your head. Cars randomly burst into flames.

Our actual transition into Midlothian (small town approx. 35 miles outside of Dallas) has been interesting. Our mail carrier drives an old '74 Chevy with no muffler. When he has mail to deliver to me personally, he sits in the driveway and honks his horn at me. Believe me, we're thankful for this. For the longest time, we weren't even getting our mail.

But even more vexing is that none of our neighbors ever came to say 'hi,' forever ruining my notion about small towns. No 'Welcome to the neighborhood,' no drop-bys. This suits Robb perfectly because, he says he doesn't want people coming around rifling through our things. Ah, yes, we've had such a problem in the past with people tearing through our things, inspecting our underwear drawers!

As part of my initiation as a professional football player, I broke two of my fingers (one finger was mangled pretty good in particular) and right hand as well as dislocating my forearm during practice. Driving home with a stick shift with broken fingers, hand, and dislocated arm was extremely painful. This all came about because one week before we left Ohio, our buddy Mark Larkin and Robb went dirt bike riding, and Mark decided to catapult his body – bike and all – from a 20-foot double jump. No one knows exactly what was going through Mark's mind, including Mark because he still has no memory of the entire day! We swapped trucks, letting Mark use our automatic while we took his standard until he healed.

So, with my career as a football player over, I thought I would try something closer to home. I tried canning. The former owners of our house left us with an extraordinary garden, and we had an abundance of peppers, tomatoes, cucumbers and zucchini. I now have a fabulous recipe for botulism salsa. I almost killed Robb, though he still didn't throw up.

I have a dream of one day owning a horse to go on the small pasture next to our house, but currently fleas (that are tearing Robb up), mice, toads, coyotes, and snakes own the meadow. The snakes and coyotes are attracted to the mice living in the tall grass. Maybe we should get a goat.

The other day I went to the store and saw a "Lost Pet" sign. The sign itself was nothing new. What was new (for me) was that it was a Lost Goat sign. Moreover, they felt compelled to give a full description of the lost goat with a picture. You know, so it wouldn't be confused with all the other loose goats milling about Midlothian. We all got poison oak. I was attacked by an angry swarm of bees while mowing the lawn. My sister-in-law, Cristi, killed our pet toad by stepping on him. Kerri thought he was sleeping for two days. Sosi (11-year-old lab mix) has a huge growth on her leg. The perils of Penny the Guinea Pig continue as Kerri continues to stuff her inside a Barbie jeep and send her flying down the hallway. Penny cannot steer – no opposable thumbs – and often crashes. She doesn't mind sitting in Barbie's Jacuzzi tub or riding up and down in Barbie's elevator, but the Barbie jet ski is alarming to Penny.

Speaking of "alarming" and Barbie, I have noted a disturbing trend when Kerri and Katie play with Barbie. Again, I blame myself. They don't have a mommy who wears dresses or much make-up. I hang out with bobsledders and football players and martial artists. But when I walk into their rooms to find multiple Barbies hanging by their necks from doorknobs and the handles on dressers, what am I to make of the macabre display?

For Thanksgiving, Kerri and I threw up all day and night with the worst flu I've ever had. While others shared turkey and dressing, Kerri and I shared a barf bucket. Robb chose this time to tell me that he secretly hoped he would get it so he could test his record.

Once again, I'm the almost-author! I had another book published, **The Code,** and it was being considered by the prestigious Coretta Scott King Award, but you have to be African American. Even though they liked the book, I was dropped as soon as they found out I'm white! Man! I finished the story for **Sports Illustrated for Women** (the whole reason for breaking and permanently deforming my pinky), then they changed editors and said they didn't think they were interested in the story anymore. How do you like that? After months of recovery – do you know how hard it is to change diapers with a broken hand? And do you know how often Tommy kicked my hand? – I managed to write a women's sports book, **Atta Girl**, pecking at the keys with just my left hand.

Hope your year was a little more healthy and a little bit happier than ours. ☺

Help! Help! Help! …..errrr, I mean, Ho, ho, ho!!!

Your Friend,

Alex

On Hope and Faith

Life is a series of connected coincidences. Just as there are random acts of kindness, there are random events that can sometimes link us in unthinkable ways. My dad, for example, was in the Pentagon when it was hit by the American Airlines plane overtaken by those rat-bastard, cowardly terrorists. Where the plane struck was, among other places, an empty office where my father was supposed to be sitting. The Defense Department's Office of African Affairs was to have been in that office space, but a delay in renovations – by one week – had left the office empty.

Our relief and gratitude was brief. On the very plane that struck Daddy's office was a wonderfully warm, dear, and amazing woman named Dr. Norma Sterle. She was a great family friend for years and years and had actually made a point of visiting Daddy before boarding that plane. It was and is a miracle/tragedy that has not escaped our attention.

The Unconquerable Marshall Allen
...and his rise to the top

By the 1970s, Marshall was a fighter – a boxer. He was a pioneer – the first black fire fighter in Salt Lake County, Utah. By the 1990s, he was a leader – commanding fire fighters.

On July 2, 2001, just months before the United States would be turned upside down by the attacks on September 11, Marshall's world would forever change as well. The early years of his life, so helpless and turbulent, were long gone as Marshall had grown to be 6'4" and, at one time, over three hundred pounds of solid muscle. He was a leader among the other fire fighters in his company, and he reasonably expected to become battalion chief within a matter of years.

But other things were stirring inside of him as well. He was suddenly making life changes. He decided to become a vegetarian; he'd taken an interest in voice-activated software, believing this technology to be the "way of the future."

It was on the morning of July 2, 2001, that he began dismantling his wife's computer. The inner workings of computers fascinated him, and he was constantly installing new hardware. Always the consummate perfectionist, he was greatly agitated when he discovered he'd fried Mary's computer. He quickly reinstalled and scavenged new parts for the CPU and motherboard so that it would, at the very least, boot up, hoping to hide this fiasco from his wife until he could replace the processor. Then, out of frustration, he decided to go for a relatively short bike ride.

The bitter irony was that Marshall, the all-around athlete, actually didn't want to ride on that day. But he made himself get out of the house and get away from the computer business that so irritated him. The irony would be that he had taken up cycling because both he and his good buddy, Al Jones, had decided their usual pick-up games of basketball were getting too dangerous. It was too tough on the joints, and cycling would be better. And the irony would be that he went cycling on that day to clear his head and make things "better."

And, of course, the true irony is that it did.

"I was installing a new processor," says Marshall, "and didn't read the directions. On an old system, you could run 'em without the coolers for a few seconds, but it was just too hot on these processors, and they burned up in a few seconds."

Out on a rural road, Marshal tried to bunny-hop over a branch in his path and crashed. There had been a storm the night before, and branches were everywhere.

Of all places, he crashed into a deep ditch, hidden from plain view, and hit so hard, he was instantly paralyzed. Essentially, his very large body was folded over his shoulders and head, and he lay helplessly on the back of his neck and upper shoulders. He lay in the ditch for over an hour, bitten by fire ants and sure that this was where he would die. He could only listen as car after car passed him, completely unaware that he was there and in such need of aid.

That, he would say, was a kind of hell all its own, knowing help was out there, but no one could not see him. Wasn't that the way with his depression and anger?

Then a man who had not taken a day off work in over six months chose that day to take his wife out. It was also that day that their babysitter bailed out at the last minute, leaving the kids with them - the same kids who, looking out of the back of their car, would be the only people to spy Marshall's bike. The little boy, always made to wear a seatbelt, had been up out of his seat on this day that his parents were still frustrated and flustered over the babysitter situation. So, on this hectic day, perched on up his knees, he saw a bike down in a ditch. He loudly announced the bike in the ditch to his parents. Only when his sister craned her neck to see the bike did she also see Marshall. The little girl shouted, "And there's a man, too!"

When the children's warning cry alarmed the parents, they stopped their car and found Marshall. But what they couldn't know was just minutes before they stopped, Marshall had given up. The man who never conceded defeat under any circumstances, the man who could never be stopped physically or mentally, had shut down just moments before.

The impact of the hit combined with the size of his body had snapped his neck. He lay where he hit, his body essentially folded over his head and neck, pinning him to the ground.

Already, his breathing was labored. Only by using his neck muscles was Marshall able to control and manipulate his airway. As he contemplated his dire situation, he came to one very definite conclusion: He didn't want to die this way. He didn't want to have the elements, maybe animals, pick away at him. And he concluded that dying in a few minutes was far better than dying over the next few days. So, with a final prayer, he exhaled, relaxed his neck muscles, and allowed his body to roll forward.

The result was immediate and twofold. Yes, he had successfully shut off his own air supply, as he intended, but he also suddenly realized, "I can't go out like this." But now he was screwed. He remembers thinking, "That's what you deserve, dumbass!"

Though Marshall had children, they were not his biological children, and he wondered and thought about children in those final moments. He thought about Mary and her children and suddenly recalled conversations he had many times with his fellow firefighters at the station house. When death came knocking, he had always said, he would fight to the end.

"I'd always said when the Grim Reaper came, there would be claw marks on the walls from me resisting!" Marshall Allen would not go out easily. As he remembered his own words, he bowed up. "I said to myself, 'You've been talkin' all this noise and now you're just giving up?' And from that moment on, I tried to straighten myself up."

But you can't jump in the ocean and then decide you don't want to get wet. This revelation was a little too late. As his wind pipe crumpled beneath his immense weight, he prayed again ... this time to live. Then the car stopped.

As a result of the McDowell family stopping, a second car would stop – an EMS officer on his way to work. Once 911 was dispatched, the fire fighters who would respond to the call knew him.

"I knew as soon as I saw his figure that he was Marshall," said Fire Chief Donnie Pickard. He almost laughed. "You know ... it's Marshall." Few men had the size that Marshall did, and even lying on the ground, face down, Pickard knew who he was.

Marshall had taken to stopping by the Ovilla Fire Department, a small "combination" firehouse of both volunteer and paid fire fighters, on his long bike rides. "He would stop by to visit, refill his water," Pickard recalled. Since Marshall and Al had stopped playing their intense basketball games, Marshall enjoyed both the challenge and solitude of long bike rides and had taken to the less traveled country roads between his home in DeSoto, Texas, and the more rural routes.

As Pickard stepped into the ditch, Marshall instantly recognized his voice. "He was face down," Pickard said, "but he knew it was me. He said, 'Donnie, I hit a stick.' A stick. And he said, 'Donnie, get the ants off of me,' but there were no ants. I think it was something to do with the paralysis."

Later, at the hospital, they would discover that, in fact, there had been ants. Fire ants. Many of them. In Marshall's clothing. All over his body.

"It was really hot that day, I remember that," said Pickard. "There were three of us who went out on the call," he said of the 911 call. According to Pickard, Marshall was the consummate professional, even as he lay face down in the ditch. Ordinarily, Pickard might have stayed with the victim, explained to him what was happening. Instead, "Marshall knew exactly what was going on, so I was able to take care of landing the helicopter."

"We had to move him to a field where there were some horses. It was the only place we could get the helicopter to land." While Pickard and the local rancher opened the gates, caught the horses, and stalled them in the nearby barn, the others stayed with Marshall.

"Marshall had just come by the station," Pickard remembered as he watched Marshall life-flighted from the open field. What were the odds, he remembered thinking that a stick, a measly little stick, could take down such a mountain of a man?

Pickard was just one of dozens who would sit and ponder the what-ifs. What were the odds that his friends, the very men he would frequently stop to talk with at the Ovilla fire house, would be the same men to send him on his way to the Baylor Medical Center? Or that later, when he was in the hospital, a letter addressed to him would bring incredible happiness – a letter from a biological daughter he never knew existed. Today, many friends and family say that his daughter needed her daddy as much as he needed her.

After almost sixteen years, Talaya Jefferson had no idea Marshall even existed. One evening, for reasons known to no one, Talaya's mother, Patricia Norwood, called her into the kitchen to inform her that the man she was named after and believed to be her biological father was not. In truth, her real father was a man named Marshall Allen, a fire fighter in Fort Worth, Texas. Then, her mother went to bed and died during the night, leaving Talaya with the quest of finding her biological father.

That her mother would reveal this information before her death, Talaya believed, was an act of God. This was divine intervention. And –

miles away, as Marshall lay in the hospital bed, friends and family gathered around to pray, certain beyond any reasonable doubt that what happened to Marshall was an act of God.

Right after he prayed, right when he realized he had to live, help arrived. Only when he realized the true seriousness of his medical situation, that he would never walk again, did he learn that he had a daughter who had been looking for him. But Talaya had actually been looking for some time. Without either parent, she and her half-sisters lived with a relative of very modest means. At that point in her life, all she could do was write letters to daytime talk shows, hoping one would help her locate her father. It would not be until she was an adult, after Marshall's accident, that she would locate him.

But why, after fifteen years, did Talaya's mother suddenly reveal this secret to her daughter? Why did it take the letter so long to get to Marshall, arriving right when, some could argue, he needed her most? And how was it that Talaya would find her father when she needed him most?

Why? It is a word that has been asked again and again … but never by Marshall. Even as he crashed, he never asked 'why,' but instantly began analyzing everything. Admittedly, he was distracted and frustrated about the fried computer. Something as insignificant as a stick sent Marshall crashing head first into a ravine and wrought-iron fence. As his body made contact and folded over his feet, still locked into the pedals, fell unnaturally over his body.

"I saw my legs fall like water after being slung out of a bucket. By looking up toward my forehead, I could see my legs lying motionless still astride the bike. Instantly, I attempted to push myself on over, but my arms wouldn't move away from their position close to my handlebars.

"I had 23 years experience as an emergency medical technician. Countless car wrecks, falls, motorcycle accidents, and, yes, bicycle accidents, in addition to hundreds of hours of classroom work studying anatomy and physiology, as well as mechanism of injury, and reading and rereading 700-page EMT manuals for certification and promotional examinations left no doubt about my condition the instant it happened."

As he stared at his own legs and digested what had happened, Marshall, the consummate professional, came to grips with what was really going on.

"My first words were "No, God, no." But of course within a few seconds, I knew that this was in fact the case. I was paralyzed from the shoulders down.

"The good news was, as I quickly realized, I was able to breathe on my own. I attempted to scream for help a couple of times, but because of my restricted air and my diaphragmatic breathing, it wouldn't allow anything with any volume. Not to mention the fact that anyone close enough to hear me was close enough to walk by and see me in the ditch. I decided to save my breath.

"I don't remember how many options I considered, but within a few seconds, it was painfully evident that nothing I could dream up which even approached practical would be of any use. In fact, there was very little that I could dream up that I could actually do. And then, the cold reality of my situation came over me.

"My realization was this: I was on a lightly-traveled road in the country, just an hour or two away from dusk. No one knew exactly where I was since I had more than one route (and none of my family had ever gone with me). What little traffic was going by was looking ahead on this two-lane road and not down in the bar ditch. I began to accept the probability that I was going to lie there for as long as I could hold my airway open and then collapse, suffocate, die, and be ravaged by the small woodland creatures in the area until some construction worker widening the road tripped on one of the long bones of my skeleton.

"Several things went through my mind. After I had tried everything reasonably conceivable to no avail and acknowledged what was so likely to be the outcome, I simply gave up. I resigned myself to the fact that this was it. I realized that I had never known before this incident how my life would end, and I was disappointed, sad, and angry.

"I was disappointed because of all the things I could imagine that I would miss. The children developing, graduating, marrying, parenting. I knew I would never be promoted to Battalion Chief or even ride on a fire truck again. I thought about my coworkers and Big Al. I knew I would never see Mary again. Mary and I had had our moments, but I loved her.

"In the ensuing months after our wedding, one of the things that I considered over and over again was whether I wanted to die first, which would leave Mary with the suffering and loneliness, or if I wanted to go second, which would be such a cruel irony. There I would be, at the end of my life, having finally taken the plunge, as it were, and then this person would be snatched away from me, and I would spend the last period of my life the same way I started, alone without the one person who ever possibly cared about me.

"Things have a funny way of working out, and my dilemma had been solved for me.

"I was sad because I was leaving the only existence I knew. I was angry because I felt shortchanged. Between the things I had always intended to do and the things that I wanted to do but didn't because I thought they were too dangerous, I was missing out on quite a bit of excitement, learning, fulfillment, whatever you want to call it by falling off of my bicycle during a workout.

"I had always wanted to do three things but did not by using what I considered my better judgment. I always wanted to skydive -- what a rush that would be. I had always wanted a motorcycle (and came close twice). And I had always wanted to build and fly my own airplane. This last desire was something I had not given up on and was still considering perhaps after retirement.

"I say to you now, if you want to do something passionately, be safe, be careful, be reasonable, but do it before you trip over the ottoman in the front room and find yourself a quadriplegic.

"I thought about all the things I had done during my life, intentionally or accidentally, which were far more dangerous than the circumstances that placed me in this ditch. As a boy and young man, I found myself in several situations that could easily have been fatal. As a firefighter for 23 years, I found myself in several situations where the circumstances unexpectedly shifted and placed me in mortal danger or situations where I calculated the odds and the cost versus benefit and, then, rolled the dice.

"I decided that there was no point in delaying the inevitable. I decided that rather than listening to the animals chew my flesh, I would accelerate the process by relaxing my neck muscles and suffocating myself. I would accept my fate and face it like a man. I would make my father proud and complete the prognostication of the man who was possibly my namesake, Marshall (Doc) White.

"Marshall N. White was an African-American Ogden city detective and a friend of my parents. He was killed in the line of duty attempting to salvage the future of a young man who had made a terrible mistake, but had not yet passed the point of no return. Doc approached the youth and attempted to convince him to turn himself in. But, instead, the young man aimed what I recall to be a deer rifle in his direction and pulled the trigger.

"The good detective held on for several days, and what I actually remember was that apparently several white college students from Weber State College went to the hospital and donated their blood in an attempt to save his life. Remember that this was the late 1960s, and such a selfless interracial act was not the norm. My parents always made a big deal of that aspect of the incident. I specifically remember my mother saying things like, "Those white kids from the college lined up to put their blood in a black man's veins."

"And so I closed my eyes and said a prayer that I was taught as a boy in Catholic school, the act of contrition. I released the muscles on the back of my neck, which allowed my head to roll forward and my chin to rest just ahead of my left armpit (remember that my cervical vertebrae were disjointed), which completed the obstruction of my airway like crimping a garden hose. The airflow stopped, and I knew that this was it.

"Now the problem with committing suicide by strangulation (especially for someone in good physical condition) is that you have several minutes of completely lucid reflection. Obviously, I thought about a great many things in the next few minutes. All of the usual past, present, and future. I also thought about two things unique to myself. I thought about all the times when sitting around the station that we discussed or I heard other firefighters discussing what would happen if. If they got trapped. If they were mortally wounded. If they were so severely burned. If they were relegated to a vegetative state. And, of course, generally speaking, the macho thing to do was pull the plug.

"But I remember, vividly, always, thinking or saying if I spoke that whenever the Grim Reaper came for me there would be claw marks on the walls as I scratched and fought to hold on for one more day. I thought about how my peers would remember these brash statements and that my actions were so much less admirable and requisite of so little fortitude (any puss can pull a trigger, but few men can walk away).

"The other thing I thought about was that how even though I wasn't the most ardent Catholic, the ideals with which I had been inundated as a child were a part of me. One of those was the concept of mortal sin. It seemed contradictory that I would say a prayer before committing what I knew to be an irrevocable offense."

When he thought about family, friends, and the way he'd always led his life, Marshall said, "I knew that I had never given up on anything in my life. I knew I had never backed away from a fight. I knew that I had always been resilient. I knew long odds were nothing new to me, and the greater the obstacle to be overcome, the greater the sense of achievement. Basically, I decided that Marshall Allen could not go out like that. So I pushed.

"I attempted to push my nose right into the ground by rolling my head back. And with a little effort, I was able to push the weight of my body back a couple of inches to open my airway slightly. Ironically, I couldn't get my airway open as widely as had been the case prior to my little experiment, and I vividly remember thinking, 'No better for you, dumb ass. That'll teach you.'

"But I would breathe to the best of my ability as I would hold my throat open until the only muscles in my body that still had sensation (those in the back of my neck) screamed and begged for mercy. I decided that when I died (I still had no reason to believe I would be found), the look on my face would not be the passive expression of quiet subjugation but the grimace of a fighter throwing his most powerful punch. I wanted the world to know by looking on my face that my first words to the Grim Reaper were not 'I'm ready,' but 'F- you.'"

* * * *

Everyone knows where they were on September 11th. For Marshall, the irony would be that while Fort Worth had been so progressive to begin training its emergency responders for a possible terrorist attack and that while Marshall had had a foreboding about terror on American soil, he himself would be lying in a hospital bed, fighting for his life.

Following his accident, the wound to his neck was left open. "The staples came out," Marshall explained. For days, Mary had been complaining to the hospital staff that Marshall's pillow and the back of his head was soaked, but no one appeared to be concerned.

In fact, spinal fluid was leaking out. "I started having headaches," Marshall recalled, adding that if he lay on his right side, he could not hear out of his left ear. "My brain was lying against my skull."

When Mary finally saw the open, gaping wound – one that let her actually see his vertebrae, "she went ballistic." Marshall almost smiled. He was taken back into surgery to replace the staples, and it was during that time, they believe, that he contracted spinal meningitis. In his weakened state so soon after his initial accident, he was also placed on blood thinners and a variety of medications that left him weaker than ever. Several friends who had marveled that Marshall survived the first crash feared that meningitis might kill him. Again and again, his doctors and attending physicians would comment how his previous exercise and eating habits had most assuredly saved his life. But as strong as he was, he needed help.

As the nation grieved on September 11th and the days that followed, Talaya found her father. Slowly, with Al holding the phone against Marshall's ear, father and daughter began to talk. The world was spiraling out of control, and Al was a constant by Marshall's side.

Marshall may have been broken, but he was determined not to be defeated. So he dutifully began rehab. He tolerated the poking and prodding. It was not a physical violation, because he felt next to nothing, but it was an invasion of his personal being. Still, he endured it all with the hope of cell and nerve renewal, muscle growth, anything.

He stayed true to the rehab regimen. He was encouraged by the constant stream of firefighters visiting. And, of course, Al. Al was always there. One day, while Marshall was awaiting transport to rehab, Al met him outside. It was a beautiful day, and Al said something about missing being able to "run around together" with Marshall. Marshall didn't miss a beat.

"I said we could probably go, and as long as he brought me back, who would know?"

Without another word, Al doubled back to the parking lot, started up his beloved Monte Carlo SS, and brought it around to the front. He lifted his 300-pound friend out of his wheelchair, carefully placed Marshall into the car, tossed the chair into the back, and took off.

"We didn't say anything," Marshall said. "We just rode around."

It is a day that Marshall recalls fondly. Just to be away from the hospital, to drive around the city and see that, in fact, life had otherwise remained the same for the rest of the world, gave Marshall a tremendous and much needed sense of normalcy.

Normalcy had been completely redefined for Marshall. And, worse, the much hoped for expectations of recovery were beginning to fade.

Protecting God's Green Earth

Marshall was not alone in the sentiment. By 2001, there were a number of families who were dealing with the children (born in the year 2000) who had severe mental disabilities and/or handicaps. While these families have asked for anonymity in this book, it is fair to say that many began to label certain neighborhoods as "hot spots" where certain diseases or disabilities were more prevalent.

In May 2001, the administration was in bed with big industry and some of the nation's worst polluters. More and more pro-industry regulations were being set and, many times, unbeknownst to most Americans. For example, it was on New Year's Eve 2002, when the Bush Administration released a statement about weakening clean air standards. (3) By all accounts, everything seemed normal to those with good health. But in 2001 in Midlothian, it was an Erin Brokovich movie all over again.

More families were speaking out, but it was animals breeders and ranchers who first raised the red flag. Animals were dying prematurely, and top-notch bitches, mares, and heifers were giving birth to animals with severe birth defects.

Decades prior, Sue Pope moved to Midlothian with her husband, Ralph, on a gorgeous 70-acre farm and started breeding Arabian horses. Unbeknownst to the Popes, Holcim, mere miles from her home, had begun burning hazardous waste. Suddenly, her previously healthy Arabian horses developed a host of medical problems. They quit breeding, and when the mares did get pregnant, they delivered stillborns or badly deformed foals. Some developed cancer. Sue lost two-thirds of her lung function and developed primary immune deficiency, and Ralph got cancer.

Sue and a man named Jim Schermbeck founded an environmental group called Downwinders At Risk, and it was Sue's first taste of Texas politics. Despite her declining health and those of her neighbors, despite the personal testimonies of other people she had never known, TXI was able to double the amount of hazardous waste it could burn in the kilns. The small town of Midlothian was taking in hazardous waste from other states and other territories such as Puerto Rico that didn't want to burn these toxic chemicals in their own backyards.

By 2001, it was clear that Ellis County, the county in which Midlothian sits, had exceeded the ozone standards permitted, and a move was in place to see that the EPA note this and place Ellis County in a non-attainment status. Although environmentalists demanded a 50 percent reduction in dangerous emissions, they compromised to just 30 percent. But never was it more clear what an industry-friendly state Texas had become than when TXI and another cement plant sued. They claimed that stricter requirements would have meant their obsolete kilns must be replaced, an expense they couldn't afford. TXI further argued that if the state would let it burn an additional two to five million tires along with its already hazardous mix, it would install "new technology" that would reduce nitrogen oxide emissions by 30 percent or more. Still – and here's the rub – TXI didn't actually want to be held to this commitment by any kind of law. TXI claimed that it could meet the new standard voluntarily if the state would just kick in some funds to underwrite the technology.

Say what?!?

But this meant that TXI/Midlothian would only be the second cement plant in the country to combine tire burning with hazardous waste. No one – not scientists, doctors, environmentalists, cement plant workers, and everyday citizens – knew what the long-term ramifications of this would mean.

While cement manufacturers in Europe were using pollution reduction methods in their kilns, Texas plants were busily doing everything they could to get around those pesky expenses of pro-environment technology.

Holcim had applied for a new permit for more burning. Things were – no pun intended – heating up. Then came the pivotal moment. While combing through an open records request on the Holcim permit, Jim Schermbeck found a memo by Texas Natural Resource Commission employee Eddie Mack that detailed the state's prior knowledge of the advanced technology before it granted Holcim a permit that allowed the company to double its capacity.

The memo read: "We're going to be raked over the coals for this. This may mean that [Holcim] has to install state-of-the-art controls, since the technology they're using isn't getting close to their represented emission rates."

For years, Jim Schermbeck and his group had known that the cement plants had been bullying state agencies and getting away with far too much, but the memo was proof. It would be the beginning of a landmark lawsuit, but, at the time, all I knew was that Tommy, my little boy, was getting sick, and we couldn't figure out what was going on.

Chapter Four

Christmas 2002

Dear Friends and Family –

It's that time again – the world according to Robb. It's a dark and bleak place. For our newer friends, let me explain. Robb opposes holiday letters that spread cheer and happiness. He insists that people really want to hear bad news. I relented, no longer writing our joyous happenings, and now relay only the really crummy things that have happened to us so that, in comparison, yours might be a brighter and happier holiday. It is our gift to you.

I sprained my ankle in March chasing after Tommy when he was in his phase of breaking out of the house and running to the creek. It still hurts today. Katie got bucked off of our horse, Star, and still carries a scar on her back. We are lucky she was not trampled. Sosi (our lab mix) died, and, very recently, I discovered that Pete, our new black lab, has been eating Nala's incontinence pills. So, she's pee peeing in her sleep, and he's turning into a camel. Kerri caught me creeping into her room acting on behalf of the tooth fairy, and Tommy has discovered that if you spray enough Windex on something it turns blue. We are all finally recovering from some kind of horrible sickness that went around our small town. Tommy went to Emergency twice with pneumonia, and Robb was the most sick I have ever seen him since we've been together. But just one day after his fever broke, he wanted to go fishing. To test whether he could stomach a car and boat ride, he smeared a four-inch-thick layer of peanut butter on a pancake and chased it with a Dr. Pepper. He became ill – but still went fishing. He still hasn't really recovered. We all call him "Lunger." (Still, his non-vomit streak holds to 1991).

I got a phone call from a publishing house that wanted a book about out of control puppies. I agreed to do this, but it occurred to me that I needed an out of control puppy. Robb opposed this idea. That was how we got Pete. He sleeps on Robb's side of the bed.

I wanted a horse to ride in our corral; Robb wanted to use it to ride his dirt bike. I found a horse named Star. Star has been with us for about six months now. He is so cool. But he seemed a little lonely, so he came to us with one of his goat friends. I thought it would be a good idea to get another goat. While Robb opposed this idea, we let him name the goats as he is a pretty good animal name giver. Their names are Zipper and Cookiedough. Cookie is pregnant, so we should have one or two little kids running around soon enough. We also have a barn cat and two guinea pigs. Robb made me swear to no more animals. I'm thinking a pony will be good for the spring.

Two different neighbors have been robbed while I was home. The neighbors are thinking about starting up a Neighborhood Watch, but I don't think I'm invited.

Zipper rammed Kerri in the tummy, and now she won't go into the corral alone. Star bit Cookie on the rear end, and she turned around and hooked him in the eye with her horn. It was a bloody mess. Just try to find a veterinarian who makes house calls on a Sunday in the Bible belt. Then, two weeks later, Star was down with colic. I learned how to use a twitch stick and put a tube down a horse's neck filled with mineral oil. Star is clean as a whistle. Inside and out.

Nala and Pete caught a skunk. Before I realized what happened, they were all over me. I had to give them three baths *each* with De-Skunk shampoo and a tomato bath. They still stunk. I managed to inhale some of it and then had to go teach kickboxing. It was okay until I started to sweat. I kept asking everyone if they could smell me. Initially, they'd said 'no,' but as I began to move around, I was politely asked to stop doing so and instruct from the other side of the room.

Tommy knocked over a display of videos in the grocery store when he took off with the grocery cart and rammed it. He thinks he's a goat.

Our trip to Yellowstone and the Allred family reunion were combined. The sites were amazing; seeing family was great. But Robb determined that we could save a bundle of money if all we ate were sandwiches from a cooler. For 10 days, 3 times a day, all we ate was bologna. Katie actually started crying at one point when she thought she was going to have to eat another sandwich. It was then that Robb picked up his current favorite phrase, "We're not the Rockefellers," because I finally had enough and tried to buy something other than a sandwich at a gas station. Yet on the way home, he stopped and bought himself some jerky. ("This is the good stuff, Alex!") Seven dollars for a tiny bag of "good stuff." That little pit stop cost him a steak dinner for me and chicken fingers for the kiddos at the very next restaurant. Six months later, Katie still won't eat a sandwich.

I got a bunch of beautiful candles but can't ever keep them lit because Robb doesn't like candles and blows them out then plays with the wax. I swear, he's worse than Tommy. He won't eat at Chili's or Olive Garden or the International House of Pancakes because their commercials are wayyyyy too happy. Also, he has a severe distrust of men with beards and couches with floral print.

I got such a bad case of poison oak I had to get two steroid injections, and my right arm still has scars. It was three weeks of agony. But in the throws of my discomfort, I was able to rethink the entire U.S. prison system. As I lay awake at night in extreme agony, I realized this is what we should be doing to our worst prisoners—roll them in poison oak, turn up the heat, and offer no comfort. Then, years later, as a repeat offender is being chased down by cops and finally cornered, instead of cuffing him, a big baggie of poison oak and sumac shall be pulled out and smeared all over his face. *Take that!*

Robb hooked Pat (Robb's brother) in the back while fishing, and the two still carry the belief that if they go off fishing for eight hours but it really only feels like an hour then, by golly, it is just about an hour.

Pat is really no different from his brother and has been involved in a series of events at work he and his buddies call "Feats of Strength." This involves contests between those who can grow the most facial hair, shock each other with electric prods, or hold up 20 pound weights for extended periods of time. Pat has put his tongue on a 16-volt battery and gorged himself all in the name of becoming "Feats of Strength Master." Robb isn't much better. He's trying to bring back the Box Hat –a look that immediately drops his IQ 20 points, causing small children to stare and women to snicker.

Potty training Tommy was no fun, Pete keeps bringing me dead snakes, and we've had a large coyote stalking around our property – I think he wants my goats. It is very distressing. I've tried to convince Robb that he needs to run around and urinate on all the trees near the barn to ward off any coyotes.

Finally, I am being sued by a kid on a motorcycle who had no motorcycle license, didn't own the bike, wasn't wearing a helmet, lied to the cop, was actually ticketed for the accident, has four witnesses who are testifying AGAINST him, and has a prior record of assaulting a police officer and disorderly conduct. Ah, the U.S. legal system at work!

I'd like to tell you that we love Midlothian, my dad and uncle built an awesome barn for Star and the goats, and that things are great, but that would break from tradition. Let's just leave it at this: Have a better year than we had!

Love,

Alex

The Unconquerable Marshall Allen
…and his rise to the top

Beyond being born on May 14, 1957, in Arizona, Marshall doesn't really know much about his birth or his birth parents. He was told that his mother was very young and very white. Based on information provided by the person he considers to be his real mother, Obelia Allen, it seems that both parents were in college and that Marshall's biological father, an African-American, was a basketball player. Historically, the big jock on campus could always get the pretty girls. In looking at Marshall, this scenario is quite plausible.

At birth, he was immediately given to the Children's Aid Society, a Catholic adoption agency, and within a year (though no exact dates are known) was adopted by a nice white family that was under the impression that Marshall was white. Whether it was because the Catholic Church believed he was white or because he was so light-skinned that his birth mother listed him as a Caucasian baby, we'll never know. What is known, however, is that as soon as the adoptive family determined Marshall was black or, at least, not all white, they returned him. Marshall would be returned a second time by a second white family for presumably the same reason. Interestingly, some 41 years later, Marshall made the trek back to Ogden with his wife, Mary, to the Children's Aid Society. His "file," he discovered, was upstairs in a backroom, and although he was not allowed to physically touch it, he was allowed to ask questions. Unfortunately, the only question the worker was permitted to answer was the reason that he was returned by the adoptive family: "Couldn't afford." Sometime after his return, he was sent to a foster home in the southern Utah area.

What bigger event in life can there be than one's own birth? For that very reason, we love to hear the details of it and hang on every word as gospel, probably making much more of the event than it really was. My own children like to have me retell the hours, even days leading up to their births.

On a personal note, I can say that I had three men sign in to claim me at the hospital's maternity ward on the day I was born. It turned into a family joke: Alex had three fathers. In truth, my father was away on military temporary duty (TDY), so when I was born in the US Army's 77th General Hospital in Frankfurt, Germany, two other men – Col. "Uncle Scotty" Wilson and, ironically enough, my Godfather Felix Henderson – signed in so that my mother would have visitors to offer congratulations and hugs. Moreover, they could report back to my daddy about our status.

Marshall Allen has no such jokes. He didn't have people lining up to claim him; instead, people kept returning him. His adoptive father,

Morris Allen, a man for whom he holds the greatest respect, did not even meet Marshall until he was adopted at the age of two years.

Prior to that, the details are sketchy. The family who first fostered Marshall (after he had already been returned by the adoptive family) was clearly interested in the monetary benefits, not the child. That fact was demonstrated by a police report of a call to the local authorities from a neighbor who was distressed by a child's crying. She explained that while she frequently heard crying, she never saw a child.

A sheriff's deputy discovered Marshall, unwanted and locked away in a closet, filthy and feeding on a bag of Oreo cookies. The year was 1959.

For several years prior to that, Obelia Allen had prayed and prayed for a child. In fact, she had been praying for years. Unable to have children of their own, both Obelia and Morris were delighted when they received a phone call that an infant (six weeks old) boy was in need of a home. Named after his new father, Morris Allen, Junior came home and lived as an only child until another call came. While the Allens were pleased to have Morris, Obelia had made a pact with God. "She told me on several occasions that as they were looking for a child she promised God to take whatever child he sent her way no matter what was wrong with him. And, as a result, she took me when no one else wanted me."

As it turned out, the caseworker who rescued Marshall from his foster family had also been the caseworker for Morris Allen, Jr. Not sure of what else to do, she placed a phone call to Obelia and, as Obelia saw it, it was not her place to say 'no.' It was two days before Marshall's second birthday when he became an Allen. Suddenly, he had a mother, a father, and a little brother.

He grew up in Ogden, Utah, in a modest home with his mother, father, and brother. They were black Catholics living in white Mormon country in the 1950s. Not surprisingly, young Marshall began to form very strong opinions of the world.

"I don't know when I was christened a Catholic, but I do know that my adoption was handled by a Catholic organization," Marshall recalled. "As a consequence, my parents converted to Catholicism, and I attended parochial schools.

"Growing up in the Catholic Church and a Catholic school, I was given no choice but to acknowledge Christianity as a fact of life. Most of the prayers I was taught as a child were completely cryptic to me until I became a man and really considered the words.

"There was one aspect of Christianity, however, which I simply could not accept because I was living the contradiction daily. I didn't know if it was an outright lie, or someone's oversight, or if I was some sort of freaky exception to the rule, but I did know for sure that God did not love me equally with all his other subjects. And since God didn't love me equally, this explained why his mortal lieutenants were so cruel either actively or passively."

Early in his education, Marshall discovered the different ways in which students were treated, often based on skin color and economic status. In truth, there was no way his parents could have afforded the cost of sending their two sons to a private Catholic school. But the family was fortunate to have a sponsor who allowed the Allen boys a better, more formal education.

"I really believe it was Dorothy Browning," Marshall said. To the young Marshall, she was an old woman who had taken an interest in the Allen family. Dorothy Browning was the presumed descendent of John Moses Browning, the son of Jonathan Browning, creator of a family of innovative military rifles and a member of the Church of Jesus Christ of Latter Day Saints. But all Marshall knew of her was that "she always drove a Cadillac. She also thought my father hung the moon."

In the early 1960s, Morris Allen detailed vehicles, and Ms. Browning was a client. But she was much more. She was a guardian angel, a Santa Claus, and an unseen champion behind Marshall's early successes. For example, one day when the Allen boys were very young, two bikes mysteriously appeared at their front step. In their early teens, two more bikes appeared along with miscellaneous gifts and, of course, their sponsorships to a private school. As long as Dorothy Browning was alive, gifts and academic sponsorship continued.

"When she died," Marshall said, "so did everything else."

Dorothy Browning was one of the few adults and certainly one of the few white adults Marshall could trust and like.

For the remainder of his academic career in Utah, Marshall was labeled a troublemaker. Although it was Marshall who was repeatedly protecting himself against groups of white boys and despite the fact that adults outside the school found him to be polite and courteous, Marshall would continue to have "problems" with school officials and fellow white students.

To have priests and nuns repeatedly judge and mistreat him put a certain damper on his own feelings about religion. "I knew that God was not in every person, and I saw that God was in very few, including those who professed Jesus' teachings most ardently. I experienced individual abuse, like being slapped so hard by one of the nuns that in the time it took me to walk home her handprint was still plainly visible on the right side of my face.

"By the time I was in my 20s, I went to church occasionally for various reasons, but it wasn't to profess my unquestioning faith in God. I had seen so many terrible things happen to so many people, including myself, through no fault of their own, and over which they had absolutely no control, that by the time I was even in my mid-20s, I concluded that no other human being could tell me anything about the world.

"I never got to the point where I was convinced that there simply was no God, but I did get to the point that I felt like I knew as much or more about the reality of life as anyone in a pulpit. As I grew older, I knew for sure that I had helped to save more lives, bring more lives into the world, and watched more lives slip away than any of the men and women preaching to me. I never told anyone that I was an atheist although, like many people, I defined myself as an agnostic. Some, who didn't know the difference, probably defined me as atheist. As I saw it, by acknowledging the possibility, I considered the probability but saw no proof." Not yet.

Marshall wanted to blend in, be normal, and be accepted. But as he grew, more confrontations would arise. Some, he readily admits, he instigated. Most, in his view, were born out of ignorance, prejudice, and intolerance on the part of others. He was young, yet already he viewed his elders with suspicion.

But almost 30 years later, Marshall was sitting at Station 17, reading about the Hubble Spacecraft and pondering the vastness of the universe. Suddenly, just days before his crash, he was reconsidering our world, our Creator, and our existence.

"What I could not have foreseen was the unfolding of a series of events beginning with a catastrophic accident that would lead to my acceptance of the unseen based upon blind faith in the inexplicable."

When he crashed, he prayed.

For Marshall, the man who was always in control and who was suddenly paralyzed, the years 2001 and 2002 would be about faith, friendships, and an indomitable spirit that even he did not know he possessed.

Prior to his accident, Marshall slowly became a vegetarian. The once calorie-consuming, ravenous carnivore decided meat – particularly beef – was too difficult for the system to digest. (This would certainly be true once he was paralyzed). And even more mind boggling was how, when, and why he began dabbling with voice-activated computer software.

From the moment he became a fire fighter, Marshall had found his calling. He even enjoyed the shifts no one else did. He liked being a swingman, a position in which a fire fighter, typically a new recruit, works at whatever station needs a body. While most recruits hope to "find a home," Marshall enjoyed rotating around the city. He liked working the ambulance shift.

In fact, it was one of his first ambulance runs in Utah that made a very deep impression on the then 21-year-old firefighter/EMT. The call was to an unusual address, an isolated stretch of highway outside Salt Lake County. Marshall and his partner, Richard Black, found a young woman standing alone with her toddler daughter. A domestic dispute had resulted in the young woman and child being dumped on the side of the highway by the husband/father.

"At some point, things became violent, and her husband pulled over and put them out. In the dark. In the field. I don't recall how we were summoned, but obviously someone saw her and made the phone call. The mother had some minor injuries on her face but was in fairly good shape. The little girl was physically unharmed but obviously traumatized and worried about her mother."

As Marshall's partner began his evaluation of the mother, Marshall reached out for the little girl. To his surprise, the girl hurried into his arms, laying her head on his shoulder. During the ride to the hospital, the little girl clung to Marshall.

"By clinging to me in her hour of need," Marshall shared, "she made me feel like the king of the jungle." It was a scenario that would play out many times in his mind as the years passed. He was a protector. But on this fateful day, Marshall was startled to discover how emotionally difficult it was to release the little girl from his arms once they arrived at the hospital.

"To disconnect physically from the only person who had ever needed me up to that point in my life was difficult. As one of the nurses pried her away from me, I was transformed from the king of the jungle to a lukewarm dish rag. It was all I could do to keep my face straight and my eyes dry until I could get back to the safety of the darkness.

"I didn't know when or where another human being would need me again, but I did know that if being a firefighter had anything to do with it, I would be there."

His accident and paralysis were not going to stop that. Ever.

In his bed, paralyzed, Marshall considered consulting Eddie Burns, then a deputy chief with the Fort Worth fire department.

"I was talking to Eddie and said something along the lines of, 'Is there any way I could come back to work?' I was thinking about my sense of worth, my identity. That was a large part of who I was and, all the sudden, I was looking at not having a job, not being a firefighter."

Marshall understood and operated voice-activated computer software, and Marshall had a job.

In January 2002, almost six months after the accident, Marshall began working as a fire inspector for the department.

"It was typical of Marshall," Kent Worley, a captain with the Fort Worth fire department recalled with a laugh. "When he was in the hospital, he was making us feel better! We'd feel sad coming in, but when we left, we were laughing with him. That's just how he was. And is. I'm not sure I would have had the gumption to go ahead, but he never complained. He'd tell us that he was coming back. You know ... we weren't so sure. Then, here comes Marshall. He showed us, became a state certified fire inspector, and was working again."

Marshall's success is a testament not only to his incredible strength of will and positive nature but also to the Fort Worth fire department. Firefighters, many of whom had second careers as contractors or home builders, came in droves to redesign Marshall's house, ripping up the carpeting to replace it with hardwood floors, creating wheelchair ramps, widening narrow doorways, and creating a chair-friendly bathroom. But during this time, before Marshall had his customized chair, it was Al who picked Marshall up every morning – literally – and took him to different locations. In part, it was a job that very few other men could handle alone because it required lifting a 300-pound man in and out of a car throughout the day. But it was also a job that no one else would dare ask for. Marshall and Al were a team. They were and are brothers.

"I always say," said Marshall, "Al's closer to me than my real brother."

Although Morris Jr. was adopted before Marshall, he was the younger brother and, as a result, was given preferential treatment. At least, this was Marshall's initial belief. But by the time Marshall was about six or seven years old, he began to realize something was wrong with his brother.

At a very tender age, Marshall saw a despairing difference not only in the way they were raised but also in the expectations their parents had for each of them.

The rules in Marshall's young life were simple: he was not to let anyone bother or pick on Morris Jr. Nor was he allowed to upset Morris

Jr. Despite years of abuse by Morris Jr., Marshall could never retaliate. In later years, Morris Jr. would be arrested for assaulting a police officer and again on murder charges. Though Morris married and had a son, drugs continued to plague him. Eventually, time and patience eroded the already tumultuous relationship, and Marshall lost contact with one brother only to find another – Al Jones.

But, once more, Marshall would have to test himself as top dog.

He had relocated to Fort Worth, Texas, and had been accepted into the fire academy along with 20 other men. In keeping with the tradition of the fire department, tom foolery and hi-jinx were par for the course. Each time the instructor stepped out of the classroom, grown men became children. Their favorite game was to take the bandages used to teach first-response and first-aid, wind them tightly into softball-sized missiles, turn off the light to the classroom, and beam the missiles at each other. Massive bruising and raucous laughter ensued. The rules were simply that there were no rules. Only Al Jones appeared to be off limits because, really, what man was going to hit a 6'5," 240 pound man who clearly didn't want to be hit? Who but Marshall?

With great precision, Marshall hurled the bandage ball, and there was a collective gasp as it nailed Al in the chest and dropped to the floor. For a moment, the two men just stared at each other. Then Al crooked a finger at Marshall, beckoning him to come closer.

"What? Am I not a man?" Marshall recalled thinking. Though he had not yet begun training as a powerlifter, Marshall was still a very large man and one who was not used to being challenged. He stepped forward.

"He picked me up and body slammed me down on a table," Marshall said. "We've been friends ever since."

In 2002, Marshall and Al were driving around downtown Fort Worth, making fire inspections. Marshall was paralyzed, awaiting the battery-operated wheelchair and custom van and driving lessons that would allow him to drive himself, so he depended on Al to drive him to the various locations around the city until then. Marshall maintained his position within the department, and Al was selected to be his escort for no other reason than he was probably the only other man who could have physically picked up and manually transferred the 300-pound Marshall from car to wheelchair and back again.

It is an afternoon that Marshall can remember with great detail. As he and Al made the rounds, Marshall suddenly became aware of a problem. He had an accident and though he could feel nothing, there was no missing the smell. Instantly, Al was on the phone trying to solicit help, including a pit stop to one of the stations. There, some fire fighters saw

Marshall and hurried forward. Unaware of what had happened, they just wanted to see their old captain. "But it was pretty obvious," Marshall said, noting that the men politely acted as if they were completely oblivious to the situation.

The minutes stretched on and on until Al decided to drive back to Marshall's house and take care of matters himself. It was, Marshall said, a quiet ride home. But as they stopped at a light, both men trying to act as though nothing were unusual, Al pointed toward a building. "Say, man," he began, asking about what kind of fire code regulation would be required for the particular structure.

Without hesitation, Marshall rattled off various codes and the protocol required for making such restrictions. When he was done, Al nodded thoughtfully, and Marshall returned to his reality after this momentary respite and added, "Pretty smart for a man sitting in his own shit, huh?" With that, he turned away, once again fighting the depression that had been with him since his teenage years but now, since July 2, 2001, had only deepened.

Protecting God's Green Earth

In Midlothian, the unthinkable was occurring. State law permitted our biggest polluters to self-report and self-regulate. The EPA and TCEQ (Texas Commission on Environmental Quality) were not winning the confidence of concerned citizens who were watching more and more questionable permits assigned to the cement plants and steel mill in Midlothian.

There were growing concerns that the air monitors set in place in and around Midlothian were turned off and on around burning schedules. Rumors swirled that the cement plants were given a heads up when inspectors would roll into town, allowing the cement heads to make adjustments for the inspectors' visit.

When interviewed in the Fort Worth Weekly in 2002, former mayor of Midlothian Maurice Osborne, who would go on to manage communications and government affairs for TXI, rebuked any adverse affects TXI or hazardous waste burning could have on the general public. "I've told Sue [Pope] and others to bring me proof, scientific or medical proof, to substantiate such claims, and I'll be the one to lead their cause. But no one yet has come forward with any proof that this cement plant is the cause of their health problems." It was an effective argument given again and again and again. With an industry-friendly legal system, state agencies falling on the side of industry, scientists actively ignoring science, and state politicians supporting hazardous waste burning, it seemed as though no real data was being collected, much less analyzed.

It was easy, then, for Osborne to simply identify the cedar trees and allergies as the culprit of upper respiratory problems, pointing out that his own family was healthy (4).

In my own journal where I fastidiously recorded everything about my children, their cute little sayings, the goofy things they did, I also recorded every conversation I had about Tommy's health. I repeatedly questioned Tommy's doctors about his health without answers. No one knew what was wrong with him or why he was continuing to get bronchitis and pneumonia. In fact, I did not yet understand how wide spread upper respiratory diseases were, how many children were disabled, or that a certain neighborhood had been labeled a 'hot bed' for leukemia, brain tumors, and chromosome abnormalities.

I didn't know that a lawsuit against one of the cement plants was in the making. I had no idea that history was in the making, nor did I know that one of my best buddies, Gina Bates, grew up in Lawrence, Kansas – the same small town as Erin Brokovich – or that they, too, had once been run-around buddies. It was just another crazy coincidence that was about to morph into something huge.

What I did know was this: I liked Midlothian. The people are warm, sincere, and family oriented. We were making friends with many who worked in the local industries. Our new friends and neighbors were (and are) actively involved in sports, church functions, and community gatherings. By all accounts, it was a great place to raise a family. And for me, an Army brat who had lived in 18 different places while growing up and never knew the feeling of living in a home town, this was home.

Chapter Five
Marshall's Family

Marshall's journey to becoming a firefighter, like so many of the roads he's traveled, did not come from planning, but rather from chance. Before he would find his calling, he would also become a boxer, a bouncer, a model, and a movie extra.

It began with schoolyard fights. One such fight occurred when Marshall was in the eighth grade. Typically, he and his brother, Morris, would walk home after school, but one day, Marshall was pleasantly surprised to see his mother sitting outside the school.

Hoping to secure the front seat before Morris, Marshall broke into "a dead run" and jumped into the front seat. As they waited for Morris, two or three of Marshall's classmates and football teammates approached the car, telling him that the football coach wanted to speak to him. While Marshall was loath to give up his position in the car, and told his teammates "I'll talk to him tomorrow," his mother, knowing that they had to wait for his little brother and completely unaware of the coach's real motives, instructed him "to go see what the man" wanted. Marshall obliged and walked right into an ambush; waiting around the corner of the schoolhouse, out of his mother's view, a group of boys waited to beat him.

Instead, Marshall held the advantage against the group of boys, and as his "friend," classmate, and teammate led him around the corner to allegedly meet with the coach, his yet untrained fighter instincts kicked in. Some thirty years later, as he lay in a ditch, it was he who offered advice and instructions to the on-call firefighters. "Even in the most dire situations," Marshall said, "I have found that I'm able to slow my thought process down and see clearly and, more importantly, think clearly." In a scenario that would play out again and again in his life, Marshall felt time compress as even the most harrowing events suddenly moved in slow motion. Such was the case with the fight against the ambushing boys.

"I saw something to my right in my peripheral vision close to my head and instinctively ducked. I saw every punch coming." In turn, he unleashed a fury of his own until all the boys backed off, leaving Marshall to stand toe-to-toe with none other than the coach's son. It was a fight that would continue until it had wound itself back in front of the school with a gathering of mostly students (except for the football coach standing nearby with his arms crossed). In the midst of the fight, Marshall had not noticed, because he was busy, that the school principal, "a Sacred Heart nun," stood at the second floor window of the school, watching the affair.

Also in attendance was the coach who had remained still as long as his son appeared to be in control of the fight. But as the fight turned and Marshall took control, two things happened. The coach stepped forward but not before Obelia Allen had stormed across the schoolyard and jerked her son off of his feet.

She was one of six children, essentially taking over the domestic duties when her mother died when Obelia was just nine-years-old. Her father was a hard "religious zealot," preaching the Gospel during the Great Depression and the Jim Crow era in the deep South. By the 1960s, she continued to harbor great distrust of white people, but she would not stand by to watch her boy be beaten while white adults looked on. It would be one of the first and last times in Marshall's young life that he could recall his mother "standing up" for him.

Placing Marshall behind her back, she turned on the coach and poked a finger into his chest, demanding to know why it was he would allow boys to "fight like dogs." But the coach appeared unfazed and, pointing toward the second-story window, stated that he had the Principal's Blessing on this.

Momentarily speechless, Obelia made the coach a promise. When she got home, she told him, she would tell her husband of this incident, and "you'll need any blessing you can get."

The next day, Marshall and Morris, Jr., did not go to school.

"I assumed that they were afraid for my safety and would keep me at home for a few days until things cooled off, but that afternoon my father did something that he only did two or three times in my entire childhood. He came home early." When Marshall saw that his parents had put on their church clothes, "I knew that my parents were going to the school." Marshall and Morris, Jr., went with them.

It was a well-orchestrated he-said-she-said between the principal, the coach, and Obelia Allen as the Monsignor listened intently. In the end, it was the Monsignor who offered the suggestion that Marshall take boxing classes. As a child, he offered, he had also been picked on and learned to defend himself. But for Morris, Sr., no amount of training could prepare Marshall against an ambush from multiple assailants. For this reason, Morris, Sr., had major concerns, and he expressed them to the Monsignor.

It was a rare moment for the Allen boys as Morris, Sr., shared personal information about his own upbringing. Unlike the white Monsignor, Morris didn't get private boxing instruction but learned his craft at 16 when he lied about his age to get into the Civilian Conservation Corps "with other unemployed sharecroppers who were desperate to make some sort of honest living." Instead, he would fight for monthly stipends, giving little to no consideration about the opponent's size or strength. He never lost a match.

The Monsignor interrupted. "Do you have a point?"

"Yes. If I ever hear of anything like this happening again to one of my boys, I will be back, and you and I will meet on that same parking lot, and I will stomp your guts."

With that, both Morris and Obelia stood in unison. They had said what they had come to say.

"For the second time in my life," Marshall said, "I felt important to my parents. I felt like they actually did love me in their rough sort of way."

Still, by the age of 14, Marshall understood that there was a double standard with the good Sisters at St. Joseph's Elementary School. Under the guise of religion, any treatment of a child could be justified. As a minority, and one who was there only through sponsorship, his support system was supposed to come from the educators, but all too often, they failed him.

He knew that he was adopted and that it was only because of a bargain Obelia had made with God that he had become an Allen. He knew that his brother, Morris, Jr., was favored, though he did not quite understand why. But, most importantly, he learned not to question his role within the family structure. A quiet anger began to grow inside of him. On that day, however, it had been enough that his parents had dressed in their finest, arranged a meeting with the school officials and made a stand for Marshall.

A few days after that meeting, Marshall was kicked off the football team and told to turn in his uniform.

In 1972, after Dorothy Browning died, the Allen boys went to public school and there, for the first time, Marshall felt asense of camaraderie among fellow students. Quite unconsciously, Marshall found other black students. Or, they found him. While most of the skirmishes between Marshall and his new friends and other members (mostly white) of the student body were minor, his reputation as being one of the "rough boys" grew.

Going into his junior year, Marshall got a surprise when he and his friends entered the basketball gym for regular practice. His old football coach from St. Joseph's was standing in the gym with his son, the very kid who had ambushed Marshall. They were in the process of entering the public school system and had ideas of Junior trying out for the Ogden High School basketball team.

At the age of 16, Marshall had grown several inches and stood at six feet. He'd begun boxing, put on weight, and -- newly armed with his "rough boy" friends - had an arrogance that his old coach was unfamiliar with. But there was something else. It was what the coach could not see. The quiet dissatisfaction that he'd known to be in Marshall as a boy had grown into a smoldering fury as a young man. So when the coach turned to Marshall and said, "Allen, you probably don't remember me," he could not have known the response he was to receive.

"I told him, 'Yes, I remember you, Coach, and I should still be pulling my foot out of your ass.'"

The gym erupted into adolescent taunts and laughter as Marshall strode onto the bleachers and calmly pulled on and laced up his basketball shoes. It was his first act of outright defiance, but beneath the bravado, there was something else that only years later Marshall could articulate. The rage was brewing.

As Marshall walked by him, before climbing the bleachers to be with his friends, he had a perfect picture in his mind. It was as clear as any picture he might see on a movie screen. "I fantasized about cutting his throat and standing over him as he begged for mercy and bled to death."

Junior did not make the basketball team.

By 1978, life had changed considerably for Marshall. He graduated from high school and found a release for his power and temper in the sport of boxing. Throughout high school, he had taken local instruction from a man named Linnard Holsten who would unwittingly play in an instrumental role in Marshall's adult life. But it would be Chappy Hyashi, a 73-year-old Hawaiian-born Japanese gentleman who trained Marshall in the "sweet science" as they headed for the Olympic Training Center in Colorado Springs, Colorado.

Chappy Hyashi, a retired lightweight, had begun volunteering his time to young men in Salt Lake City when he discovered Marshall Allen – a raw, high-energy, intelligent youth who, under the guidance of Linnard Holsten, had only recently begun to channel his aggression and understand his potential.

When Marshall moved from Ogden to Salt Lake City, Marshall changed boxing clubs and began to fight under the direction of Chappy. Between such positive role models and excellent coaches, Marshall began to thrive. He won bout after bout, slowly earning a reputation among both fighters and coaches.

One of greatest challenges came when Marshall was to fight a giant Tongan at the Utah State Fair. The first time Marshall laid eyes on the Tongan, he voiced concern to his coach. But Mr. Holsten said, "That's okay, Mr. Allen, he puts his pants on just like you do."

To the still-developing Marshall, however, there was no comparison. "Yes, but he wears much bigger pants than I do!"

In the ring, the Tongan was the first to strike. "He hit me in the hip so hard," Marshall recalled, "that I said if he does that shit again, I quit!" But under Mr. Holsten's steady guidance, Marshall ultimately won the decision and won his first serious battle.

Together, the two went to Colorado Springs with the hopes of making the U.S. National team.

Neither could know that in another year (December, 1979), Russia would invade Afghanistan, causing the U.S. to boycott the 1980 Olympics held in Moscow, Russia. It was a devastating blow to the U.S. athletes who had fought so hard to make the national teams. But Marshall would never know this disappointment.

Since graduation, Marshall had been working at the Mountain Fuel Supply Company, reading gas meters while he trained with Mr. Holsten, but he was on a temporary leave of absence for his trip to Colorado Springs. On the morning of the final day of the regional boxing tournament championship at the Olympic Training Center, Marshall had other things on his mind. He was to face off against Al "the butcher" Salamanca, another large fighter with an even bigger reputation

"I was in the lobby of the hotel getting some last-minute pointers from a boxing coach from Oakland." Marshall said. Although Marshall had previously knocked out some of the coach's athletes, the man was happy to discuss strategy with Marshall as to how to take on The Butcher. It is a testament to Marshall's character that even one-time adversaries are compelled to engage with him.

While they talked, other men had entered the hotel to discuss Marshall Allen: Chic Paris, a fire chief for Salt Lake County, Utah, and Tony Montoya, the director of the Police Athletic League team in Salt Lake City.

"I don't know what conversations he had with Chappy," Marshall said of Chic, but all three men had discussed the young athlete's potential as a fire fighter. Without warning, Chappy approached Marshall while he ate breakfast. "He came over to my table, leaning over my plate and asked me in no uncertain terms, 'You want to be fireman? I make you fireman!' But given the fact that Chappy was given to blurting statements that made absolutely no sense to any of us [fighters] and the fact that I was mulling over the prospect of fighting Al "the butcher," I pretty much blew Chappy off with something like, 'Yes, sounds great.'"

Marshall knocked The Butcher out in the second round but would be beaten in a decision match in Biloxi, ultimately ending his run for a national title. But fate had other ideas and on the very day that Marshall was to fight The Butcher, he was approached by a large, well-dressed, well-groomed white man. Charles "Chic" Paris stuck out a hand and said, "I understand you want to be a fire fighter."

Marshall enjoyed boxing and would continue to fight throughout the years, but at that time, it was an unsteady, uncertain profession, and Marshall was looking for something he could rely on. While he loved the physical and mental demands of boxing, the prospect of becoming a firefighter was too thrilling to turn away.

Subsequently, while Marshall turned his attention to the new and exciting prospect of firefighting, a fresh batch of U.S. boxing hopefuls traveled to Moscow, Russia, in early 1979, months prior to the Afghanistan invasion. Ironically enough, it was the same time I was living in Moscow. As the daughter of a U.S. Defense Attaché, I lived in a country that suffered at the hands of communist rule. As an American youth, living without television (beyond Russian propaganda and soap operas), shopping malls, movie theaters, fast food, and anything else Americana was difficult.

The U.S. boxers gave the small American community something to cheer about and broke up the monotony of sunless skies and frigid temperatures. As one who still holds dearly the memory of the boxers coming to Russia, I marvel at the possibility that I almost met Marshall in 1979.

(The U.S. Hockey team, the very team what would do the unthinkable at the 1980 Lake Placid Olympic Games by beating the Soviets, also came to visit that year. Both visits from the boxers and hockey players resulted in a rare dinner for the Americans living in Moscow. We dined on steak!)

Marshall, meantime, had returned to Ogden to Mountain Fuel Supply and decided to become a fire fighter. Never had he wanted something so much. Although he'd never considered the profession of fire fighting, suddenly it was the most important thing in the world. He began calling on the chief again and again.

"I was naïve regarding the government structures and politics. I thought that I was applying for and being hired to a specific fire department. My mother and father had always taught me that when you were interested in a position, you had a responsibility to make the hiring party know how interested you were in the job. You did this by regularly checking in with that person so they knew that you had not lost interest. With so much at stake, this meant that I should call on the fire chief daily to see if my paperwork was in the process."

He drove everyone crazy. He would return from reading meters and, at every opportunity, would run up to the office to use the phone to call the chief. He would drive to Salt Lake City when he could and continuously made both his name and face available to fire department personnel.

"By the time I finally quit my job at Mountain Fuel Supply in anticipation of being hired on the Salt Lake County fire department, the office staff knew my voice on the telephone, and they knew that I was definitely interested in the job."

He relocated, moving to Salt Lake County to live with his Uncle Bob and Aunt Babe. He would walk some 40 blocks to the main fire station, which housed the administrative offices for the Salt Lake County fire department and none other than Chic Paris.

He pawned all his belongings, including his beloved 35 mm camera. He was, among other things, a budding photographer, but as time wore on, he needed money to sustain himself.

Before leaving the Ogden, Marshall had also worked part-time as a bouncer at a local nightclub. There, he was extremely popular for both his size but also for his following with the women. Months prior, a coworker had mentioned that Marshall should seek work with a talent agency. It was a remark he had quickly dismissed, but suddenly unemployed and living off of the kindness of his aunt and uncle – something he did not intend to do – he revisited the idea.

"I was reasonably certain I could remember the name of the agency and the contact person." It was his master plan to simply walk in off the street and announce that a coworker thought he should contact them.

"In a development befitting the stupidity of my arrival and announcement, the owner of the agency looked at me for a moment, called his partner in and said, 'I think we can make it work.'"

Within weeks, Marshall would be running up and down the mountainside of Park City, Utah, dressed as an Indian in the movie, *The Deerslayer*, starring Steve Forrest, John Anderson, and Ned Romero (from *The Last of the Mohicans*). It is also the movie where actress named Madeline Stowe got her start. With a wink, actor Marshall likes to say, "Yeah, I gave her her start. She was a good kid."

The Deerslayer is based on James Fenimore Cooper's classic novel from *The Leatherstocking Tales*, and Marshall played the "blue Indian." To his friends and family, he is most easily identified as the biggest, leanest, most muscular Indian. To the director of the set, the blue Indian would best be known as the infernal extra who kept outrunning the horse in the scene where mounted Indians as well as those on foot were to travel quickly across the swift moving creek bed. The scene was intense, as the Indians returned from a raid, stealing a neighboring tribal princess.

Swept up in the moment, even in the final cut, it is Marshall who first arrives on the other side of the creek, beating the horse.

In the movie, Marshall is seen multiple times, fighting, running, dying, leaping, and outrunning equine. When I ordered the movie online, my own children – respectively 7, 11, and 13 at the time of viewing -- giggled and pointed every time Marshall made an appearance. Today, they know him as the soft-spoken man who offers hugs and lets them pilfer through his change purse. As the "blue Indian," he is large and looming, scowling and menacing.

"Ha! There he is! There he is!" the kids screamed at the scene where he and his fellow Indians tower over their prisoner, arms folded, daring the white man to move.

It is the same scene that Marshall recalls as troublesome. The director's instructions had been simple. All Indians were to crowd around, looking down into the camera, arms crossed. They were to scowl. *Scowl! Scowl like you really mean it! Scowl harder!*

But for Marshall and the other "Indians" – and not one man was actually of Native American decent – it was difficult to conjure such menacing glowers as they were having the time of their lives.

As a point of interest, by the second week of filming, the only real Native American on set declared "this is bullshit" and walked off the set, leaving African-Americans and Mexicans to play the roles of Mohican and Huron Indians.

Years earlier, Marshall had taken a field trip from Ogden to Brigham City, near the mouth of Logan Canyon, where he and his classmates visited the Intermountain Indian School, an "upward bound" program for Native American youths.

Initially, the school had served as a Nushnell Army Hospital during WWII, from 1942 to1947, treating wounded soldiers. But when the city of Brigham pushed for its own hospital, the land and building were donated to the federal government. Then, the year following the hospital's closing, President Harry Truman signed off on a bill proposing an Indian School. The $3.75 million reconstruction job allowed for Navajo children to attend the Intermountain Indian School. The K-12 institution opened its doors to 542 students in January 1950.

The Navajo children, bused from Arizona, were chosen because that tribe had the most school-aged children. It seemed the perfect solution as the building already had its own medical facility and printing press. On the Navajo reservation, there was not enough water or resources to provide for the children. It was, by all appearances, a win/win. In 1954, 24 students graduated from the Intermountain Indian School, and the next year, the graduation rate was an impressive 188.

But by the 1970s, enrollment was so low that students were bussed in from nearly 100 different tribes. The school was renamed the Intermountain Inter-Tribal School. And again, it seemed like a great idea on paper. But a number of growing problems began to plague the school. Clashes between different tribes created unrest on campus. Critics complained that the school was designed for the sole purpose of imposing white views and the white culture on Native Americans, whose cultures had all but been wiped out by the white man in the first place.

Additionally, finding funding from the federal government and qualified educators to teach was an on-going problem. Eventually, the school was closed in 1984, and a portion of that land, 17 acres, was deeded back to the city of Brigham City. Today, the building facility serves as a business center, and the dormitories have been turned into townhouses. The land was turned into a golf course, and the school is a memory. (5)

For Marshall, the memory of the Intermountain Indian School is that "it looked like a prison."

Even at a young age, Marshall was struck by the fact that the students – boys and girls from very different Indian cultures – were all lumped together. "When we were going through the different buildings," Marshall said, "I was just struck by the idea of all these kids, all of a certain race, rounded up or being shipped there. To me, that just reeked of segregation." As he walked through the hallways, peering into each classroom, he had an uncomfortable sense of walking through a zoo, "and the kids were all part of the zoo exhibit."

"I remember the Indian boys. I don't know whether they were Navajo or Yute, but they all looked pissed off. Even as big and tall as I was, I felt like if I said or did the wrong thing, I would get my ass whipped, and it stuck with me that this, the way they were all put together, was not right."

As the "blue Indian," however, Marshall was having the time of his life. Each day on the mountain as the "blue Indian" was a new adventure. One day, tired of running around the mountain, he reasoned that he could probably make a good Indian on horseback: never mind that he had absolutely no experience on a horse; it seemed like a good idea. So, during a break, with no one in sight, Marshall spied a lone horse and leapt on – bareback. He emulated the motions he'd seen the other professional riders do but was quickly bucked off. Again, Marshall jumped on, and, again, he was bucked off.

"That happened two or three times. I figured I was obviously kicking him in the wrong place." So, once again, leaping on top of the well-trained horse, Marshall chose another place to kick. "And I found the GO! switch."

This time, the horse took off with Marshall hanging on for dear life. They tore through the trees with Marshall ducking low-hanging branches and clinging against the animal until, at last, they'd made a complete circle, coming back almost to the exact place they'd begun. "Then, he threw me off anyway." When he realized no one had seen a thing, he scampered away, vowing never to try that again. "He [the horse] may still be standing there as far as I know."

From the beginning, Marshall had been on cloud nine. As soon as he was introduced to the casting agent, "we went outside, shot a couple of Polaroids, and he hired me on the spot for $20 a day on one condition. He cautiously informed me that I had to shave my facial hair and my 16 chest hairs in order to play a Huron Indian. Let me just say that I spent the next four to six weeks running around the mountains above Park City, Utah, in a wig and loin cloth with 12 other guys all similarly attired. I would show up at the Hilton at 5 a.m., no problem. From there, they would take us out to the location, give us our costumes, do our make-up, and feed us three times a day and then pay us $20 a day. At that point in my life, I had absolutely never had life so good, and I wasn't even a fireman yet!"

He was a black man running around in a loincloth, pretending to be a Native American Indian. Briefly, that was his reality. But to become a firefighter was completely implausible. Or, so he had once thought.

How could he have known what the fire department would mean to him? In many respects, he could not truly know until he was paralyzed. He would not really know the trueness of his place in the Fort Worth Fire Department until his injury. Yes, he was rising in the ranks. Yes, he was earning respect. But there was something much deeper.

On the day of his accident, it was Big Al who had to make the phone call to Obelia to let her know what had happened to Marshall. Her husband had died and her other son, Morris, Jr., was in prison. Again. "I'll never forget it," Al recalled. "When I told her there had been an accident and Marshall was paralyzed, the first thing she said was, 'Who's going to take care of me now?'"

But at the very same time, his brothers and sisters of the department were rallying around him, already plotting how to redesign his house to be wheelchair friendly and to create a fund to cover his expenses.

He was adopted into the Allen family, but in the hospital he discovered his true brothers and sisters with Big Al leading the way.

It was in the fire station, his true home, where Marshall learned about giving and sharing and trust and … an enormous amount of tomfoolery.

As an example, the sister and brothers of the FWFD learned that Al, although he is a firefighter, doesn't want to rescue cats. He'll climb roofs, battles raging fires, and rescue men, women, children, and dogs. Just don't ask him to save a cat.

"On account of the attack," he explains.

We were sitting around a table at Starbucks, a full house: Big Al Jones, his son, Christopher, though nicknamed Duckey, Marshall, Marshal's daughter, Talaya, a coffee buddy, Stan, and I. Almost immediately, someone bites.

What attack, we wondered.

"A cougar," Al begins, telling us how he's responded to a 911 only to have a cougar leap out of a window. The battle spanned the front yard, man vs. beast, while others apparently – to Al's way of thinking – looked on. He strangled the cat, yelled in pain, and fought for his life. Finally, "I drew out a hunting knife from my boot," he began. Talaya and I both raised eyebrows. A knife-wielding fire fighter? "For such occasions," he continued.

Ahh.

He was able to finish off the cat. It was, he assures us all, horrible.

But there are instant problems with this story as Stan, Talaya and I trip over each other to sort through the events. Rogue cougars in Ft. Worth, Texas?

"Tell us the story, Daddy," Talaya laughs, looking to Marshall for clarification.

"There was a cougar," Marshall confirms with the faintest of smiles. With the Marshall/Al tag team routine in full swing, there was no way Marshall was going to say anything to detract from his buddy's story.

"Gee, you'd think we would have heard that on the news," someone says.

"What can I say?" Al shrugs. "It was a horrible, horrible thing, and I fought for my life."

"You were attacked?" I persist.

"Tell us the real story." Talaya is looking at her father.

"…by a cougar?" I go on. Stan is smiling.

"C'mon, Daddy," Talaya presses Marshall.

"I had to go to the hospital," Al says.

"While responding to a 911?" I ask.

"I could have died," Al goes on.

"And this cougar was someone's … pet?" I ask.

"C'mon, Daddy," Talaya laughs. All eyes are on Marshall. No one can trust Al as far as – collectively – we can throw him. Marshall is our rock. We can believe what Marshall tells us, but he refuses, simply offering a very pleasant, non-committal expression.

"Do you really expect me to dispute the word of my best friend?" he asks.

"Did you get a medal for this act of bravery?" Al is asked, but he sniffs at the suggestions.

"I was just doing my job."

For the next ten minutes, we hear about Al's lifelong aversion to cougars, as he'd also come across them during his tour in Vietnam. Ah, yes, you know, all those stories about rogue Vietnamese cougars attacking American troops. Never mind that he's about 10 years too young to have been in Vietnam to witness these rogue oversized cats in the first place.

As it happens, Al did respond to a 911. A very large, elderly woman had fallen down and, unable to get up, had called for help. But she'd panicked when the fire fighters were about to move her and began screaming. Apparently, this is not an uncommon response. Nor is it uncommon for house pets to become protective of their owners.

While Al and other fire fighters were readying to lift the woman on count, Al was suddenly attacked from behind by a small but angry housecat.

Al whirled, grabbed his commanding officer, and planted the officer between himself and the cat for protection, but the damage was done. The cat had bitten clear through his boot, and Al had to have a rabies shot. Over time and subsequent retelling of the event, the housecat had grown to significant proportions. The bit about the hunting blade in his boot was a necessary evil because his buddies back at the firehouse love the fact that Big Al was taken down by an itty-bitty kitty.

Most humorously, Marshall offers another perspective to the story. As Al leapt around the woman's small bedroom, his fellow firefighters simply stood watching. "You know," Marshall chuckled. "Al is so full of it, they were just waiting to see what he was doing." Certain that there was some kind of joke being played out, everyone stood around and watched while Al was terrorized by a small but angry housecat.

Cat rescues are not just in the movies. Nor are the constant, non-stop practical jokes at firehouses. Just as the movies depict, fire fighters are overgrown kids. They are rambunctious. They are pranksters. They are brothers and sisters who love one another and love to tease and torment each other.

But when firefighter Bruce Rogers, a man who caught and peddled rattlesnakes (and their skins) in his spare time, was caught casually strolling around the firehouse in an apparent search for something, much of the station house humor was lost.

Uh, Bruce? What are you looking for?

Bruce had trapped and contained a specific number of live rattlers, but, once at the station where his truck had been parked, he discovered he was missing one snake but didn't dare tell anyone.

Watch any Hollywood movie with firefighters, and, however far reaching, however dramatized, the one accurate portrayal is that of the firehouse antics.

Wrestling matches, water buckets, short-sheets, hidden personal items, and the taking in and letting out of hems to convince other people they are either growing or shrinking were all par for the course for fire fighters. And any kind of sabotage was also considered excellent strategy.

A favorite place of sabotage was the phone booth, a small room at the firehouse designed for private phone calls while the fire fighters were on call. Rigged doors, wet floors, prank calls were all commonplace, but trapping a fellow firefighter in the phone booth was just good fun. During one such phone conversation, firefighter Laura Jenkins was talking to her would-be husband. Laura would later be the fire fighter who discovered Talaya's letter at the station and brought it to her captain while he lay in the hospital bed, just weeks after his accident. Only a few words into the letter, she had stopped, asking, "You sure you don't want to read this on your own ... later?" But Marshall would urge her on, leaving everyone in the room stunned by the possibility that Marshall suddenly had a biological daughter.

As the only female in the house, Laura had learned quickly to hold her own. And her abilities as a firefighter would prove essential to the way Marshall dealt with female officers.

She had been sitting in the private room when a dead snake, saved from an earlier call in the day, was tossed into the room with her. Preserved for such a moment, a thoughtful fire fighter had saved the snake.

Laura panicked and began screaming to get out of the then blocked door of the tiny room.

There are frequent stories in which Marshall was part of dragging, taunting, or sabotaging someone only to have the house captain turn a deaf ear. If he didn't see it, it wasn't actually happening. As long as no one got hurt, there was no problem. When Marshall became acting captain, there were many times he entered a room as nearly a half dozen men suddenly froze. Seeing no blood but only mischief in the eyes of his men, he'd simply turn and leave the room.

For the few women on the force, it was important that they hold their own. Laura Jenkins was such a woman. One of Marshall's protégés, she quickly earned a reputation as a thick-skinned, quick-witted, and fully capable fire fighter, defying and denying any beliefs that a woman could not make a strong fire fighter.

When it was suspected that something dead was in the station's attic, only Laura was willing and able to climb into the rafters to investigate, her legs hanging out. Feeling around with her hand, she discovered and latched on to the tail of a dead rat. But as she had been feeling around for the dead animal, the boys below had been goosing her. The payback was wielding the dead rodent and threatening to toss it on someone. The tough fire fighters recoiled in horror, and Laura was crowned Queen of the firehouse.

But the status of legends belongs to Marshall and Big Al.

To "Take s Spin" took on new meaning with the big men. "Pretty much," Al shared, "Marshall and I were the only two in the city taking the guys for spins."

Indeed. There were not too many 300-pound, muscle-bound fire fighters running around Ft. Worth, Texas.

"It started," Al said, "with Craig Cox. He was kind of a smaller guy." He was 190 pounds.

In yet another firehouse prank, Cox had strategically created a puddle of water just outside the phone booth at the station. "He sabotaged the booth," Al said. "He knew that every night I would take my shoes off after 8 o'clock." Al recalled how he stepped outside the booth, saturated his socks, and saw red.

"Like I said, I knew it was him, so I sought him out, picked him out of the group, and …" the spin.

Catching Cox at the knees with one hand and just behind the neck with the other hand, the hapless victim was then hoisted into the air like a bench press. Then, turning faster and faster and faster, the 190-pound man was twirled into nauseated oblivion.

The next spinning victim was 230-pound swingman Darrin Partridge. While the crew was out testing fire hydrants, the young swingman began taunting Al – a frequent occurrence with new recruits. An overgrown child himself, Al was often an easy target, and Darrin couldn't resist.

"He found some cockleburs and started throwing them at me while I was twisting hydrants. It was funny to him, and I couldn't get him to stop, so I tussled with him and, in the midst of it, got him in the spin position."

Marshall and Al had begun working out every day, both men in the best shapes of their lives, both well over 300 pounds, but after "tussling" with a 230-pound man on the grass and sidewalk near a very public hydrant, Al was nearing exhaustion.

"The truth of the matter was, the officer in charge made us quit, and I could have kissed him for it. I was pretty much exhausted, and Darrin was just starting to have fun."

Darrin's version of the story, however, is slightly different. Both men agree that Darrin had been throwing cockleburs in Al's boot and on his clothing when Al wasn't looking. Both agree that Al accused and Darrin denied the throwing of the cockleburs.

"Then I pushed it," Darrin said. "He caught me [throwing cockleburs] in one clean swoop, one hand behind my knee, the other up by my back." Al jerked him off his feet, but his voice remained eerily calm. "He said, 'I asked you and asked you to stop.' When he asked me if he needed to tell me again, I said, 'No, sir. If a man can pick me up like that, that quick...'" Darrin reasoned this was not a man he wanted to mess with. But he was already in the air; there was no turning back.

The spinning became a running joke within the department. As part of an initiation to the department, new recruits were often encouraged to agitate the giants, or they were simply set up to be the next victim.

In the case of new recruit Todd Breedlove, it was the promise to drive the fire truck. They were working in station #26 when Todd walked up to Marshall and said, "Marshall Allen is a pussy."

Not far away, "I saw D.D. Clark and Willis Anderson and knew they set him up," Marshall said. To the recruit, Marshall said, "Son, I don't know what they promised you, but I hope it was worth it." And he hit Todd on the side the head with the portable radio.

It was the ultimate dare, the greatest feat. Challenge Marshall Allen, if you dare.

Chapter Six

Christmas 2003
Greetings!

The annual Allred holiday letter has always been a bad one. Yes, bad because we like it that way. The tradition started in the late '90s when Robb reviewed one of my letters with disgust and announced no one wants to read happy news. People want to hear the bad stuff, thus lifting their own spirits. To prove him wrong, I wrote everything that went bad that year – and the letter was a hit. But we don't need to tell you this year was tough, filled with tragedy and heartbreak. The fall of the Saddam Hussein statue was good to watch but at a great price. It's hard to find things to joke about. As war broke out, my father (ret. Col. Marc Powe) was handpicked by Gen. Colin Powell to work alongside General Garner for the Organization for Reconstruction and Humanitarian Affairs in Baghdad. After a three-month tour, he did manage to come home just before his father (my Daddydaddy) died. Nonetheless, we will try to recap some of the old flavor of Christmas letters past with the trivial mishaps of our lives.

The year 2003 has been the year of the animal. After 6 ½ years with us, Kerri's beloved guinea pig, Penny, died. Robb made us all promise that there would be no more animals, but after some time, Kerri was ready for a new pig, and we brought Cinny home. Cinny was with us for less than 48 hours before Tommy got her out to play with her and played a rousing game of 'roll on top of the pig' and accidentally killed her. Our big male goat, Zipper, continued to ram us until we had no choice but to sell him. Neighbors sat outside on lawn chairs in their driveways close to dinnertime just to watch me try to feed that stupid goat. No amount of kickbox classes could keep that goat off me!

Apparently, if you move between a (psychotic) billy goat and his herd, this is perceived to be a threat, and the goat has no other recourse but to attack. They really should tell people these kinds of things before letting said people buy said goats.

Finally, we got rid of Zipper and the two baby goats, Sugar and Ginger, keeping Cookiedough. But the barn was empty, so we got a new horse. An 18-month-old gelding Quarter horse name Lightning came to us with the wild, unbridled enthusiasm of a young, untrained horse. He kicked the goat, bit, and charged, but the day he leapt over the fence was truly a bad day. I was weeding around the outside of the fence, and Lightning was having a hissy fit because I was feeding the weeds to Star and not him. Finally, I moved over to the corner of the fence and said, "Okay! Here!" and bent over to pull some weeds just for him. Ker-klunk! Ker-klunk! Ker-klunk! Sounds of pounding hooves, moving in my direction, resonated in my ears, and then in s-l-o-w motion I watched as Lightning sailed over me, landed on the street, and turned. He looked at me; I looked at him. Somewhere in the distance, crickets chirped. Then, the 45-minute battle of getting the nice horsey back into the corral began. Of course, this occurred on possibly the hottest day in Texas, and Robb was not home. Just as I got Lightning back to the corral gate, Tommy came tearing out of the garage, yelling. Lightning whirled around and flung me across the driveway and ran up the street again. When Tommy charged out, he also let Pete, the Labrador, out who chased Benson up a tree. Benson is the kitty cat who came to us with Lightning and is named after the kind people we got Lighting from. (It took Robb three days to figure out we got a new cat. We run a "Don't tell if no one asks" policy around here), Kerri ran out crying because the cat was up the tree, and Tommy got sticker burrs all over his feet. I caught the horse, caught the dog, cleaned Tommy's feet, saved the cat, and went inside to call a horse trainer. A week later, Lighting went to charm school. It worked because he is very charming!!

  One day after leaving kickboxing, I heard a faint mew from a car and made a joke to my friend/kickboxing buddy, Audra, that there was a cat somewhere. Sure enough, she had a stowaway – a kitten that had crawled into her car somewhere in Oklahoma. The kitten traveled in the middle of summertime from Oklahoma to Texas on a Saturday and was still in the engine block on Monday morning. Dehydrated, slightly injured, scared, and hungry, he was finally lured out sometime on Tuesday. We named him Sooner (He is from Oklahoma after all) and brought him home where he quickly bonded with Cookiedough, the goat. Sooner and Cookie sleep and eat together and will be featured in an upcoming book entitled, **Top Ten Cats**. It took another week for Robb to figure out that Benson and Sooner were, in fact, two different felines.

  Being the conscientious animal owner that I am, I sent Benson and Sooner to be spayed/neutered, but nerve damage was done to Benson, and she was paralyzed for almost a week. So she lived in the house with us. Robb hacked away from allergies but, remarkably, never said "no" to her coming inside. By God, I think we're wearing him down. Pete was on high-alert – ready to attack at any moment.

  Nala got hit by a truck and survived. Cookie had two more babies named Skittles and Nutmeg, but Nutmeg is doing things to his sister that a nice goat really shouldn't do, so he must go away. Pete caught and half-ate a squirrel, leaving the carcass where Kerri and Katie stand to catch the bus. Kerri's gag reflex is alive and well.

Tommy was diagnosed with asthma, and Kerri gets motion sickness on her school bus. We replaced the carpet with hardwood floors and got a barn for our hay. I did this, of course, when the penny-pincher was gone (Robb went elk hunting). What with all the animals, this was a needed purchase, but as that monstrosity of a two-story barn was being delivered, I had to ask my dad, "You think Robb will notice it?"

Tommy had to be taken to the doctor's the day before Thanksgiving because he stuck a bead that was supposed to be part of his Native American headdress for the 'big dinner' with the Pilgrims in his ear, and Katie stood up in the middle of her cafeteria at school and announced to everyone that Santa was NOT coming, but no one should panic because her billy goat had a beard and could fill in for Old St. Nick. By the time the phone call came from a teacher, I was made to understand that Katie announced Santa IS a Billy goat.

I ripped the door handle off the van when the door got stuck – the same van on which I banged up the rear bumper and broke the rear windshield wiper. While I was busy trying to recover the credit card bill so that Robb would not see how much it costs when a cat goes paralyzed, I discovered that someone stole our credit card identity and placed a $2,000 charge through E-bay on gift baskets and was forced to show him the bill. I stood firm, prepared for the explosion, but I believe he imploded. I heard a small ticking sound. A little part of him died. For the holidays, I believe I will be buying him a burial plot. Always look ahead, I say!

The power went out while I was working on a manuscript, and I lost almost 50 pages, and Kerri is going through the worst hormonal 10-year-old change possible. I swear, I never knew a person could whine the alphabet. Katie is going through a phase of cartwheels . . .every annoying second of the day she does cartwheels. Cartwheels to the dinner table, cartwheels to brush teeth, cartwheels in front of the T.V. Tommy won't stop singing, "Did you know the Muffin Man?" at top volume and tries to incorporate the word 'poop' anywhere he can – even with the Muffin Man. That's just wrong!

Robb is so deeply invested in Fantasy Football that the only way I can get him to focus on anything is to talk football. "Robb, it's third down, and the opposing shower in the guest room has been broken since July! Now, if we put our first stringers on the line and go for fourth and goal, victory can be ours! We can do this, Robb. Hut, hut!" Tommy broke a very valuable Russian vase, Nala scratched Tommy, Kerri punched Katie in the tummy, Kerri has announced she doesn't want to eat meat anymore, and Katie refuses to wear "girl" clothes. The shower still doesn't work, and the toilet gurgles whenever I do laundry.

Here's to another year!

Alex

A Little Bit of Faith and Hope

It is the weirdest thing. Robb, after years of being the consummate bad boy, is suddenly talking about the church where he was reared. *What's that about?* Church people are coming around, and it's really irritating. I mean, if you want to believe in God, that's great, but one should never push beliefs on other people. I've never liked it when people knock on my door or give me flyers or otherwise intrude in my space with their beliefs!

This new, strange person who calls himself my husband asks, "Well, how else are they going to reach you if they don't reach out to you?"

Crap, I don't know! But they don't need to come to my house! If God really wants me that badly, I once sniffed, He should find a better way to reach me.

The Unconquerable Marshall Allen
...and his rise to the top

By 2003, Marshall had found his groove. Always fiercely independent, Marshall began making plans as soon as he began to feel strong again. "When Marshall said he was getting a van," Al recalled, "I thought he meant it was going to be something to fit his chair." Marshall's chair, built to fit Marshall's frame, is large.

But Marshall had no intention of being "driven" anywhere. Not if he could drive himself. For some time, Al had been picking him up and taking Marshall everywhere. In the beginning, Al literally picked Marshall up, and when Marshall was finally outfitted with a chair, it was Al who lifted both Marshall and his chair in and out of various vehicles. But when the Texas Rehabilitation Commission helped Marshall get his own hand-operated vehicle, Marshall regained his independence.

As a result of his accident, Marshall can only flex his hands upward. "My fingers don't work at all, and I have limited sensation in my arms and fingers." But with tenodesis splints, Marshall is able to perform day-to-day functions, including maneuvering his van. With a brace fitted to the steering wheel so that his arm can never fall away from the controls and his other hand fitted to the door, controlling the accelerator and brake, Marshall is in full control.

Initially, Marshall was fearful. But he began taking driving lessons, and "once I got enough confidence," Marshall said, "I took the driving test, passed it, and starting driving around the neighborhood. Once again, Al facilitated all that."

But the new-found freedom came with a price. One day, while driving himself around, Marshall became too comfortable with the sensation of driving, and old memories clouded reality.

"I made a left turn," Marshall said, "and fell over." How often we all forget or do not recognize how much we use our core strength just to hold us upright in a car. Something so small, so minute as making a turn in a car, was nearly disastrous for Marshall. With no stomach or back muscles, he fell over in the chair, and, without a driver, the van lurched over a median and crashed into a pickup truck.

"A kid. It was a kid," Marshall recalled, the pain still evident in his voice. While no one was hurt and the damage was minimal, Marshall almost hung up his keys, vowing never to drive and never risk hurting another person again. "I really beat up myself."

After Marshall moved back home, after his fire fighter buddies had remodeled his home to accommodate the chair, Al and Mary took on the job of caring for Marshall. This included heavy lifting, bathing, and dressing to name but a few tasks. And always, Marshall told his wife that if it ever became too much for her, he would understand if Mary wanted "out."

There were two very distinct things about Mary. She was strong, and she was strong-willed.

When he met her, he knew her as Mary Alice Martin, a woman who had charmed him one day with a grace and beauty he found unusual. He watched her from afar as she offered to help a delivery man and knew he wanted her phone number. Later, he would learn that she was the sister of Dallas Cowboy legend Harvey Martin.

Drafted in the third round of the 1973 NFL Draft, Harvey became part of the famed Doomsday Defense alongside Randy White and Ed "Too Tall" Jones. He had a tremendous career, setting multiple records, including titles such as four-time Pro-Bowler and co-Super Bowl MVP in Super Bowl XII (sharing the title with Randy White). Until the end of his career with the Cowboys, Harvey was one of the most popular and celebrated players on the team.

Briefly, he had his own radio show and ventured into a number of businesses, but things quickly unraveled after his retirement from the NFL. It seemed as though everyone wanted a piece of him -- or, rather, of his financial pie. Mary, especially, became accustomed to a certain way of living and all the benefits that came with having a celebrity brother, and she was not afraid to use this sub-celebrity status. Many doors were opened for her simply by using his name.

Without the steady demands of the NFL, Harvey began to look elsewhere for excitement. By 1982, the FBI questioned him about his involvement with illegal drugs, and though he was never formally charged, a cloud of suspicion hung over him as well as a few other Cowboys during the summer of 1983 when an F.B.I. wiretap was used to ensnare drug users. Coach Tom Landry sent Harvey to rehab in 1983, but he continued to abuse drugs and alcohol. In 1996, he was arrested on cocaine and domestic-abuse charges following an argument with a girlfriend and spent the next eight months in a court-ordered rehabilitation program.

Bankruptcies also haunted him until – out of rehab -- friend and former teammate John Niland offered Harvey a job selling chemicals. And for the first time in a very long time, it appeared that Harvey was back on track. He spoke to grade school children about the dangers of drugs and did public service announcements. All the while, he was continuously hit up for autographs and for business partnerships. (6)

It was during that time that Mary met Marshall. And it was during their courtship that Harvey once pulled Marshall to the side and thanked him.

It wasn't just Mary but many people around the Martin family who grew accustomed to, even expectant of, preferential treatment due to Harvey's fame. During the 1970s and the early 1980s, the Martins lived large. By the 1990s, Harvey had two children: a son, Devincent Roberson Martin, and a daughter, Chase Martin.

Mary had four children: sons Simeon and Delbert Knight and son Rashaud Mitchell and daughter Marical Mitchell. The children's fathers were well acquainted with Harvey's business ventures. Or, Harvey had worried, they wanted to be. For Harvey, Marshall Allen was a breath of fresh air.

The imposing firefighter, of similar size and strength to Harvey Martin, was not the least bit interested in Harvey's celebrity status or bank account.

"He shook my hand and thanked me," Marshall said. It had meant a lot to him that his sister had found a man who did not want or need his money. "What was I going to do with it?" Marshall shrugged. "I had my own."

In the earlier years, Harvey had taken care of Mary. Although there were men in her life, her brother's financial and celebrity status afforded her the lifestyle she desired. The fathers of her children, however, did not. Neither paid child support, and Mary struggled financially after Harvey battled his own demons and eventually succumbed to pancreatic cancer. Keeping up with her bills, keeping food in the refrigerator, and even keeping the electricity turned on had been a challenge. Once she was with Marshall, there were no red carpet affairs, but she and her children were well provided for. Marshall had become a stabilizing force in the home financially, but he was also a strong, positive male role model for her children. When Mary fought with her children, it was Marshall who stepped in and played mediator. It was Marshall who provided the kids with cars and sound advice on money management. He was, in every sense, the father Mary's children had never had but had always needed.

During their courtship, Marshall had not worried about his relationship so much with Mary but with the children. Falling in love with a woman with four children was a large responsibility and one that most men would have shied away from. But the children were special.

Marshall recalled a particular date with Mary for which he'd arrived early. Mary's hair was still wet as she ran around, only partially dressed, yelling at the kids to finish homework and get ready for bed. At one point, in the middle of her tirade, she noticed that her third son, Rashaad, was standing around. When he said he didn't have any homework, she told him to "get a book and read!" But in the chaos, she forgot what she told her son to do, and on her return trip down the hall, yelled, "Take a shower and get ready for bed!" As she yelled at the children to prepare themselves for bed and finished dressing herself, she caught sight of Rashaad again. "What are you doing? Go read a book!"

Casually, Rashaad walked over to the bookshelf near where Marshall sat and perused the small library. When he selected his book, he lifted it and nodded toward Marshall. "I guess I'll read this in the shower."

Marshall admired and tried to adopt Rashaad's philosophy for survival: if he wasn't particularly interested, he let it slide. Sometimes, however, Marshall and Mary went toe to toe. And as the years passed, they went toe to toe more often.

"They [the children] knew what was going on," Marshall said of his arguments with Mary, adding that it was always important to let his children know where they stood with him. Although they were not his biological children, he was just as committed to them.

In the years leading up to the accident, the relationship between Marshall and Mary had become volatile. They were arguing with growing frequency and intensity, and it was unclear if this was a storm they would be able to weather or would even want to. By Marshall's admission, they had stopped talking to each other. Both were tired of the constant arguing.

But when Marshall needed his wife most, she was there. However strained their relationship had been prior to the accident, Mary put that behind her and focused on what needed to be done. Over time, however, exhaustion won over, and she knew she needed more help.

It came in the way of Richard, a quiet, unassuming man who began arriving at Marshall's front door at 5 a.m., like clockwork, offering Marshall both a friendship and the kind of care that cannot be measured. And, more important than dressing or feeding, Richard loves Marshall's powerfully-built yet ever-puppyish Rottweiler, Caesar.

Richard Kapscos served in the U.S. Navy and is a Vietnam veteran. He is a man of many talents, and he is perfect for Marshall, who continues to be fascinated by his caregiver. Both politically and religiously, they are opposites and often engage in a delicate banter. While Marshall goes head on against most people, these two share a more respectful and humorous on-going debate.

Richard is also a man who offers relief to Caesar. He wrestles with the dog and prepares him, as well as Marshall, for their outings. Even more amusing is the fact that Caesar understands that "Daddy," a.k.a. Marshall, is no good at throwing and completely refuses to bring any toy to Marshall. Richard is a far better toy thrower.

Small in stature, Richard is powerfully built. During the Vietnam War, he acted as a radar operator, guiding missiles and tracking ships and submarines. In the civilian world, he has worked as a typesetter and a format editor for a newspaper; he learned to make sausage when he worked as a meat processor in Wyoming.

As soon as Richard prepares Marshall for the day, each goes his own way, both headed to their full-time jobs. For Richard, it is always another day at work. For Marshall, everyday is a new challenge: another jackass parking in a handicap spot preventing him from finding a place to park, another adjustment to maneuvering his chair, another opportunity to listen to whatever signals his body might be trying to send him. Often times, he could be injured and not even realize it. Only when he feels strange prickling sensations, senses heart palpitations, or begins sweating does he know that something is wrong. It is all new, often frustrating, and always challenging.

Oddly, paying attention to his body brings a sense of normalcy to him.

Marshall had always struggled.

In the days and weeks leading up to his accident, Marshall could feel himself spiraling out of control. After verbally assaulting a female sheriff, he turned on her male counterpart and challenged him to take off the badge and gun. He was ready, he said, to "stomp his guts out."

He was tired of the day-to-day grind, of people not doing what they were supposed to do, of sub-par work ethics, of the ridiculous protocol, of the behind-the-back talk, and of arguing with Mary. He was beaten down by the senseless death he saw on the job. Life, death, and everything in between were sucking the life out of him, and no one could know how hard it was just to function throughout the day. Worse than all of the external problems was the incessant internal struggle. Not just all of his waking hours, but even after sleep took over.

But he was Marshall Allen! He was superman. He was Godzilla. To many, he wasn't a man but a machine. He was supposed to be able to handle everything, and the constant pressure to do just that was consuming. So, one evening, as he was driving home, he'd set his cruise control at 70 mph. Of this he is sure because setting the control was his daily practice. He even passed a Dallas County Sheriff's cruiser, certain of his speed. But when the cruiser fell in behind him following him through the city of Grand Prairie, Marshall became watchful.

As soon as he reached the Dallas city limit, the sheriff flipped on the lights and pulled Marshall over. Suddenly, the speed limit dropped to 60 mph.

Marshall watched as a female officer approached his vehicle from the passenger side, and as soon as she informed him that he was going 75 mph, he called her "a damned liar."

Within minutes, there was backup and another exchange, only this time it was with a male sheriff who, among other things, asked Marshall, "Do you have a wife and a daughter?"

Before that, the sheriff never questioned or commented on Marshall's speed. At that point, speed had become a moot point.

"I knew what this was about," Marshall said. He had been through it many times. He was the big black guy, and the female officer was the helpless white woman in need of protection. So when Marshall responded that "yes" he had a wife and daughter, he hardly batted an eyelash when the sheriff said that perhaps he would follow Marshall's wife and child around for a while just to harass them and see how he liked it. At this, the sheriff added, "We don't like our women being treated that way either." It was the "our women" comment that caught him.

"That was when I said, 'Well, I'll tell you what I'll do. If you'll take off that badge and gun …'" and the threats began. Even as Marshall retold the story, he squeezed his eyes shut as though he could see it all replay before him again. Later, when he called Mary and told her, "I did it again," what had scared him was not that he would have really followed the sheriff into a nearby parking lot or that he wanted to beat him to a pulp, but that he was actually frightened by the rage he felt. He could see himself driving a fist through the man's face, crushing the bones. He could imagine grabbing a fistful of hair with one hand to hold the guy's head in place while he pounded it with the other. He could picture the gushing blood and the devastation that would befall that poor, misguided sonofabitch, and it was incredibly satisfying.

It was an image so clear in his mind that it was only after the sheriff walked away that Marshall understood and feared his own rage. The sheriff wrote him a citation for speeding and for displaying both a current and old registration sticker on his windshield. Later, Mary had to appear in court as Marshall lay paralyzed in a hospital bed. While the registration citation was dropped, Mary paid the speeding fine. But there, on the side of the highway on the evening Marshall was pulled over, the ticket hadn't mattered. Marshall was both thankful and lucky the sheriff walked away. Perhaps the sheriff could recognize an enraged giant, or he was blissfully unaware of the danger that loomed. Whatever the case, Marshall was sent on his way and both men had been given a gift. But Marshall was losing control. He could feel it.

Statistically, Marshall has always been aware of his odds as an African American male living in America. A disproportionate number of African American males had (and continue to) done time in prison. Even as a child, Marshall was aware of the challenges he faced.

"But I had the good fortune or blessing of having not one but two primary positive male role models during my formative years. They were similar in so many ways, but different in enough areas that they complemented each other": his father and a man named Linnard Holsten, his first boxing instructor and mentor. Combined, the two men taught Marshall poise, manners, and composure. Fighting was always to be a last resort but an important measure when appropriate.

By the time he was just 21-years-old, Marshall had been hired as the first black firefighter in the history of the Salt Lake County Fire

Department. A year later when he moved to Fort Worth, Texas, he was one of a very small number of black fire fighters.

"As a consequence, I was being judged and evaluated differently than any of my Anglo contemporaries. And I knew that, for many years after me, young black men and women would be compared to the standard that I set.

"It never occurred to me to become a fire fighter. It never occurred to me that I could. I had never seen a black fire fighter before," Marshall said.

More than a decade later, Marshall would experience one of the greatest moments of his professional career. As he and his crew returned to Station #22 from a routine call, they decided to "buzz a school."

"We had this thing where we would go by the schools and turn on the sirens and air horns." Marshall smiled at the memory. "We used to like to play around with kids. They loved it!"

So on this particular day, Marshall's crew pulled up to an intersection and stopped at the stop sign. As they pulled to a stop, the crew could see three small children standing on the corner on the driver's side of the vehicle. Two boys, one black and the other white, and a little white girl all gawked at the enormous fire truck. The two firefighters in the front seat (Marshall and the driver, Scott James) had a perfect view of all three kids and waved.

"The little black kid did a double take as he looked up into the fire truck," Marshall recalled of the little boy, "and then pointed directly at me and said something to his friend." It was like one of those scenes in a movie when all the external sounds fade away, and they heard the little boy say clearly, "when I grow up, I wanna be just like him."

Scott James, the truck's engineer looked back to Marshall and said, "That's gotta make you feel good, doesn't it?"

"That really choked me up," Marshall said. "And later, I used that experience as a great example of the purpose of Affirmative Action. You know, I always say it's [Affirmative Action] not about giving someone a job, which is what the nay-sayers always point out, but when I was growing up, I never saw a fire fighter who resembled my father. Once you get a few people like me in that position, it occurs to other people like that little boy that they can be a fire fighter. That's the bottom line."

For Marshall, the stunned expression of that little boy at the intersection was more than a child realizing his own dream. It was about all the possibilities of a dream.

From the first day Marshall joined the force, traveling between stations as a swingman, it was "game on." Each new crew brought new challenges. During lunch one day at Station 14, after he had been with the department almost a year, a fajita buffet had been laid out for the men. It was a typical day; the conversation was filled with barbs and jabs at one another, including old jokes.

"And at some point, someone gave a few examples of their favorite jokes, and the topic turned to how jokes could be applied to various groups," Marshall recalled. As he prepared his plate, assembling a fajita, he was wary. This kind of open forum had a tendency to lead toward more unpleasant or distasteful subjects. Station 14 was what was termed a double company station, which meant it housed a pump and ladder truck and was also the battalion headquarters. This meant that, on any given day, 10 firefighters were assigned as swingman and that there were a number of different personalities in the mix.

"The odds that someone would crack an off-color joke were pretty good, to say the least. And given my familiarity with these particular individuals, inevitable." Almost on cue, it came.

Its messenger was a large, burly individual near 6'2" and close to 300 pounds by Marshall's estimation. "He was the prototype of the ex-high school football champion with his ever-present cigar and crew cut. Suffice to say that this guy was not afraid of anyone or anything. With good reason."

The joke was posed as a question: What three things can't you give a nigger?

Answer: A black eye, a fat lip, and a job.

"I would say that you could have heard the proverbial pin drop. The table was dead silent. Everyone, including the lieutenant, the captain, and the battalion chief were waiting to see how this first-year rookie [meaning me] would respond."

The idea of beating the man came to mind. Feelings of rage blistered inside of him. As mere seconds ticked off, a number of thoughts occurred. If he struck, he would surely take a beating, but he was not afraid of that. Instead, he worried about being fired. Even worse, "I would be fired as another hotheaded, intolerant Negro who could not fit in. I would be one more example used against the next two generations of young men and women attempting to occupy one of these positions."

While Marshall weighed his options, he pretended not to have heard the statement. He merely continued to build his fajita while he silently stewed. The silence, he said, was deafening.

"When I could no longer stand the tension, I stopped what I was doing and looked up and around the table at my fellow firefighters with a slightly surprised look. Then it hit me! I said, 'If that comment was aimed at me, you are absolutely correct.'"

For a moment, his audience was stunned. For those who did not know Marshall, they could not have known what was coming, but those who did, "knew I damn well would not accept this stereotype for myself or anyone else."

Marshall finished his fajita and said, "There isn't a son of a bitch here who can give me a black eye or a fat lip. And as for the job, I outscored every other candidate who took the test. Nobody gave me this job. I took this job, and it's mine."

Without another word, Marshall went back to his lunch.

"After just a moment, the tension lifted, and three of the individuals at that table seemed genuinely pleased with the way I handled the situation. Without missing a beat and acting quite matter-of-factly, I went back to my lunch.

"Prior to that day, I had never had a fajita, and since that day, I have enjoyed many but none quite as much as the first."

Protecting God's Green Earth

Our lives were changing, though I hadn't really realized it at the time. I just thought we were in some kind of bad cycle.

I was sitting in the emergency room in Dallas, awaiting Tommy's release. My little angel had an oxygen level so low they would not release him until he had at least 80 percent of his lung capacity in check.

In 2002 when Wendy's founder Dave Thomas died, Wendy's headquarters requested that I write the in-house obituary to be shared with all employees. It was an honor to be trusted in this manner, and I made it my mission to make the obituary both warm and loving but accurate. In that same year, I heard back from Jenny Craig, founder and CEO of the mega-weight loss corporation. She told me that in over twenty years of interviews, mine was the most accurate and enjoyable story about her she'd ever read. A true feather in my cap was an interview with Bill Willis, one of the first black athletes to play in the NFL and one who had flat out refused to talk to press in the latter years of his life. He'd refused ABC Sports, ESPN, and Sports Illustrated but had spoken to me.

I had two things working in my favor. I always read back notes to my subjects, and I'm a good listener. Not so long ago, I was interviewed by the *New York Times* only, I later discovered, to be misquoted. How irritating.

Over the years, with too many interviews to count, I've only had a few people imply that I misheard. Usually, this happens when they belatedly realize they don't like how they presented themselves. I don't mishear anything. People mis-speak, but I don't mishear, so I heard him perfectly when Tommy's attending physician told me that it was the air in Midlothian making Tommy sick.

Out of habit, I picked up a pad of paper and pen and jotted down what he said. Almost instantly, he frowned, asking that I not put anything in print. From the moment I picked up my pen, he backpedaled. I could not yet know how many doctors, educators, city officials, and residents would do or say or NOT say anything to keep the dirtiest secret a secret or prevent themselves from being held liable. Having lived all over the U.S. and abroad, having lived among capitalists and communists, socialists and idealists, I've never been anywhere where such a deep and dangerous denial ran a town. The obfuscation was surreal.

Chapter Seven

Christmas 2004

Greetings!

Ah, the holidays. A time for good cheer, well wishes, peace, and love. It is a time when loved ones typically send letters telling of fun-filled times in the year past, of milestones and celebrations. Sleigh bells ringing, carolers singing . . . stop. You'll find none of that here. This, my friends, is the un-Christmas letter. It is the letter telling of mishaps, fumbles, and foibles. A miscalculation of chemicals in the pool sent the children screaming, their eyes stinging, dog poop flinging, car doors dinging. This is our holiday song.

No one wants to read about all the great things happening to other people. You want the stinging, the flinging, and the dinging. No singing, no ringing. And so, this is our report of woe from 2004 – making you realize how much more you have to be grateful for. It could always be worse; think of the dread: you could live with us and be an Allred.

The year started with a bang: a bunch of boards fell on our box of freshly wrapped Christmas ornaments. Who sets a box of breakables next to a stack of boards? Oh, yeah; it was me. I went on to sprain my ankle, lost a toenail, and had to have a crown put on a cracked tooth. Robb's shoulder came out of socket. Katie's best friend (also a Katie) accidentally socked her in the eye with a baseball bat, and I witnessed the horrendous murder of a large field mouse by Sooner, the cat. It is why we got a cat, but, geez, the torture went on a might too long. Even the other neighbor cats were beginning to complain about the rat screams. Our horses and goats escaped from the corral when the gate wasn't properly latched – this while both Robb and I were out of town. Mercifully, neighbors came to the rescue. It didn't help matters, however, to have neighbor Sarah hide behind a tree announcing to everyone that Lightning (admittedly a little frisky) is a "crazy horse."

Our goat, Cookiedough, was pregnant, and I didn't even realize her condition. I just thought she was carrying a little too much in the mid-section. Having kids will do that to you.

The only males she's been around were our gelded horses, a neutered cat, Robb, and her three month old son, Nutmeg. Of the five, no one appeared to have the interest or ability. But, in May, Cookie had twins – one boy, one girl. The girl, Cinnamon, is still with us, but the inbred boy had to go. Interestingly, the inbred girl appears to be our smartest goat yet.

Kerri finally got her braces off and went through four retainers in a little over one month, repeatedly sitting on them and leaving us to wonder about *her* level of intelligence. How many times can you sit on a retainer? It was Katie's turn, and she went to the periodondist to have mouth surgery before getting her braces. She was heavily medicated and began hallucinating. She's an ugly drunk. We hope to use this to our advantage in talking about alcohol and partying when she's a teenager. "Katie, honey, we've seen you drunk, and it's ugly. Your friends will party with you once – once."

Katie went through a phase of calling me Aunt Trudie – no one knows why – but has given that up and is now calling me Captain Weasel Pants (which can be really embarrassing in public). Tommy relates to everything in life by way of his computer game – Age of Empire. Recently when Robb was burning a pile of leaves and fallen tree limbs, Tommy listened to the fire crackling and mused, "dats what it sounds like when I burn down my enemies' castles." At school, we've learned that all he really wants to do is "wrestle, tackle and, spin." Who doesn't? But when he's hopped up on his asthma medication, it's hard to control the impulses. He tackled another kid during an unscheduled fire drill. What with all the bells and mass exodus from the building, the excitement was more than he could handle.

While some friends went to Jamaica, we watched their three children, Bentleigh, Braiden, and Brooks, for a week. Although they are great kids, add them to Kerri, Katie, and Tommy and we were one hectic house. Each night as I tried to get six children to bed, check homework, and prepare backpacks, Braiden insisted on reciting from the New Testament while Brooks and Tommy argued over Secret Agent Barbie. Yes, while Robb was still reeling from the fact his son is playing Secret Agent Barbie, Tommy announced his deep desire to have and to own his own Easy-Bake Oven. He wanted to make "wee-nilla cakes" for everyone. Robb said **no way** would his son own an Easy-Bake Oven.

It's purple and pink, and Tommy makes a mean wee-nilla cake. With sprinkles.

Pete, the Lab, hurt his tail and couldn't wag it for a while. Benson, the cat, went up a tree and was stuck for over 22 hours. Distressed, Kerri called the fire department, and to our great embarrassment and surprise, they came out and rescued the stupid cat. Be at peace to know, it was a rookie who was forced to go up the tree – in full gear – after the cat, and no other emergency calls had come in. And, yes, we have pictures. *National Geographic for Kids* is going to do a feature on our cat, Sooner, who thinks he's a goat and has sent a photographer to come out to the house. We've added a horse named Snow to the Allred herd – all events occurred while Robb was in Colorado hunting. Oh, the irony of a hunter being overrun with animals.

I understand there is a need for hunting in some parts of the world, but I try not to think about it too much. I've never liked the idea and have fantasies of evening the playing field a little more. It goes something like this: Brrring [cell phone actually reaching Robb in the middle of nowhere]. *Hello?*

Hi, honey. Are you there? Your camp is set up and you're ready to hunt?

Yup.

Well, then run like hell, honey, because I've sprayed doe scent all over you, and you're about the sweetest smelling thing out there right now. I imagine there are about 20 bulls bearing down on you right . . . Robb? Honey? Are you still . . .?

Argghhh!!!!

Don't forget your gun! Oh, and have a good time!!! Love you! [click]

The rain just won't stop, and we've sustained roof damage that costs more money to repair than we have, but the very good news is that while my father was here to build library shelves in the study, we discovered a mouse in the house, so we don't even think about the roof anymore. What are those stupid cats doing anyway? They are killing the toads which would help eliminate the giant horse flies that invade us and ignore the mice! But you can't explain strategy to cats because they just don't care!

Our guest shower is still broken, the toilet still bubbles when laundry is being done, I got ripped off by a former co-worker, and Tommy is going through a phase of answering the phone and hanging up without telling anyone. But at least he keeps his clothes on now. Nala, the shep/boxer mix, caught another skunk, and I experienced the on-set of heat stroke while running 14 miles with a friend/neighbor. Robb declared we would have a movie night – just the two of us – and picked out "an oldie but goodie." *Fried Green Tomatoes? Some Like It Hot?* No. *The Texas Chainsaw Massacre.*

But not all was lost for the year. I had a new dog book come out, and a lifelong dream was realized. I ran a marathon. The goal was to run – never walk at any time – the entire 26.2 course. After three knee surgeries, I never thought it possible to put that kind of pounding on my almost 40-year-old joints. But with my running partner, and our amazing families, we journeyed to San Antonio for the big event. This is something I have thought about for at least two decades but never thought possible. The night before, my Kerri (daughter) and I walked to the end of the hotel and looked out the bay window from the high-rise. My hope was to show her the historic city of San Antonio and . . .oh, look, a huge billboard for a Gentlemen's Club. Gentlemen, my arse.

Never mind. The moment was mine! Miles 1-14 were fun as my buddy and I chatted away and got to see our families at mile 13, complete with my sister, Michelle, running alongside us taking pictures. But my running partner and I soon separated as she is not carrying quite the luggage in the ol' caboose I am, and I got to listen to music Michelle and Mark Larkin gave me as a gift, and for the next six miles, I jogged along happily enough. No stopping, no walking. By mile 23 when the theme song of 'Rocky' came on, I was recharged. I began waving to everyone, talking loudly, and thanking everyone from the police officers directing traffic to the people handing out water. At mile 25, I turned down a new street to see my family again, and as Katie stepped off the curb to join me in my final mile, my heart was soaring. People were clapping and urging me on. 'Rocky' blared, and I was flying, man! The wind was in my hair! I was just minutes – mere minutes – from a dream come true. This was what it was all about. Strength. Determination. Grit. Perserv... "Um, Mommy," Katie said next to me as we blazed down the street toward the Alamo dome. The finish line. The end of an incredible journey. Things were streaming by. "Uh, not to hurt your feelings, but . . . I'm walking."

Wham.

Another dream tarnished. I looked to see that Katie's short nine-year-old stride was perfectly matched to my *blinding* speed.

Love,

Alex

Of Faith and Divinity

Other than my running times, life moves at a blinding speed. People come and go, things that seem so important in the news today are nothing tomorrow, and no one seems to blink twice as laws and history and traditions fade away or are removed or destroyed. There seems to be little consequence or, rather, because we cannot immediately see a consequence to our actions, humans are doing and saying and singing and wearing things they should not. So, as we blaze forward into oblivion with nary a concern, it seems unlikely that there is such a thing as divine intervention.

It is 2004 and the drug cartels in Mexico run the country, Roman Polanski is living happily in Europe, wife beaters and pedophiles dwell among us, and OJ Simpson is playing golf.

What sucks is that good things happen to bad people and bad things happen to good people, and if you're looking for things to even out at the finish line, you better never run the race because it ain't gonna happen. Sometimes, life just sucks, and no amount of praying or believing is going to change that.

The Unconquerable Marshall Allen
...and his rise to the top

Shortly after Marshall had been released from the hospital, his stepson, Delbert, was determined to make Marshall's life as normal as possible. "He wanted me to sit on the couch," Marshall recalled. But no sooner had Marshall been seated on the light-colored couch than his bowels released. That morning at the hospital, the nurse's aide had not only neglected to put a diaper on him but underwear as well. As Marshall described it, "It went everywhere." He was devastated.

Instantly, people were moving Marshall and cleaning the mess while Marshall apologized profusely. Larry, a young man who had grown up with Marshall's kids and had been visiting that day said, "Oh, that's okay, Mr. Marshall. We poop, too!"

Today, Marshall can recall the incident with some humor, "but at the time, that was it for me. I was depressed. I was ready to go. I didn't think I could live like this."

As if on cue, Al arrived and put Marshall back into his chair. Still determined to make Marshall feel some semblance of normalcy, Delbert said, "Say, man, you haven't been in your truck!"

Knowing how much Marshall loved his truck, Delbert then wrestled the much larger Marshall into his truck and drove his stepfather around Dallas and Fort Worth for nearly two hours.

Marshall, so devout and resolute in his determination to "suck it up" and "be a man" about his depression and growing rage would ultimately have to learn to look to others for help. The irony is, of course, that he had made the decision to seek help before his accident.

The first time Dr. Ann Marie Warren saw Marshall less than a month after his accident, she was worried. "He had such a physical presence!" Almost immediately, she recalled thinking, "This is going to be challenging."

She believed that not only would he have some of the challenges that many individuals face after a spinal cord injury, his sheer physical presence and self identity that had likely been built around that might result in more walls now that he was facing such a physical. She was in for a surprise.

Dr. Warren, then a licensed psychological associate with her Master's degree in psychology, worked closely with her colleague Dr. Lance Bruce, director of the Spinal Cord Injury Service Baylor Institute of Rehabilitation, to help Marshall to accommodate psychologically to the changes resulting from the accident. Dr. Bruce, long recognized as one of the foremost experts in the field of spinal cord injuries, has gained national recognition for the Institute.

At the time of Marshall's accident, Dr. Warren was relatively new in working with individuals with spinal cord injury, and when she was first hired to work with the spinal cord team, Dr. Bruce was initially hesitant. However, he soon changed his opinion, "because she has a way of putting people at ease." Spinal trauma patients are typically angry – angry at themselves for making a mistake that ruined their lives or angry at the circumstances that left them paralyzed. It is all-important that they be able to acknowledge the sudden life changes facing them and to begin to open themselves to accepting help to deal with those changes. Neither Dr. Bruce nor Dr. Warren accepts denial. For this reason, Marshall would be a man they would remember for years.

Initially, Dr. Warren had feared Marshall would have a significant struggle with the psychological impact of this type of injury and that it would take months just to knock down some of the walls he had erected. "But you were so forthcoming," she told him during a meeting when they met years later in the hospital's cafeteria. "You were so comfortable with letting all the emotions out."

"People always assume," Dr. Bruce said, "that people are depressed because of the accident." Marshall is their shining example of the opposite. With his accident came a willingness to talk about other things – things much bigger than the fact that he was now paralyzed.

Although Marshall had begun seeing a counselor before his accident, he admitted that "I was jousting with her [the other doctor]. It was a challenge to see who was smarter." But after his accident, he said, "I'd been reduced to nothing." He was ready – finally ready – to talk.

One of the things Dr. Warren always tells a spinal cord injury patient that "I have no clue how you're feeling because I'm not sitting where you're sitting, so I'm not going to pretend to understand how you feel. I need for you to tell me what your experience is." It's an opening that gives her instant credibility. At once, her patients understand that she is merely trying to *understand* how they feel, not *share* feelings. She said, "We can't allow people to think that you can't ever have a bad day. We teach patients and their families how to deal with a bad day because the reality is everyone is going to have a bad day."

But with Marshall, Dr. Warren didn't have such concerns. One of the classes she conducts with family members and patients with spinal cord injuries is assertive communication – learning when and how to ask for the help that is vital to survival and sanity. Marshall, however, was more than ready to survive. He was and is willing to ask for help.

"He was so open with his emotions. He was demonstrably emotional," she said, smiling. "His vulnerability has always stayed with me. Here was this huge presence, and he was so soft inside."

But something else was happening between Dr. Warren and Marshall. Not yet having earned her PhD, she had questions about her own future, and if specializing in helping those with spinal cord injury was the right path. While all of the FWFD, friends, and family members were watching Marshall to see how he would handle his new position in life, Marshall had placed his life in the hands of Dr. Warren. "I called her my little angel," he later confided.

Like everyone he seems to touch, Marshall came to Dr. Warren at a critical time for her as well as for himself. "He validated that I could do this, that I was on the right track," she said. Marshall, she said, had a kind of inner confidence that she admired, and "he helped me with my own confidence. I realized, 'this is where I'm supposed to be and what I'm supposed to be doing.'"

One of her fond memories is that Marshall preferred being out-of-doors. "I remember you liked to be outside," she said. It seemed to be easier for him to open up outside – the place where he always wanted to be. In 100 degree weather, he studied outside for his engineering and captain tests. He worked and trained outside. He crashed and survived outside, and so it was fitting that he thrives there as well.

"How you dealt with things before," Dr. Bruce said, "is telling of how you deal with problems after." After 30 years of experience working with spinal cord injury patients, this sentiment has been proven to Dr.

Bruce again and again. So, it was no surprise to him that Marshall would indeed survive and thrive. It was how and why he excelled within the fire department, overcame so many odds, and proved himself to be a true warrior.

After two months of meeting with Dr. Warren, most often outside, Marshall and his doctor worked on a strategy. "I remember making plans for [his] returning to work. We talked a lot about energy conservation."

She worried that he would become discouraged by how quickly his energy stores were depleted. Once a man of superman status, Dr. Warren wanted Marshall to understand that his endurance for even the relatively simple activities would be difficult, especially in the first few months following the injury. "Because he was used to being pushed and working hard for hours and hours with little or no fatigue prior to his injury, I realized that much of his frustration was coming from not understanding the issue about energy conservation after SCI."

Using energy wisely was something that Marshall had to address. People with spinal cord injuries must conserve energy, and they must learn about bowel and bladder management as well as fatigue. He has to weigh and consider everything he does. For him, going into town to get a bite to eat takes as much effort as it would take the average person to pack a car for a family road trip. Even then, packing for a family of eight would be easier than what Marshall has to go through.

Marshall is not alone, and it is for this reason friends and family members of a quadriplegic are so enraged when an ambulatory person parks in a handicap spot. We know what they go through just to get to the car. Parking shouldn't be a nightmare.

"By the time I was 12 or 13-years-old," Marshall said, "I knew that things weren't right, but I didn't know what was wrong, either."

"I had to break my neck," Marshall almost laughed, "so that I could be put on 60 milligrams of Prozac!"

"And then the constant internal dialogue went away," Marshall said, adding that it was as though he was reborn. "There had been this constant gray cloud over me. From the moment I woke up, it was there. It wasn't just a battle once you could get yourself up. Depression carries over into your sleep."

"Thank God I was in the hospital," Marshall said, because his injury would ultimately lead to his diagnosis. Good looking, smart, successful, determined to "make something of myself," it is shocking to know that he contemplated suicide – before his accident. To the outside world, he appeared to be on top of the world. In reality, he was miserable.

While Marshall battled demons, Mary was with him, but others had become aware of growing problems. Dr. Warren had been working on her dissertation at the time she met Marshall, and had begun some initial research work in the area. She could not possibly know how vital she would be to his true recovery, which had little to do with his physical injuries. Today, Marshall credits her with being "the person" to properly diagnose his "real" problem – his depression.

Now, years after Marshall left Baylor, Dr. Warren is a Board Certified Rehabilitation Psychologist, is the Clinical Coordinator of the Neuropsychology and Rehabilitation Psychology Service at Baylor Institute of Rehabilitation, and is an Associate Investigator of Spinal Cord Injury. Her most recent publications in understanding resiliency after traumatic spinal cord injury is at the core of an attempt to better help individuals like Marshall with the psychological impact of this experience. Marshall remained an inspiration to her continued dedication and work in the field.

Leading up to the accident, Marshall had been under the care of psychologist Joan Lanning and, later, Dr. Jessie Ingram. Marshall sought therapy and was on a 20-milligram dosage of Prozac. It helped, but it was not enough.

"And if you stopped taking the pills," Marshall said, recalling a time that he'd stopped taking his Prozac, "it takes a couple of weeks for it to build up in your system. It is a chemical imbalance," he said. Today, he is content. Today he understands why and how he feels as he does. "But you mess up the cycle," he stopped for a moment and shook his head. "And the next thing you know, you're cursing out a sheriff."

It was a very long time ago, indeed.

Protecting God's Green Earth

The irony was that Carrie Houston was on top of the world. She was in perfect health and living a dream when she got her first teaching job in Midlothian, Texas. At the tender age of 28, she purchased her first home – a quaint ranch style house less than three miles from the TXI cement plant. The neighborhood, lined with trees, sat atop a hill, providing a picturesque view of the southern sector of Midlothian and two of its three cement plants.

Within just a few months, she began to get sick.

Her illness would be the beginning of a nearly fatal on-going health problem until she was ultimately forced to pump more medication into her body than she ever had, sell her home, leave her job, and move away from Midlothian forever.

Oh, Ye have Little Faith

It's 2004. I don't know Marshall. I don't know Sue Pope, Jim Schermbeck, Sandy Breakfield, or Becky Bornhorst. I don't know Carrie Houston. I only know that Tommy is getting sick a lot, and no one has answers. Robb and I would lie awake at night, listening to our son struggle for air. We would lie in the dark, talking to each other, listening to his ragged breathing, promising each other that it would be okay. *He'll be okay. He'll be okay. Everything will be okay.*

I don't know yet what is wrong with him. I only know that there seems to be some kind of weird don't-ask/don't tell policy about health issues. I have no faith in anything. In anything ... so as my frustrations mount, I use the only tool I have left – humor.

For years, Robb and I had been going around and around about the annual Christmas letters. Initially, his complaint had been that our newsy letter was too happy, so I changed it, but as it gained popularity, the hyper-private Robb began to protest the letter altogether. So imagine my surprise as I, bagel still hanging out of my mouth, bent over to pick up a local paper at the gas station one early morning and began reading an article on the front page, lower section, and thought, "Hmm, this sounds vaguely famil ... oh, no!"

My editor, greatly amused by the letter I'd sent him – to him – personally – chose to run it on the front page of the paper! Briefly, I entertained driving all over the town and surrounding towns to buy every paper in sight. Later – much later – we would all have a chuckle over the fact that our holiday letter had been read by thousands.

But as frustrations mounted over health concerns, I published the most outlandish article to date, fictitiously throwing my hat in the ring as candidate for president of the United States.

With Gina Bates, a former police officer, Republican (she denies this label, but, honestly, she listens to Bill O'Reily. Case closed!), mother, and shockingly outspoken citizen as my VP, we went on to outline our platform, including **opposing** the outsourcing of American jobs, the continued practice of buying all things made in China, and releasing known pedophiles from prison. A guy who molests small children is NEVER going to be a guy who is right in the mind. It seems reasonable that when able-bodied people choose to park in handicapped parking places, the American public should be able to assault these people, rendering them handicapped for a brief – but painful – period of time. This same punishment should also be given to debt dodgers.

"We're not talking about people who have legitimately tried and failed to make ends meet through accidents or mishaps. Instead, our gripe is with the people who buy new cars and plasma televisions, take trips to Disney World, and then declare bankruptcy so they may wash their hands of financial responsibility. Or people who spend all their money on Christmas presents and then tell the landlord, "Sorry, can't pay rent!" Such lack of responsibility and accountability by people is the cause of too many problems."

The article went on to outline our concerns over 12-year-old girls acting like divas (and all the parents who are letting this happen), parents who had stopped parenting in the interest of being "cool," and compromising standards for children's performance in school and athletics. The new policy of giving every kid who just shows up a 'participation certificate' encourages mediocrity in talent and intelligence. By trying to ensure that no kids get their feelings hurt or feel left out, we've instilled an overwhelming feeling of complacency and an embarrassing sense of entitlement among American children!

Everyone and everything, it seemed, was "FOR SALE." America was "FOR SALE." And it had to be stopped. This rather cheeky article was my way of dealing with what was really going on at home. Something was wrong with Tommy. Neighbors had expressed growing concerns about health, but no one really wanted to delve into what was causing the problems.

When the article ran, in its entirety, I had already moved on to another project, briefly forgetting our run for presidency. I'd also forgotten to tell Gina that the article was even coming out. When Gina called, I suddenly remembered. *Dang! I knew there was something I'd been meaning to tell her ...*

She had been receiving phone calls about the article as soon as it came out, and though she had been taken aback by the first caller, she was absolutely tickled by the end of the day. In our small town, she'd become somewhat of a local celebrity. The article was getting rave reviews, including one from her pastor, Tim Wallace. But I got a different kind of phone call.

Like something out of a movie, I heard a voice on the other end of the line say, "I have a story that I need to tell you ..." Only, unlike my previous conversation with Gina, this was not a funny phone call. Soon, I would be dragged into the unsavory world of local and later national politics. What I learned was that private business owners or city employees who asked too many questions were routinely punished as an underground of environmentalists slowly began to organize in homes of Midlothian residents. But I will be honest. When this idea was suggested to me by a school employee, I had to focus on NOT rolling my eyes. I am not into conspiracy theories, and this reeked of it.

Chapter Eight

Christmas 2005

Greetings!

Oh, sure, there were happy times in our home this year. Cute kids did and said cute things. But let's face it, even if I told you about those cute things, would you really remember them next year? No. Instead, let me start with a note about dental care.

Heed this lesson well all you parents of children who will be needing orthodontia: It doesn't matter how often you tell your kids "Don't wrap your retainer in a napkin and place it on your lunch tray." They don't listen. It doesn't matter how often their orthodontist reiterates this advice. They don't care. They will continue to wrap retainers in napkins so that they might throw them away, so that you then will have to plunge your arms elbow-deep into public waste cans and fish through sticky drinks and rotten food. Not once or twice, mind you, but numerous times. And, still, each time you will tell yourself that the child has learned her lesson. But this is a lie. There will be more days of retainer-trashing. Days like November 17, 2005.

The day played out in a painfully slow, torturous rhythm that began when my dryer broke, and I had to wear damp yoga pants to my kickboxing class. I had the flu and felt just awful, but I had to teach anyway. During class, I pulled a stomach muscle – very painful – but beat it on back to the middle school to pick up Kerri for her orthodontist's appointment. She had the appointment because, during a lunch break from her soccer tournament the previous weekend, she had decided to wrap her retainer in a napkin, place it on her lunch tray, and – you guessed it – throw it away. She then strategically waited another five hours before tearfully announcing that her retainer – her *fourth* – was in a trash can in Duncanville (20+minutes away). After I signed Kerri in at the orthodontist's as Kerri "I Lost My Retainer Again" Allred, I learned that our retainer insurance had lapsed and that a new retainer would cost more than my computer. But Kerri was saved from my rage by the doctor's decision to hold off on another retainer so that he could pull two of her teeth.

Back home, while the dryer guy determined that the motor was fried and needed to be replaced, Tommy and Katie came home from school, and Katie burst into tears. My stomach was killing me, my head was pounding, and my dryer was on the fritz. What else could possibly be wrong? Not to be outdone by her older sister, Katie had wrapped her retainer in a napkin during lunch, placed it on her lunch tray, and then dutifully thrown it away, waiting until now to tell anyone. I thought about leaping across the foyer to kill her, but my aching stomach prevented it.

Now knowing how much a retainer cost and that we had no retainer insurance, there was only one solution. So after the dryer guy left, Katie and I went back to the school and began pulling trash bags out of the dumpsters behind the cafeteria. We soon concluded that the contents of dumpster #1 – chicken, stuffing, gravy, green beans, rolls, and Jell-O – meant that it was the correct dumpster, and we rummaged through the nasty, foul, disgusting remainders of kiddy food. And vomit. No school dumpster is complete without vomit. By bag #4 (and I'm talking giant bags) and no luck, it was clear that I would have to go into the dumpster because – hindered by my stomach – I couldn't reach any further. So, cussing and ranting, I climbed inside the dumpster.

As I sifted through the sewage of saliva and goo, Katie decided to assist me further by making retching noises outside the dumpster. Have you ever been inside a dumpster? I mean really inside one, wallowing in chocolate milk, mashed meat, and vomit-soaked bread? It really, *really* stinks. And not just from days of revolting smells, but from weeks, nay, months of rancid stench that wilts your taste buds even when your mouth is closed. My eyes hurt from the putridity, and the princess was standing *outside* the dumpster gagging!

I snapped. "SHUT UP!"

We don't say shut up in my house. It's very rude and extremely inappropriate to say to children.

"SHUT UP! SHUT UP! SHUT UP!"

Trapped inside that echoing coffin of noxious fumes, I'm not sure who heard me, but I am sure that somewhere in the world a child caught in the act of wrapping a retainer in a napkin paused and shuddered.

Then, just as I thought I might faint from the fumes, I saw – perched precariously on a heap of ... man, I don't know what that was – something sparkle. I held my breath, plunged my entire arm into the abyss, and pulled out the precious retainer. *Yes!*

We drove home with the windows down. I made dinner, fed the animals, and announced that after I did a load of laundry (since I really didn't want our – well, my – dumpster clothing to ripen overnight), I was going to bed. Halfway through my Thera-Flu, the dryer stopped. Dead. And somehow, I knew the retainer was responsible.

Sometime during the dryer/retainer ordeal, Aggie, the cat, disappeared, and I feared an owl might have done her in. This has been a bad year for animals in our house. Over the summer, an owl snatched both Sooner and Benson (our previous cats) and carried them away – at separate times. So we got Aggie and Hunter. But Aggie, ever determined to come into the house, must have met Pete, the dog, head-on while I was answering the door for the dryer guy. The morning following Aggies's disappearance, I assigned the girls the task of raking Pete's area. Then came the guttural cry – Kerri had raked up Aggie's lifeless, little body. We have a new kitten now to keep Hunter company. His name is Calvin. Hunter is now named Susie because it turns out he is a she.

Earlier in the summer, determined to prove to Robb that Pete isn't the stupidest dog on earth, Pete went to retrieving school. Initially, all he wanted to do was run alongside the other dogs, which was a little embarrassing, but soon enough he was retrieving pigeons. We were pleased as punch when we picked him up from summer school until I realized that the pigeons being thrown for him to retrieve were real. And alive. It was horrible! So Patty the pigeon came home with us, clipped wings and all, and I was determined to teach her to fly again. At no time did I envision having a pet pigeon, but Patty spent her nights in the garage and her days pooping on our cars. We would carry her out and throw her into the air. "You're free, Patty!" But she's a homing pigeon, so she wouldn't leave.

She would fly on top of the garage, perch on its edge, and watch us. She would run along the roof of the house as we drove away and be waiting there faithfully when we returned. Unfortunately, one day she apparently lost her balance and fell into Pete's area. When I came home, Nala was spitting out feathers.

Cookiedough, our goat, got so fat from eating Snow's (horse) food that we sent her away to a fat farm – actually, a neighbor's small goat farm – so that she could regain her figure and her dignity. We're still waiting. We pretend she's just on vacation visiting family.

For reasons known only to herself, Katie declared she wants to be called Pinky. So Tommy now wants to be called Pokey. And Kerri was designated Pukey.

But the worst incident of the summer occurred when a little serial killer in the making came to our house and poked out our guinea pig's eye. Literally. Sparkles ultimately had to be put to sleep. It was terrible. And it was made all the more terrible by the fact that the child had no remorse.

Also over the summer, I was involved in three lawsuits. One was against the idiot kid on the motorcycle who tried to commit suicide by nearly driving into the side of my van. Anyone remember this? Two years ago, he was driving 70 miles per hour without a license on a motorcycle that wasn't his with a prior conviction for assaulting a police officer (just to give you an idea of the kind of upstanding citizen he is). Witnesses had already called 911 before our mishap, stating that he was going to kill someone. The police cited him for causing the accident, but he sued me for medical expenses (he broke his toe when he lost control of the bike and skidded off the road) and lost wages. The case dragged on for more than a year because the kid kept no-showing for court, forcing us to reschedule several times. Finally, my insurance company decided, as a matter of "economics," to settle. Meaning they paid the little weasel. Our judicial system at its finest.

The other two lawsuits involved Erin Brokovich who came to Midlothian to help fight pollution from the three local cement plants and two local environmental groups. The two groups, Downwinders at Risk and Blue Skies Alliance, recently made Texas history by winning a large settlement against one of the plants. All this occurred while I was finishing the book *Athletic Scholarships for Dummies*.

And, of course, there is the world according to Robb. Here are some examples of how his mind works: on a recent business trip, he and a co-worker went out to get a bite to eat. When the waitress came, the co-worker unwittingly ordered the same meal Robb had planned to order, which meant Robb now had to order something else. Why? Apparently, real men cannot eat the same meal at restaurants. If one guy at a table orders a meal that sounds really good to another guy at the table, the second guy is out of luck. He can't order the same thing because – according to the rules of Robb – no self respecting guy would ever say, "I'll have the same thing." Instead, he has to order something different. Who knew? It seems so clear to him, but Pinky, Pokey, Pukey, and I just don't get it.

Other rules of Robb: furniture must not have flower print, he doesn't trust men with beards, and he will never use a stall in a public restroom if a stall next to it is occupied because – as I understand it – men must never potty beside other men. Good to know.

Robb refuses to eat at Friday's restaurants and Chili's because people look too happy on their commercials. (Many of you may recall his similar boycott of Olive Garden restaurants because of their commercials depicting people laughing and enjoying themselves.) And Robb maintains that no one really likes coffee. We're just pretending because we want to be seen drinking our status coffees. Frankly, I think this is a mild overreaction to my addiction to Starbucks.

Kerri broke her foot in volleyball and then played a full game of soccer before we (okay, before I) realized it was broken. During my interview with a U.S. Senator, Katie got on the other phone and began breathing heavily, "I know what you did last summer!" Kerri came home from school one day and excitedly asked that we go to the grocery store and buy a box of chewy granola bars (which I give them as snacks for school). Apparently, Kerri had been selling her .42 cent granola bars in the cafeteria for $2 apiece. What an extortionist! With visions of laptop computers dancing in her head, she may have a lucrative career in the gasoline/oil industry – jacking up prices in times of need. Tommy then declared that he either wants money from Santa Claus or a machine with which he can make his own money. He also has decided, for some reason, to open a car dealership when he grows up. I don't know where they get this stuff.

Robb has now taken to imitating Judge Judy and is driving us nuts. He's in love with the diminutive, yet domineering 4'8," 65-year-old queen of daytime television mean. How do I compete with that?

From time to time, believe it or not, I actually forget that I'm in rural Texas – despite the fact that an owl stole my cats, that coyotes are occasionally spotted in our backyard, and that friends continue to introduce me to others as "my friend, the Democrat." Apparently, I alone represent the Democratic party in Ellis County, Texas. But reminders of where we are always bring me back to reality pretty quickly. Like the other day when, just a couple blocks from my house, I came face-to-face with three cows and a bull standing in the middle of the street. I stopped, got out of my van, and did my best imitation of a cowboy, waving my arms and yelling, "Go on ... git!" And they did git. Proud, I got back in the van and realized, by golly, I just herded cattle. Of course, I herded them onto the wrong property. Oh well, the urban cowgirl strikes again.

Still, despite our best efforts, it hasn't been all doom and gloom this year: both girls won first place in their school talent shows – Katie and her best buddy, Katie Bates, for their singing duet and Kerri for her violin solo. Kerri also became a member of the Old Time Fiddlers Association and won 4th place in a regional competition. Tommy played his very first season of soccer (asthma and all). He played defense, although he spent most of his time on the field entertaining his goalie and other defenders with his air guitar impressions. He's very excited now because he has lost two front teeth, which means more money from the tooth fairy. New books are out (and in book stores), and I've got a great literary agent.

In May, I traveled to Orange County, California, and test-drove a gravity car for Volvo and wrote about it for a European magazine. Robb went on his annual hunting trip and bagged an elk. That's his happy news, not ours, but the kids and I are getting used to the taste of elk meat. Finally, inspired by the local pollution and Tommy's asthma, the girls created and launched their own environmental website.

And so with that ... we wish you a very happy holiday, and take heart ... you could be spending it in a dumpster. Oh, and don't wrap your retainer in a napkin!

Love,

Alex

An Environmental Digression

Here's a little secret about Texas. The state has flying cockroaches, mosquitoes the size of small aircraft carriers, fire ants, and mesquite trees. The environment can be harsh and brutal, and somewhere along the line Texans mistook the term "tailgating"(a fun affair before football games in which friends BBQ and trash talk) to mean "ride hard and fast on another person's bumper at 60 MPH," which, in turn, would explain all the car wrecks, flips, explosions, and/or fender benders that surely put Texans as some of the most dangerous drivers in the world. Ah, but I digress. Despite these adverse living conditions, Texans are thoroughly enjoyable people. (Please exclude the other problem that some Texans feel the need to fly the Texas flag at equal level to the U.S. flag, which is a highly offensive act to any and all patriots of this great nation.)

By 2005, I am in a precarious situation as I have many dear friends connected to the cement plants. I love my friends. I am crazy about my friends. They are good, kind, hard working people just trying to make a living, and I could and would never begrudge them this. Never have I wanted anyone to lose a job over this mess. I have only wanted the industry to do what was right, but in the minds of many, it is hard to separate industry practice from individual workers. Not for me. I know which one is the beast.

Unafraid of Faith and the Wolfman

My grandmother-in-law, Elda Huling, was not a fan of the Holiday Allred letters. Why, she wanted to know, couldn't we simply send out a normal card celebrating the intent of the season – the birth of Christ.

What I could not tell her was as much as Robb abhorred the life-is-swell letters from friends and family, I found the 'Christ is Born' cards equally nauseating. We're all celebrating the 25th of December for one reason and one reason only. Loot. Lots and lots of loot.

To believe in God, however, is a tremendous leap of faith. Certainly, there are crazy coincidences that are almost impossible to explain. But random acts are much easier to rationalize than an idea that some higher power has set events into some sort of motion that would end with one specific desired result.

For those who are in a weaker state, more vulnerable and unable to deal with the realities and fragility of life, religion does serve an excellent purpose. It makes them feel better about themselves and their lives. But that's it. For those of us who are realists, for those of us unafraid of the future, there is but one conclusion. Life is a set of coincidences that set different people on different paths.

If you could believe in God, couldn't you just as well believe in Santa Claus? Or the wolf man? If the spirit of God can dwell unseen inside of us, can't the werewolf dwell in the national state park?

The Unconquerable Marshall Allen
...and his rise to the top

In January of 2005, Al called his friend to tell him he had prostate cancer. "The first thing I told him was not to mess around with it." Marshall insisted that Al act aggressively to fight the cancer.

In the early spring, Al underwent surgery, "and there he was." Marshall smiled at the memory. "He called, and it was my turn to get him out of the house." So Marshall pulled up in his van and watched as Al shuffled weakly from his house. "He had to have a catheter," Marshall smiled again. "We went from him coming to my house with mine ... to me going to his house to get him ... with his."

The "with his," to get a visual, was very uncomfortable: Al, shuffling out of his house toward Marshall's van, with his catheter.

In the Fall of 2005, Al had taken to dropping by Marshall's office on his off days. Prior to the accident, they scheduled their days so that they could work out in the gym together, play pick-up games of basketball, and just hang out. In many respects, the accident changed very little, and Al, once again, found himself in a seat across from Marshall's desk, shooting the breeze and discussing whatever topics entered his mind.

But on this particular day, Lyn Simmons had also happened by the office. A dark skinned man of medium build "with a prominent brow and cheekbones" who Marshall describes as a "passionate man of debate," Lyn was the perfect sparring partner for Al.

The topics of interest varied from sports to current events until Al had challenged Lyn on a scientific point. Lyn fancied himself a man of scientific knowledge, but for Al, it was just another opportunity for Al to needle Lyn in any way he could. But when Lyn was certain he had Al on the topic of carbon dating, he bowed up.

"Well, is carbon an element?" he wanted to know of Al.

"Yeah, it's the sixth most abundant element in the universe," Al answered.

Perhaps the biggest mistake people continue to make with Al is to underestimate what he knows. Like Marshall, he is omnivorous about knowledge. Both men love to read, retain, and discuss, and for this reason will often tune everyone else out, discussing a topic only amongst themselves as if no one else knows what in the world they are talking about.

"Well, do you know about how they do carbon dating? And what makes you think you can trust it?" Lyn persisted, not yet ready to concede.

For several minutes, they discussed the whys and hows of carbon dating but on this particular subject, Marshall saw Al falter and was quick to act. As part of their 20+ year Frick-and-Frack, Who's-on-First, What's-on-Second routine, they routinely double team some poor sloth, and this day was no different. Marshall quietly called up carbon dating on his computer. Al leaned back in his chair and contemplated this most vexing question.

"Carbon 14 or, as it's known, C14," Al shrugged. "It's an isotope of carbon with carbonate neutrons instead of the more common neutrons. But it's unstable. It radioactively decays by electron emission to Nitrogen 14 with a half-life of 5730 years."

Lyn's jaw went slack.

"You have to understand that in the atmosphere, cosmic rays smash into normal carbon 12 atoms and create carbon 14 isotopes. This process is constantly occurring and has been for a very long time, so there is a fairly constant ratio of carbon 14 atoms to carbon 12 atoms in the atmosphere."

Al pressed his fingertips together and slowly spread his fingers, and he pursed his lips thoughtfully.

"It's the rate of decay, or how many radioactive emissions occur per unit time, measured against how many atoms there are in a sample. This way, we can figure an exponential decay rate."

Lyn blinked.

"You measure a rate of 15.6 decays/min per gram of carbon in a living sample. But, obviously," Al shrugged, "this technique only works on dead organic materials."

Slowly, Marshall had turned one of his 20" monitors toward Al and spoon fed his buddy line by line. Marshall had been working off of two 20" monitors when the ridiculous contest of words between Al and Lyn had begun. Very slowly, he lowered the resolution on the left monitor so that the print would appear larger and more clearly. "On the right monitor," Marshall said, "I Googled carbon dating and then posted the page on the monitor on my left nearest to Al." With that, Al allowed Lyn to absorb what he'd heard for a moment longer and then leaned forward.

"You did know that I got my degree in archeology?"

Minutes ticked off the clock while Marshall attempted to get work done, but neither Al nor Lyn was ready to leave.

"They've [Al and Lyn] known each other for years, and they know that there are no surprises to be had until …" Marshall shakes his head even at the memory of it.

For the next twenty minutes, the conversations became more and more outrageous. Marshall had been quickly and quietly Googling and presenting information to Al so that Al could (and did) claim to hold degrees in a variety of the sciences, including geology and medicine. But when Lyn demanded to know, "Is that your wife or is that your concubine?" there was a loud slamming of the door from the office next to Marshall's.

Marshall's office mate had heard and had enough. But when the subject turned to the wolf man, Marshall stopped feeding any information to Al. Even Marshall had had enough, and he knew they were in dangerous waters.

Al believes in the wolf man. At least, for the sake of arguing with someone else, he maintains werewolves exist.

Tensions mounted as Al and Lyn argued about the legendary wolf man. What drove Marshall to put an end to this madness was not that Lyn was denying the wolf man's existence but, rather, how to defend himself against the dreaded creature.

Through the entirety of this ridiculous conversation, Lyn held steadfast to one position: *How do you know what you're being told is true? How do you know that you're not been duped by some larger conspiracy?*

Around and around Al and Lyn went. Marshall's nerves were on edge until Lyn's fated question.

"Well, here's the thing," Lyn began cautiously, thinking through the process that led him to his final question for Al. "What if I let you convince me that a man is the werewolf, and I use my last silver bullet … but he's the wrong man?"

"Get out!" Marshall roared. Swinging his arms at both Al and Lyn, Marshall yelled at them. "Get out!" After listening to the two argue in his office for nearly an hour, Marshall had had enough.

"Now I'm defenseless against the real world because I let you convince me …" Lyn was still following a thread.

"Out!"

Though his wolfman is purely fictional, Al has been chasing monsters for many years.

The next time we had an opportunity to talk in privacy, Al began talking about the "fun" of the wolf man. The monster had been a necessary evil for Al to joke about with other people, and Lyn had merely provided Al with more fun than he could have ever hoped for because the true purpose of pondering the existence of the wolf man was to keep people off Al.

He'd learned at an early age that through laughter and ridiculous antics, he could control what people mocked.

Today, Al confides, "It is a miracle I ever learned to read." His memories of school are not those of a successful academic. He was labeled. He was difficult. He was challenged. Yet, no one knew why.

While Marshall suffered immeasurable mental and emotional torture, living with depression, Al was not diagnosed with severe ADD/ADHD until he was 50 years. The severe combination of attention deficit with attention deficit hyper disorder had made the everyday functions of a job and interacting with other people a constant challenge for Al.

"No one knew what that was 20 years ago," said Al.

He could not understand why everything was so difficult. He could not understand why his friends and fellow students could so easily grasp something that was forever out of his reach. And when he joined the army and later became a fire fighter, he struggled daily with the everyday tasks demanded of his job, not because he was unwilling but because there were just so many other things interfering with his thought process.

Unlike Marshall, Al never adequately prepared for the Engineer test, "because there was just no way could I grasp all that material." For Al, the variety of books required for the study manual was
    overwhelming.

The reality is Al is extremely intelligent. But undiagnosed and vastly misunderstood, he struggled daily. By his own admission, he was constantly doing and saying all the wrong things.

"It wasn't malicious," he said. Even as he speaks, his frustrations are apparent. By his early twenties, he was angry. He was frustrated by other people and their lack of understanding or compassion toward him. Everyone, it seemed, was against him, picking on him, going after him, trying to break him down in some way. It was impossible for Al to understand why this was. Eventually, he would come to a final and devastating conclusion. He was stupid.

This is an astonishing admission by a man who is so quick-witted, naturally curious, and intelligent. Oh, if only the whole world was as "stupid" as Al. It is impossible to imagine Al believing such a thing. But unable to even understand himself, it was the only reasonable conclusion.

That and the wolf man existed.

When Al spun yarns of absurdity, challenged all things sane and rational, and playfully suggested the most ridiculous possibilities, he wasn't stupid. He was entertaining. He was funny. He was not stupid.

Because he was so entertaining and because he has such an easy-going nature, he is a man people are naturally drawn to. On our weekly Sunday meets, it is not uncommon for five or six people strategically to plant themselves around Al's chair, ready to engage in the varied topics of sports, politics, cars, music, and, dependent upon Al's mood, quantum physics and the social ramifications of Buddhist Monks rebelling against the Myanmar, formally known as Burma, military government. To drive home some finer point he hopes to make, Al will often proclaim himself to be a professor or former ruler of small Third World countries.

Still, no matter how compelling the subject and no matter how attentive the audience, women are a constant distraction to Al. All shapes and sizes are of interest to him. In fact, he jokes that he's spent the better part of his adulthood asking women "Not to call the police."

While sitting at a table, Al instinctively would say, "Look!" as an attractive woman approached. Also from instinct, Marshall swung his head around, caught himself, and rolled his eyes.

"I can't believe I just looked," he would say with disgust. After more than twenty years of friendship with Al, Marshall need not look. He is all too aware of Al's fascination with women. He knows about Al's propensity to say whatever is on his mind, and during the course of their friendship, Marshall has either helped his friend reign in his impulsive banter or simply not "looked!" when called upon.

According to the Natural Resource Center for AD/HD, Al is the walking poster child for adults with ADHD. Impulsive, disorganized, intense, and extremely intelligent. By the time Al was diagnosed with ADD and ADHD, he had suffered humiliation and "self-castigation," believing himself unworthy or unable to handle specific tasks.

"One of the last things we did together before his accident," Al said of Marshall, "was install a new dishwasher in my house." By Al's account, he could only stand back and watch Marshall do the actual installation. "He is such a quick study of everything," Al marveled. What is interesting, however, is Al is a very good mechanic and technician. But everything and everyday is subject to self perception, and for the man with an undiagnosed condition such as AD/HD, self ridicule is debilitating.

Marshall, Al said, "somehow tolerated me through all this."

How ironic that these two giant, gentle men, both undiagnosed – one with depression and the other with severe AD/HD – and left alone to battle their demons, found each other, befriended, and understood one another as no one else could. Only the one sitting in a wheelchair has managed to fully confront, battle, and win against his demons. Al still struggles daily.

They used to joke about how local police would react when they saw Marshall and Al, two muscle-bound, massive human beings, sauntering down the street. Livestock would get nervous as the two walked by, and they could see people do a quick weight capacity tally on the elevator as they stepped on. Nothing could possibly harm these two men. Nothing could scare them, rattle them, or defeat them. At least, this was the perception of the outside world. Yet both Al and Marshall, with two very different illnesses, could not have been more vulnerable.

To hear Al talk, Marshall "protected" him from ridicule and disrespect.

Al's social interactions with his fellow fire fighters, friends, neighbors, and women were often marred by Al-isms. Because he has no sense of restraint, no filter, there were endless incidences of misunderstandings. Or, as the National Resource Center for AD/HD explains, "those with AD/HD have a decreased ability to self-regulate their actions and reactions toward others. This can cause relationships to be overly tense and fragile."

This would explain his overwhelming need to flirt with every single woman who passes by just as this would explain why there were often misunderstandings between him and all the women out there he pesters and teases. Even as the woman feigns or actually feels irritation, she is still drawn to him. This is how it goes with Al.

"They [women] eat that up," Marshall shook his head. Because the truth is, Al is adorable. Though he is handsome, large, powerful, and full of boyish charm, he could potentially explode at any given moment. One can only imagine the sensation the two created in their hay day.

Today, he is happier, but life is a daily struggle. Like Marshall, he would not be diagnosed until he was older and had arguably suffered more than was needed. Like Marshall, his contentment comes not only from being properly medicated but also in the satisfaction of understanding "what was wrong." But just in case, he's got a silver bullet.

Protecting God's Green Earth
"Careful, kids! That sucker is gonna blow!"

I was sitting in the front row, seated between my kids, my sister Michelle, and Erin Brokovich's childhood friend Gina Bates, but all I could concentrate on was the golden snake emblem clasp that held Erin's shirt together. It was uncertain how much strain that little clasp could take before an explosion of mammary glands would overtake us all.

I'd had dinner and drinks with Erin the night before, so I'd had time to digest one simple fact: how Julia Roberts speaks in the movie, *Erin Brokovich*, is spot on to the real-life Erin. Yet somehow, as the "F" bombs are dropped left and right, she is not offensive. She's hilarious. While others would try to paint her as an opportunist, I found there was something very genuine in her environmental concerns.

Just how Erin came to work with McCurdy & McCurdy and land in our own backyard was an incredible series of coincidences that really made a body wonder. My good buddy just happened to be the childhood buddy of Erin who happened to be working with a man, Jim Ross, who just happened to be on SWAT with Gina's husband, Brian. Jim Ross just happened to get the *D Magazine* from a colleague the same day I mailed Erin a copy. It was a crazy series of coincidences that began with the *D Magazine* article written by Tom Boyle in May 2005.

Chapter Nine
Coincidence and Faith Collide:
What a Difference One Woman Can Make

Tommy's health appeared to be on a rapid decline. We had the diagnosis of 'environmental asthma' yet could not seem to control the symptoms, and he was missing too many days of school. Later, I would have to write a letter of appeal with notes from doctors to explain to the school board why Tommy had missed so many days of school. I was beyond frustration when I pulled up behind a suburban at a stoplight. *What's in Midlothian's Air?* was written on the back windows along with a website.

I followed her through the light, and when she stopped at a gas station, I jumped out and approached the driver's window, startling the woman I would come to know as Carrie Kiesling. In just five minutes of talking to her, I learned that both she and her husband, within six months of each other, developed two different kinds of cancer after moving to Midlothian. When they had an "expert" from the EPA come out to their home, just downwind of the Holcim cement plant, she was asked if she fed her family the wide variety of vegetables from her huge, lush garden – a certain point of pride for her. When she said 'yes,' she was told, "I wouldn't."

It was a horribly sobering moment for her. By the time I'd met her, her house was up for sale. But what was more evident to me was how guarded she was when I first introduced myself. It was not until she actually saw Tommy, sick and sitting in my van, that she believed me when I said I was "concerned, too!"

Through Carrie, I would come to meet a group of concerned citizens at Carrie's house to discuss how to shine a spotlight on what was happening in Midlothian.

In the world of crazy coincidences, Erin was working a toxic waste dumping case in Florida, and, as it happened, her Texas-based co-council once worked SWAT with none other than Gina Bates' husband, Brian. Gina grew up with Erin Brokovich. Well before I ever spoke to Erin, I found myself laughing with a man named Jim Ross about what a small world we live in. What a crazy coincidence!

He said, "You don't even know how wild this is." Apparently, Jim's boss had read the *D Magazine* article by Tom Boyle and had sent it on to Jim. He "wanted to help the people in Midlothian" and had been sick of hearing about how "industry always did what they wanted." He told Jim it had been a long time coming that someone set this place right. Hurray!

Jim was in Florida at the time, co-counseling a case with Erin, when he finally read the article. Coincidentally, I had sent a magazine copy to Erin's office. When they were together, Erin approached Jim first, asking, "Have you ever heard of a Mid…Midalot… Midltian, Texas?"

"Midlothian, Texas?" Jim asked.

"Yea, that's the one," she said.

Together, they decided it must be fate that they were both presented this magazine article. And the wheels were put in motion.

I met with an amazing group of people from a local environmental group called Downwinders at Risk. The idea being, of course, that anyone downwind of the plants were and are at risk, and dependent upon who you asked, this small group had made quite a name for itself. Initially, I was uneasy about becoming connected to a grassroots environmental group. Admittedly, the stereotypical image of an environmentalist – particularly in Texas – is not a good one.

The irony here, of course, is what kind of person protests clean air and water? Or, more specifically, what kind of person dislikes another person because he or she *wants* clean air or water? Yet, the negative stereotype among the less educated does exist.

When I finally met this environmental bunch, I did not find drugged out hippies but normal, everyday, walking and talking folks. Not only were the majority of them conservative professionals with strong ties to the community and family, but they were the only people unafraid to speak on what they thought was right – or wrong, as the case may be.

How many times had I been in a group of mothers talking about the air quality, but when it was mentioned that we, as a collective group, speak out about it, every last mother backed off. It was incredibly frustrating to watch parents shrink away from what was right because of possible consequences. There was a belief that high school athletes and business owners could be punished if they (or their parents) were too outspoken about the cement plants. By being afraid to stand up and speak out, however, it seemed they put their children's health at risk.

With Jim Schermbeck at the helm, a passionate, outspoken activist who possesses a cell phone with an Apache warrior cry for a ring tone, the group has been standing up against air pollution for over two decades. Had they based in Virginia, Colorado, Maine, Kentucky, California or Florida, it would not be nearly as impressive. But the truth is, Downwinders, a small band of determined citizens, withstood threats from politicians, industry, and everyday Texans brainwashed into believing that fighting for better air and clean water was somehow suspicious and anti-American.

Becky Bornhorst, head chair to the Downwinders organization, began calling me regularly. Initially, I enjoyed the phone calls because it made me feel plugged in and somehow stronger to fight for my son's health. I sometimes believe it was meant to be that Becky was my contact person. Tougher than nails intermixed with a sweet disposition, Becky is the kind of woman I want to be friends with. Smart, clever, compassionate, and active, she is also fair in her assessments and not afraid to speak her mind. Much of the legal mumbo-jumbo between the cement plants hazardous emissions and the state's compliance laws were so complicated I often felt inept, but Becky had a way of explaining things to help me understand.

When I began actively asking questions, perhaps the most influential Midlothian resident was Sue Pope. An accomplished artist and horse breeder, Sue's amazing life has been filled with joy, triumph, tragedy, and despair with, sadly, much of the more unhappy events occurring while living in Midlothian. When her horses became sick in the early 90s, it was only a taste of what was to come, and Sue would unwittingly becoming the matriarch to DAR's movement against the cement plants. This strong, beautiful woman, the consummate picture of the Texas southern bell, became our poster child for what living under the cement stacks could do to the human body.

Her son died without explanation in his thirties, and as her own health plummeted, she became more of a recluse. A Sue sighting was rare – so rare, in fact, that I would only see her about three times in six months.

Suddenly, I was trying to learn and memorize new names and faces, understand terms like SCRs (selective catalytic reduction) technology, scrubbers, and what it meant to be of non-attainment status in Ellis County, the county of Midlothian.

A meeting was held for a number of residents who had children born with mental and physical disorders. The legal team of McCurdy & McCurdy were so busy talking to residents that it was almost chaotic. Hundreds of people were excited; they wanted answers, and all were asking what they hoped Erin could accomplish by coming. Jim Ross was clear: Erin's presence would be the first sign to industry that "we've had it with their corrupt ways and in-the-pocket politicians. Plus," he said, "we get to really irritate them."

Their law firm had deep pockets. They set up containment canisters that collected eight hours of polluted air and opened a website to collect medical histories on anyone interested.

In our meeting, we tried to compare notes. For example, many of us recalled (for various reasons) that on April 20, a Wednesday, brown smoke had come from the TXI stacks. I knew this because Tommy had been at Baylor Hospital Emergency the day before and, though home and out of school, I'd had to transport him in the car to get steroids. I had noted in my journal that whichever way I drove, I was driving through what I hoped was not hazardous waste.

The group decided that we should all begin taking more diligent notes and take pictures when we saw anything unusual.

But a man in the room shook his head. "It won't work. They know you're coming now. They'll just shut down production for a while."

After Jim Ross and company left, I got word that Karen Shipp had died of cancer. Her father was still struggling with cancer, but her uncle and a six-year-old cousin had died of cancer while another family member had some terrible skin disorder. All were in Midlothian, and, to my surprise when I called Jim Ross about it, he said, "I know Karen. She's married to my cousin."

I was stunned. There were just too many coincidences, too many connections to something really, really bad.

But things were moving too quickly to appreciate the moment. Suddenly, word of Erin's arrival buzzed everywhere. The *Chicago Tribune* was calling, and television news crews were pressing for live coverage. The residents of Midlothian were, by and large, excited about her arrival while the cement heads and local politicians were unsettled. No one really knew how this would all play out, and worse, Robb and I were struggling.

All Robb wanted me to do was walk away from it all, but I couldn't. Instead, I was on local news, in national media outlets, and in dialogue with U.S. Senators. As Tommy struggled for oxygen, surrendering to peer pressure was not an option. As soon as the law firm of McCurdy and McCurdy secured its first official client, the ball was officially rolling. Still, as I met family members of those with serious problems, I began to back off. We were lucky. Tommy only had asthma. Then, Erin called me next with a very clear message: "When you do something for the morally right reason, you can't be wrong."

Then, she dropped another coincidental bombshell. One of the reasons she cares so much about environmental issues is because her brother, Tommy, died of an asthma attack when she was a young girl.

115

Here I was worried that my Tommy's condition wasn't that serious when her Tommy had died from asthma. What are the odds that she had a Tommy and I had a Tommy. What are the odds?

It was that kind of jaw dropping information that made everything click, and I knew I was taking the right path. At the time, I could not put how I felt into proper words. It felt foolish, even arrogant, but I had this amazing, powerfully real feeling that it was just meant to be. All of it. It was supposed to happen this way.

By May 15, mere weeks before Erin was to come, two more lawyers came in from California. Brian Butcher and James Drury (from Masry and Vititoe) flew in to take pictures and gather information. In the next few days, they went to Austin to scan/gather more info. They were pleased to note that the Texas Commission of Environmental Quality and other state agencies were willing to work with them as they were reportedly disgusted with TXI, AshGrove, Holcim, and Chaparral Steel.

Only in Texas could the industries actually sue the state, saying that citizens fearful about air pollution (and its long term effects) impeded their rights as American businesses by trying to control air quality!

As rumors of Erin's appearance swirled, more and more people began to contact the DAR website and the city. The more persistent citizens contacted us directly, and we began to gather information about families who suffered from asthma, cancer, leukemia, Downs, cerebral palsy, skin disorders, chromosome malformations, and upper respiratory diseases.

Across the street from the TXI property, citizens from "Cement Valley" were putting up signs and handing out flyers in hopes of making more people aware of what was happening.

Across the highway from Holcim and next to Ash Grove, another good buddy, Audra Dahl, had taken on a battle of her own. Again, it is worth mentioning that Audra is a reluctant environmentalist. In fact, she would tell you she is not an environmentalist at all. At this time, she was finishing up her Bachelor's degree at Dallas Baptist University with the idea of earning a Masters in psychology. What she wanted to do was Christian-based counseling. A deeply religious woman, doting wife and mother of two, she was also battling very serious health issues (all, I believe, unrelated to the cement plants). Between work, school, and family, she was extremely busy but always on hand to pick up her children who attended Vitovsky Elementary School on Highway 67 (adjacent to the cement plants). It was on such a day that I pointed out a sign next to the school, and her face fell. Not 500 feet from the elementary school was a sign that read *future quarry site*.

"Nuh uh" was all she could say.

"Yuh huh," I smiled, though there was truly no joy in my heart. "I'm telling ya, Audra, this kind of stuff is happening right now, right here."

Audra and her husband, Tim, moved to Midlothian because of the school system. Like us, they liked the idea of smaller classrooms, more hands-on teaching with wide open spaces. The idea that the schools could be causing more harm was unacceptable, and so Audra took matters into her own hands. As sweet and compassionate and loving as she is, you do not want her mad at you!

Two days later, she called me. She was so frustrated, she was laughing. She spoke to the Ash Grove official to discover that, yes, in fact, a future quarry site filled with the cement kiln dust or CKD (which can play havoc on the immune system) some 500 feet away from the children's playground and school was going to be constructed.

Astonished, she questioned the wisdom of this, noting how many developing lungs would be compromised by the cement kiln dust. His response? "We were here first."

If, indeed, Ash Grove was there first with a proposed future quarry site, who approved building a school right next to it? The school board? What could "educators" possibly be thinking in building an elementary school right next to a proposed quarry site just mere miles from two different cement plants? (By 2008, this same school would be flagged as one of the most toxic schools in the United States of America in *USAToday, Dec. 2008*). I have to believe they just didn't know.

More complaints came in. While the TCEQ had been enlisted to take soil, water, and blood/urine samples to detect any problems, some residents complained that everything was coming back suspiciously clean. One resident, who has asked for anonymity, had her own blood tested by an independent contractor. She no longer trusted the state to do the right thing. And, lo and behold, the results were proof positive that something screwy was going on.

"I should have had some arsenic or lead show up because I'm a smoker," she later said. "What does that tell you?" Instead, with the TCEQ, her blood work was clean. For anyone new to the area or to the realm of environmentalism, these claims might have seemed farfetched. How far would people really go to keep their image clean and continue to be allowed to burn harmful substances?

June 7, two days before Erin was to arrive, DAR members Sue Pope, Becky Bornhorst, Sandy Breakfield, Merle Ann Roten, and Reecea Henderson with attorney Jim Ross and a plethora of Midlothian residents all showed up to tell personal stories to get party status in an upcoming lawsuit before a judge in the courthouse of Waxahachie, Texas.

For a decade, DAR members had been fighting against the cement plants with little fanfare. Suddenly, the appearance of Erin Brokovich combined with an upcoming party status hearing brought out more press than the grass-roots organization could ever recall.

An official hearing to determine who could get party status in an effort to fight toxic emissions was to begin in the courtroom of City Hall. We all filed in to listen to those who hoped to obtain "Party Status" so that they could move on to the next step to fight TXI. TXI had previously stated their intentions to remove pollution controls as it was more profitable for the corporation. Never mind public health.

Ironically, when the cement plants were burning less hazardous material, a person could obtain party status if they lived within 20 miles of the cement kiln emissions. But as the cement plants became more powerful, burned more hazardous waste, became more lethal lobbyists, they narrowed the distance in which a person could fight for party status. What was once a 20 mile radius had been drastically reduced to a two-mile radius – a decision made by a state agency.

So we all listened in astonishment and grave disappointment as Sue Pope talked about how her husband was dying and now she has primary immune deficiency, autoimmune disease, and only one third lung function remaining in her only lung yet the judged ruled she was denied party status because she lived too far out. We listened to Carrie and Craig talk about how they each got cancer, and they are now terrified their children will be exposed to toxins. They were denied. I listened to story after story as each person was told their health and lives didn't matter because they didn't live close enough for TXI to feel comfortable for them to complain.

Dressed in jeans, flip flops, and a t-shirt, I hadn't thought I would speak because I live too far out. But then I listened to someone talk about Mt. Peak Elementary School being just two miles away. My ears pricked up. I reasoned that if he was five miles out, then my house was easily three or four miles out, which would indeed put Mt. Peak two miles out from TXI. Tommy went to Mt. Peak Elementary. (Mt. Peak Elementary would be another school flagged in the *USA Today* report as being one of the most toxic schools in the nation).

I also listened in disbelief as TXI maintained that they wanted to turn the controls off during the winter months, which wouldn't affect us. Excuse me? We get the northern winds – blowing right up my street, through my house, against Tommy.

A former campaign worker for Representative Joe Barton (R-Ennis) spoke up and said that she was concerned when she would take her children to the park at Kimmel Park. It was less than two miles away, but the judge shrugged it off, saying that that was the general public.

Much murmuring in the room. *What? The general public doesn't matter?*

Then she said that she was concerned about children who spend half their lives in a school that was less than two miles away.

The TXI lawyers – cloned suits – just like in the movies – protested this point, saying that this wasn't really the issue because it was about whether it affected people in their residence – I popped up. That did it. I was officially pissed. They also protested the point that kids do not spend half their lives in school. Damned near. I made my way down the row to speak out when Kathy Altman, also a lawyer, reached out to me. She is that rare lawyer who is most interested in initiating a dialogue between both parties with the hope of resolving conflict (impossible!) without a lawsuit. She leaned over and whispered in my ear, "If we've agreed that Midlothian residents could be harmed within two miles and there was a large amount of people within that radius, 'Who represents the General Public'?"

When it was my turn, I approached the microphone, and my heart was pounding. I had suddenly become a client in potentially one of the largest lawsuits in Texas, and now I was standing before a judge. But before I said who I was and how I was affected, I wanted to ask the court a question: Who was representing the general public.

Laughs echoed throughout the court. The judge gave an expected lame-o answer, but it hardly mattered. The point had been made and was greatly appreciated by the audience.

Then I launched into who I was, all about when we moved here, and Tommy. I then turned to the lawyers and said I wanted to take issue with a few things the lawyers had said. If my son didn't spend half his life in the classroom, he spent a third of his life in the classroom, and as a direct result of his school location, his health and education were in danger. I said that he was a bright and articulate boy who was in danger of failing because he missed so much school. He was a boy who repeatedly missed out on recess and gym – which was a required class. And, if he participated, it could send him to the hospital.

I said that to say the prevailing winds in the winter time would not affect us was absurd as they blew right at us and that it was during those months I drove down the back roads to the hospital seeking medical treatment for my son. I said this wasn't just about emotional and financial strain. This wasn't just about the fear of Tommy ingesting high volumes of albuterol, azithromycin, duoneb, and the more aggressive steroids the hospitals gave Tommy, but that this was also affecting his relationships with others as well as his education.

They stopped me, and the lawyers asked to see a map.

Later, I would learn the value of pressing this point, as TXI did not want to have to take on the schools and did not want any speculation that they might be putting school children in jeopardy! This was very uncomfortable for them.

As they pulled out a map, the judge said it was off the record, and the mics were turned off as we looked over the map to find Mt. Peak Elementary school. It was within a 2.5 mile radius.

I turned back to the judge and started to say how hard this has been. He interrupted me. "Raise your right hand." As quickly as that, I got party status!

I could be part of a lawsuit that would – in my mind – complain about the emissions and set forth the motion to make the industry do the right thing. What this meant at home to my George Bush loving, Republican husband was I'd crossed some terrible line, and I needed to drop the entire thing.

I had previously asked Jim Ross if I should even try, but we had agreed that there was no point because I lived too far away. Neither Jim nor I had considered the school location until they – TXI – made that horrible and completely unconcerned remark about children that just set me off.

I said, "One more thing, your honor."

Just before I went up, a "cement valley" resident had walked up and handed me a piece of paper she had from her lawsuit against TXI in 2000.

I held up the piece of paper and said, "I have here documentation of a study conducted by RMT engineers from Chaparral Steel. It was a study done that shows that winds up to 15 miles per hour affect people as far as three miles away. Winds up to 20 miles per hour affected people up to five miles away. And so on. As soon as I said this, the head TXI lawyer popped up. "I object to this," and the judge shot me down.

"I understand," I said. "I just thought you might want to reconsider the people you denied who live within five miles." Again, I was dismissed, but as I turned around, the entire courtroom broke into applause, and, for fun, I pumped a fist.

When I walked over to Jim Ross, not sure what he would think about that; he murmured in low tones, "You go, girl!"

Chapter Ten
Marshall's Law

By 2005, Marshall sometimes dreamed he could still walk, but the dreams were fewer and further between. Though he continued to work with the fire department, he missed the action and camaraderie of fire fighting, the sounds of the fire truck.

Since he joined the department in 1979, Marshall was an important fixture. From 1979 to 1986, Marshall worked as swingman. Certainly, he put in much more time than most firefighters do as a swing, but Marshall actively requested to stay on the swing list. He enjoyed the rotation, but when he realized he could make more decisions to help his fellow fire fighters, he decided it was time to pursue a promotion. Success followed quickly after he moved from the swing shift.

In 1986, he became an engineer and was assigned to Station 26 for four and a half years, taking and passing his lieutenant's test in 1991. As lieutenant, he was assigned several crews that were considered more difficult or challenging than others. Whatever the hope, that he be forced out or that he inspire change, the crews began to excel under his direction. While Marshall speculated that he had been blessed with good people and good crews, the growing sentiment was that the fire department had been blessed with a very good officer. His first assignment was Station 20, a well-staffed house but one in need of consistent leadership. Almost instantaneously, Marshall melded with the firefighters. In the next two years, he would be transferred two more times to lend support to other stations before officially settling in at Station 17 as captain in May 1996.

He was a positive force, but few people understood the turmoil he'd undergone in recent years. By all accounts, Marshall was a happy man. The practical jokes were endless. The firefighters' release comes in tormenting and teasing each other during their downtime. It is their way of coping and appreciating life all at the same time. Just like in the movies, these overgrown madmen short-sheet each other's beds, throw rubber snakes, have water fights, make prank calls, and continuously test each other in any and every form of physical and mental harassment -- until the next call comes.

To the outside world, Marshall was the picture of ultimate control. He had it all. Power, intelligence, confidence, courage, stamina, good looks, and a cool demeanor. By merely standing next to them, he empowered his crew. So, understandably, there was general surprise during one call when Marshall Allen got on the radio asking for "lift help."

After responding to an EMS call, Marshall and his crew found a grossly overweight female in need of medical attention and transport. "But she was too big for the three of us to move." When another company arrived for backup, "we literally pulled her down the hallway on a tarp between all of us." And, together, the fire fighters had to remove the stretcher from the ambulance to make room for the woman to be placed on the floor of the vehicle.

No sooner had he returned to the station than Marshall started getting phone calls from various station houses, the first being from Captain Mark Foster at Station 28. "I just wanted to know what in the hell Marshall Allen needed lift help for," Foster had laughed.

Marshall was the ultimate swingman, able to handle whatever came his way.

But it was not just the fire fighters in Fort Worth who were aware of the physical prowess of Marshall and his friend, Big Al. Other departments were acutely aware, particularly during the annual Mayfest tug-of-war contests between all the departments in the Dallas/Fort Worth metroplex area. With Al and Marshall each standing over 6'4" and 300 pounds, Scott "Tiny" Cole at 6'3" and 300 pounds, Todd Bagby at 6'6" and 270 pounds, and Darrin Partridge hovering at 300 pounds and acting as anchor, Fort Worth could not be beat. After all, the five men alone weighed a combined 1500 pounds. Yet, to everyone's surprise, Dallas had soundly beaten Fort Worth during the tug-of-war contest.

The contest had taken place over the murky Trinity River in Fort Worth's Trinity Park. In a best two-out-of-three competition, Fort Worth's department had been confident.

"There was no way they were going to beat us, but they did. Two out of three times," Marshall almost laughed. "We couldn't figure it out."

Worn out after the second round, the Fort Worth team slid down the embankment to the river and the Dallas team drifted away from the rope. "That's when we saw what had happened," Marshall explained. Their side [Dallas fire department] had backed up to a parking lot" where they had tied their end of the rope to a guard rail post and feigned pulling while Marshall, Al, Darrin, and the others simply tired themselves out pulling against asphalt, cement, and metal.

"I wanted to be mad," Marshall said later. "But I just couldn't. It was too funny."

Over time, Marshall had learned how his size impressed and/or entertained people. He was superman. He was super swingman.

When visiting any of the stations Marshall once worked, one must expect endless stories of Marshall's heroics and playful antics.

Did you hear about the time that Marshall lifted up a bus filled with people?

Roars of laughter filled each station as the stories of Marshall grew. Most revel in upping the other with bigger, grander Marshall stories.

"But there was that one time," Darrin laughed, "I was a new guy at Station 26." It was during a time when Marshall was into power lifting and all that went with the competitive sport – including shaving.

"I walked into the bathroom, and here stands this huge black man, 330 pounds of solid muscle, and he had shaving cream on his chest and on his legs." Darrin instantly put up his hands and began slowly backing out of the bathroom, reassuring Marshall, "I don't see or know anything."

As soon as he got out, Darrin said, he couldn't wait to share what he'd seen. But little surprised anyone about Marshall. He was known to be the "master" of messing with people. "He would spend hours arguing the sky was not blue when–" even as he spoke, Darrin's frustration was clear—"the sky is clearly blue!"

Marshall was a neat freak. Marshall loved to debate. He loved to challenge people both physically and mentally. "He was just this monster," Darrin said. A monster that had to be fed regularly. "He was constantly eating! He would always bring a breakfast, which always had a cinnamon roll, then eat lunch and dinner, but he would always buy an extra plate at dinner. Then, about 10:00 o'clock at night, he would eat the other dinner. But he would eat another full meal about 2 a.m. He had like five percent body fat," Darrin said, adding that it was a challenge for Marshall to keep weight on. "It was a little startling when you don't think anyone is up and you get up to get a drink of water at 2 a.m. You walk in the kitchen, and there's this huge guy sitting at the table, in the dark, eating."

Did you know that Marshall once ate an entire busload of people?

As Marshall moved up the ranks, becoming captain, he was beloved as both "one of the guys" and respected as a strong leader. With obvious glee, men reported stories of being in mid-prank only to have Captain Allen walk by. Two men would be sitting atop of another: one man might be hanging by a foot from a bunk, two others would be squared off, each armed with pitchers of water, but in all scenarios, everyone would freeze as Marshall entered. Silently, Marshall would assess the situation, say nothing, turn, and leave, saying, "I'll be in my office."

He was the very same captain who also implemented new rules and regulations, though not intentionally. More than once, Marshall would make a call as acting officer at a fire that would later become a standard procedure of operation. As more than one fire fighter would say, Marshall was ahead of his time.

During his time with the FWFD, he implemented new ways of managing emergency situations and introduced new department protocol. To this, he simply says, "If I saw the need, I did what needed to be done."

One of his first instrumental decisions in the department came about not through thoughtful planning or necessity, but out of a sense of decency. When a call came in to his station telling him that there were oxygen cylinders in a structure fire, tensions were instantly heightened. "We couldn't get there in time and the Battalion Chief was delayed as well," Marshall said. "It was a long ride for us, and we would be the last unit in."

The caller reported "a big one." Even over the radio, it was clear that the scene was chaotic and becoming volatile. The first person on the scene was an acting lieutenant who "was completely overwhelmed." The lieutenant also happened to be a female fire fighter, new to the department, and completely on her own among the good ol' boys.

"It was not only beyond her control, it was also beyond her ability," Marshall recalled. As other companies arrived, no one stepped up to take charge. Rather than containing and controlling the scene, it was spiraling out of control, and the oxygen cylinders were going to blow.

Marshall's engineer roared through the streets, sirens blaring, but they just couldn't get to the scene fast enough. Inside his truck, everyone grew anxious as they could hear an increasingly agitated voice over the radio.

Marshall couldn't stand it. He understood what was happening. The lieutenant was going to be left to hang. "I felt sorry for her," he said. "Because she was a female, they were letting her sink. No one was stepping up. But it was more than that." Listening to the radio transmission, hearing the distress and chaos, Marshall picked up the radio.

"It was so stressful," he said, "but I made a decision. I couldn't stand listening to the chaos and potential loss of lives."

As he poised his thumb, he was about to break protocol. An officer was not allowed to read and react to a scene without being physically present.

"Aw, screw it," he said, and his engineer peered at him, asking, "You really going to do that?"

"I have to," Marshall nodded. "Somebody's got to do something!" And he depressed the button.

He began barking out orders, and by the time his company from Station 22 arrived, things had settled down, and the scene had been contained. There was no loss of life. But it was an experience that stayed with him throughout the remainder of his career with the department. He was greatly disappointed by the inaction of his fellow fire fighters and by the fact that they were willing to have property and possibly lives destroyed to teach the "female" a lesson.

"I was afraid that I might have embarrassed the people I worked alongside, but I never asked anyone on the crews what they thought, and no one said anything." Silently, he worried what people thought. "One of my doubts was that I'd been too cocky or aggressive to try to take control over the radio. I imagined that I'd really screwed up." But, again, no one said a word.

Almost 15 years later, Marshall made a startling discovery. The radio transmission of that evening was used as a training tool for new recruits, and it had been considered "an exemplary act" that saved lives.

Ironically, when Marshall was hurt, this same female lieutenant sat with him several times at home, allowing Mary to go to work. So long ago, he had broken current policy and began giving orders over the radio because "it wasn't right to let her handle it all by herself. There was nothing right about it." Years later, she had felt the same for him.

There were other runs and many more opportunities when Marshall exhibited the forward thinking that changed policy, saved lives, and reduced property damage. While he had no intention of setting new standards or changing existing rules, if he could make his crew more effective and efficient, he would break the rules.

In one instance, Marshall's company responded to a call, fully aware that Station 7 had been called first. "But I knew we were closer," Marshall explained. "And our engineer knew we would be there faster." So rather than sit back, Marshall began a verbal exchange between the two companies. To "jump a run," that is, to take over a call that was initially dispatched to another company was not against regulations but "could also turn into a pissing contest to see who could get to the fire first. Not to mention the fact that if you're not actually first on, you have left your primary territory unprotected for no reason."

But by getting and staying in constant contact with Station 7, "we were able to ensure that we really were closer, and everyone knew what was going on."

Again, this radio transmission was later used as a training tool in the department's classes. As more Marshall laws were enacted, there was a buzz within the department of Marshall's certain rise to Battalion Chief. Though this is a statement Marshall plays down, many within the department or those since retired echo the sentiment, "He was on his way up!"

But no one knew how every day was a struggle, how "it was just so hard to get up in the morning." At the mere recollection of those days, Marshall chokes with emotion. No one knew of his own personal hell.

He was Marshall. He was supposed to be invincible. Superman really does have his kryptonite. He was in the business of saving lives, offering help and hope, but it was not in his nature to ask for it. There was some societal double standard in play as well. Big, strong men were not supposed to need help or to feel beaten down. For these reasons, he suppressed his feelings of despair, and he did whatever he could to make sure no one knew how he struggled.

Then three things rocked him in such a way that even his tough-guy exterior began to crumble. "First, I bombed the captain's test," he said. Previously, Marshall had set records within the department for his grades, excelling in both the promotional exams and physical tests. "Then Battalion Chief Robert Cockey died." This was a man Marshall greatly admired. He was a man Marshall believed he could look to for advice and come to with questions. When Cockey died suddenly of a heart attack, it felt to Marshall as though he'd been personally assaulted.

The final blow was the death of a young man Marshall knew, the younger brother of a woman Marshall had dated. When the two dated, her little brother had followed Marshall around. He had been a great kid, and Marshall was fond of him. But, as life happens, he had not seen or really thought about the boy in years until the boy's sister, an ex-girlfriend, sent him a card containing the obituary.

As a swingman, he'd personally attended horrific accidents that left its victims maimed, mangled, and many times dead. But they were nameless.

For whatever reason, the succession of bad news was more than Marshall could bear, and in 1994, "I had a nervous breakdown."

Superman was knocked flat.

But that same year, on July 4, 1994, a woman named Patricia Norwood decided, for reasons no one knows, to call her then 15-year-old daughter, Talaya, into the kitchen. There she explained that the man Talaya had always believed to be her father was not. Her real father was a man named Marshall Allen who was a fire fighter in Fort Worth, Texas.

That night, Patricia died of heart failure, leaving her still shocked teenaged daughter to find her the following morning.

After Talaya and her sisters were taken to North Carolina to live with another family member, Talaya began her search for the father she had never met. During the summer when she was 21, she began an internship with a brokerage company and was able to use its massive network to locate three Marshall Allens in North Texas. She was desperate to find him. In earlier years, she wrote to the Montell Williams and Oprah Winfrey shows for help.

She wrote three letters to three men, hoping for a hit. Two of the Marshall Allens immediately contacted her, letting her know they were not the man she was looking for. One of those men stayed in contact with her for some time, feeling sorry for the young Talaya. The third Marshall Allen, however, did not respond. His letter had arrived at the fire station just after his accident.

"A couple of my fire fighters came to visit [in the hospital], and Laura brought the letter with her," Marshall said.

Firefighter Laura Jenkins was "like a daughter" to Marshall. It was, he would later say, only fitting that Laura was the one to retrieve and read the letter to him. But as she began to read, she stopped at the first paragraph, suggesting that Marshall might want to read the letter privately.

"I told her to go ahead," Marshall recalled. Slowly, Laura read on. "It said, 'Hello, my name is Talaya Jefferson. I hope you can help me in my search for a missing family member. First let me tell you a little about myself ….'"

Almost instantly, Marshall knew he was the man she was looking for. "She was looking for her daddy." Never had he any inkling that he had a biological daughter, yet now he knew as he listened to her letter. She was a three-sport athlete, going to college on an athletic scholarship, majoring in psychology. But it was the tone of the letter that gripped him, and there was not a dry eye in the room. To everyone's disbelief, the young author of the letter was writing simply to see if Marshall Allen, this Marshall Allen, had known a woman named Patricia Norwood.

"Around July of '95, I began to search for my father," Talaya explained how she'd come to write Marshall the letter. "The first search consisted of a U.S. search. I received a response from them about two weeks later stating that they could send me a list of Marshall Allens in the United States for a fee of $59. Me being fifteen-years-old and living with my grandparents, I could not ask for or afford $59. So that is when I decided to try on my own. For the next six years, I sent letters, e-mails, and made phone calls to any and every Marshall Allen I could find. I even wrote letters to such talk shows as Sally, Jenny Jones, and Montell Williams. A couple of the letters that I sent to Montell Williams were reviewed. I don't know what else became of those letters. I never received any responses from any of the personal letters I sent out. I received a few responses from the e-mails, but as you can probably already tell, none of those was the e-mail that I was looking for.

"On August 11, 2001, I decided to take a shower after a long day's work. Just at the point where the shower gets to feeling really good, my phone rang. My youngest sister was on the line. She said 'Talaya, what are you doing?' I said, 'Keyona, I am in the shower.' She said, 'I think you need to get out of the shower.' I said, 'Keyona, I will call you back.' But she said, 'No, I have someone on the other line that you need to talk to.' Thinking that she had one of her friends on the line, I said, 'Really, Keyona, whoever it is can wait. I have suds all over me. I will call you back.' That was when a man's voice, a man's very, very, very deep voice came over the phone, 'Talaya honey, this is Marshal Allen.' I said 'Excuse me, this is who?' I thought someone was playing a very cruel joke. He said, 'This is Marshal Allen. I got your letter.' I asked him, 'Did you understand my letter?' He simply said, 'Yes, I did, and I believe that there is a very distinct possibility...' That is when my heart stopped beating and my knees got weak. Everything that I had ever dreamt about, my most miraculous of dreams had come true. The moment that I had waited for my entire life was at that moment happening to me."

With Big Al holding the phone up against Marshall's ear, he heard his daughter start to cry. "Talaya said something like, 'I've got a thousand questions and I can't think of anything!'"

In the days to come, Marshall and Talaya talked two or three times a day, and they talked about everything. But when Talaya sent pictures of herself, the deal was sealed.

"She just looked like me," Marshall beamed. "I *knew* I had a daughter!"

"Of course," Marshall added, "I had to call her and tell her I saw her. Then I gave her a website that had some pictures of me so she was able to see her daddy."

Unbeknownst to Marshall, Mary, an employee of American Airlines, arranged to have Talaya fly to Dallas.

One day, Marshall said, "everyone started showing up in my room": his mother-in-law, his children, Mary, friends. But when his eldest son, Simeon, walked in the room, Marshall immediately noticed the young woman behind him.

Earlier, when Marshall had seen the pictures of his biological daughter, he'd become speechless, and Mary teased him. "For the second time in my life," Marshall said, upon recognizing the young woman, "I was speechless. I couldn't think of anything to say. All I could do was open my arms."

Talaya raced forward and fell into his arms, crying. While flashbulbs exploded around the room, others were scrambling for Kleenex. Marshall had found his daughter. But he instantly apologized to her, telling her he was sorry.

"She finally found me, and I was all broken up and paralyzed. I was always so big and physical with the other kids. I was a fun guy. But she found me when I couldn't do anything."

He could open his arms. Both physically and metaphorically. He could open his arms.

Talaya hardly noticed anything else. She hadn't cared about his physical condition. She had been afraid that he would be dead or would reject her.

"He is the best thing that could have ever happened to me. I thank God that He has performed a miracle for me. I think that God planned for the two of us to share our lives together. Because He knew the perfect timing for the both of us. You see, only one month before my father received my letter, he was injured in a bicycle accident, which resulted in paralysis. My life was also changing. My senior year was about to begin, an event that was jeopardized due to financial problems, and I could not make the tuition payments. Both my father and I were going through emotional, physical, and mental changes. We both needed someone. We needed each other."

In his own words, Marshall has pondered the role we all play in each other's lives and how much we truly need each other. He had always been big and strong, and he slipped nicely into the role of savior, fire fighter, protector. Happily, from his wheelchair, that role has not changed. By 2005, he continued to be sought after for council from injured fire fighters to administrators to friends and family. He encapsulates a kind of inner peace few people ever realize – an amazing feat because the road he's journeyed has been difficult. He's the ultimate swingman.

Chapter Eleven

Town Hall Meeting
& The Fall Out

I'd been working on an article when my niece, Colette, some neighborhood children, and my daughters, Kerri and Katie, burst into the study. At once, they were all screaming and wildly pointing. The only two words I clearly understood were "Tommy" and "breathing" – or, rather, "not" breathing.

I was on my feet, running down the hallway with a horde of kids behind me, giving me direction. As promised, Tommy was lying on the floor in between my bedroom and bathroom. He was so red he was almost purplish.

I'd become a seasoned pro about remaining calm (always for Tommy's sake) and hooking up our nebulizer machine in mere seconds. Without instruction, Kerri, now 12, knew where to find the steroids and how to set Tommy up. And, with hand holding, steroids, cool clothes, and time, we could often work him through the scariest part of a severe asthma attack.

But this day was different. This day was even worse than all the other times I had to rush him to Emergency. This time, he was turning more purple within seconds, and this time, he wasn't making any noises. He was simply powering down.

I screamed instructions, scooped him into my arms, and literally peeled out of my driveway. I pleaded for help. Please don't let there be any children or animals or cars in my way. *Please don't let there be any police. Please don't let anything happen to Tommy. Please let me get there, please let me get there, please let me get there!*

We were flying down the back roads to the Waxahachie Baylor Hospital, and I can't honestly say how fast we were driving. It wasn't fast enough, I can tell you that. I was begging and pleading with all the forces of the universe when I heard Tommy's little voice.

"Can a little boy die of this?" His voice was raspy and scared, and I instantly snapped at him.

"Don't be ridiculous! Of course not! You can't DIE from asthma, Tommy! That's stupid!"

I was mean and terrified and desperate. He couldn't believe he could die! He had to think there was no way death could happen. But I knew better. Erin's Tommy died of an asthma attack while camping.

When we got to Baylor, I didn't bother with the parking lot and roared up to the entrance. There had been a car accident with two bleeding victims inside, but Tommy sailed right by them. I think the combination of my wild expression and my purple son spoke to the staff.

In all of my life, including the time my sister and I were on the plane going down over Tunis, Tunisia, I have never known such terror.

In the car, speeding down the back roads, prepared to make any deal with any life force there was just to let Tommy live, I was the most lonely and terrified I've ever felt. What was worse, there seemed to be no answers. When I did press for answers, I was rebuffed, and, through my job as a journalist, was warned to back off. There was, I realized, no power to the people. Whatever was poisoning Tommy was big industry all the way.

Eventually, Tommy's oxygen level was restored, and after plenty of rest and more medication than I was ever comfortable with, he could go home.

Tommy's scare was another reason I was happy Erin Brokovich agreed to come, that several prestigious families or powerhouses in Dallas were willing to fund our fight, and that I had become allies with the likes of Jim Schermbeck, Sue Pope, Becky Bornhorst, Sandy Breakfield, Reecea Henderson, MerleAnn Roten, and everyone else with Downwinders.

The cavalry was coming.

When Michelle, Gina, and I, with kids in tow, arrived to help DAR members set up (and claim front row seats) at the convention center where Erin was to speak, we were greeted by a group I did not recognize.

A table with two or three people had been set up so that they could hand out anti-Erin literature. But people didn't know it was anti-Erin literature. They saw a huge sign that made promises of a better Midlothian, and citizens eagerly lined up to get color glossy pamphlets and provide personal information, complete with phone numbers and e-mails. Later, we would hear again and again from people who were furious they had been duped into giving personal information, believing they were actually giving it to Erin and the law firm she represented. Instead, it was believed that the information was used by supporters of the cement industry.

Downwinders at Risk had quietly set up a table around the corner, just outside the town hall meeting. Foolishly, we were thinking people could pick up materials about the environment if they wanted to.

The *other* table led people to believe they needed to sign in. Only when reporter Howard Witt from the *Chicago Tribune* tipped us off to what was going on did we put a stop to it.

In the end, when Erin arrived and even made fun of the material being handed out, it was clear that the hundreds and hundreds of people who attended were not buying what the others were selling. There were so many people who came with cancer, asthma, Downs, birth defects, and skin ailments, the crises were overwhelming.

We sat next to a woman named Sue Ellen – a nurse whose 14-year-old daughter was so sick she couldn't leave her breathing machine to come watch Erin. After learning about her daughter, Michelle talked her into speaking with the press. A continued problem in Midlothian is and has always been that people are afraid of retribution. They do not want their neighbors, friends, or co-workers to see them speaking out, so they remain silent.

As the room filled up, people were talking to one another, almost comparing notes.

Oh, yes, our neighbor's son was just diagnosed with leukemia.

Oh, really, where do they live?

Oh, yeah, that's a bad place for cancer.

Many people brought pictures of loved ones who were unable to be there because of poor health or, sadly, because they had already died. There was a picture of a young girl who had just died of a rare cancer that moved to her heart, so her family brought a huge portrait for Erin to see. A man with a brain tumor spoke to Gina while Michelle fell into a conversation with a woman who had had autoimmune disease and some other funky problems no one understood.

For so many people, it was healing just to be there and talk. But when Erin came in, there was so much hope, the air was electric. She introduced herself as the director of environmental research at Masry & Vititoe and with Jim Ross an environmental lawyer of McCurdy & McCurdy; she further explained she was here only to discuss the concerns she had heard expressed by a number of Midlothian residents and how an investigation into the contamination and health effects in the Midlothian area might be helpful.

If people came to the meeting in hopes of catching a glimpse of the Erin Brokovich from the movie, they were probably disappointed—though the gold snake-emblem pennant that appeared to hold her enormous assets together was no less impressive. But she was very low-key. There was no foul language, no fist-pounding. She was heartfelt and gave the message that knowledge is power. She said things like, "let's find out" and "let me help you." She made fun of the anti-Erin material passed out and cracked several jokes about herself, her cleavage, and others. Truly, she was engaging and charming. She received rave reviews from everyone in attendance and even the anti-Erin group was happily relieved. No one was slammed; no one was defamed or challenged.

A great giggle point for Gina and I came just before Erin's entrance when the room was filling beyond capacity, and the fire marshal needed to make an announcement that there were too many people standing in front of the exit doors. We were already at capacity, and people were still coming in. He approached Michelle (a very blonde, very busty woman) and said, "Um, Ms. Brokovich?" Gina and I erupted into peels of laughter.

While Erin signed autographs, graciously listening to the heartbreaking stories of too many families to count, I milled over to Jim Ross who stood with his arms folded across his chest and said, "This is the hardest part right here."

Erin is a rock star, only her fans aren't screaming music fans. They are desperate and scared, sick and powerless normal folk. They are hurt, damaged, and angry. For that reason, Erin is incredibly patient and listens intently to each story.

Two days later, I was approached at a soccer game and braced myself for what was to come. A friend and coach who worked at one of the cement plants said, "You must think we're a bunch of dumbasses."

I shook my head. No, I don't. I've just always believed that the employees of the cement plants are just like the citizens of Midlothian. We don't really know what is going on. But before I could answer, another parent said, "I hope they gather a lot of evidence that shows they're polluting the air."

The coach piped up. "They won't." We all looked to him.

Why not?

He said, "Because we ain't doing anything wrong." He went on to say that his plant had very, very strict rules and regulations regarding safety and the health of their employees. He ran down a list of all the things they have to do to be in regulation. Then, he looked to me and said, "What I wonder is... does everyone who is against [the plants] think we're all a bunch of dumbshits for staying somewhere that would be dangerous?"

I was so glad he asked that question again.

I said "no." What I hoped for was that when Jim Ross and Erin Brokovich, along with their team, discovered and revealed the truth, the employees of all the cement plants would then be able to go back to their own employers and say, "What the hell?" I know and like so many people who work at one of the three plants and can honestly say I wouldn't hang out with people I thought were stupid or thoughtless. But there had been a common thread in town. Only when a family member got sick did people start to wonder and ask questions. Until this, the prevailing thought was, *Well, I've lived here for 20+ years, and I'm fine so …. There must not be a problem.*

It was then that the coach's wife weighed in, saying, "Yea, look at Enron. You think their people all knew what was coming?"

Even his wife opposed the air quality controls being turned off, calling it "a bunch of bull," but she also wondered how many cases of cancer and asthma and other diseases in the area were all being blamed on the cement plants. It is a valid argument, but the one thing that no one seems to be denying was the number of medical health issues in Midlothian were staggering.

Less than two years later, I would be asked to help out some friends while one underwent medical tests. When I asked what was wrong, he replied, "You know how you're supposed to look to see if you have blood in your stool?"

Never in all of my whacky adventures or unusual jobs – I was once a giant Gingerbread Cookie man, a loader for UPS, and a daily mucker of a 16-stall horse barn -- have I ever had an employer or teammate suggest that I periodically check my stool for blood. I said as much to a professor at a local community college who confirmed, "Oh, yeah, I have a student who cleans out some of the [cement] bins and has had the same issue." Additionally, there are lots and lots of nose bleeds. Because of the heavy metals that the employees of cement plants are daily exposed to, it is a common practice in the industry; sure enough, he had blood.

He was put on the Family Leave Act until his blood work came back clean and he returned to work. Case closed.

By mid-summer, there were party status hearing meetings held so that we, as a group, could decide how to proceed. For people like Wendy Hammond, a Dallas-based environmental lawyer, who had been going against TXI for years, this was business as usual. But as I listened to talk of possible court costs, deadlines, and that TXI would have something called "discovery," which essentially allowed them to know everything about us and our families during the process, I was worried. This all sounded very time consuming and exhausting. Then, one man spoke about his cousin, an employee of TXI, who suffered from boils and blisters through steel-toe boots; and I heard about the Estrada family whose little girl had lung damage—they lived near "cement valley"—and I felt that I couldn't quit.

On July 13, 2005, Wendi, Sue Pope, and Becky Bornhorst, among others, sat in mediation with TXI all day long. By 5 pm, TXI sent forward a list of conditions that were so ridiculous, it was offensive. Instead of agreeing to limit the burning and release of hazardous waste into the atmosphere, they offered to establish a website for citizens to get online and see how the air quality was. But as evening fell and Wendi and Becky prepared to walk, TXI finally agreed to our conditions.

Downwinders had asked that pollution controls be run year round. It was a first! TXI had never agreed to the demands of the public before, so when they did, Becky reported, mouths dropped open.

Instantly, some were suspect. After all, the whole purpose of their permit request was to take *off* controls. Why agree to keep them on year round? But TXI countered by saying that they would simply need to make emissions a bit higher, but that was more cost effective, and they would keep the controls on year round.

As it turned out, there had been a side business deal between other companies that would allow the burning of millions of tires in one year – on top of all the other lovely things, such as lead, mercury, benzene, and arsenic.

In the months to come, while members of DAR patiently explained terminologies to me and I learned about air monitors, I was also learning a lot about my neighbors. Since Erin's appearance, people wanted money and had visions of winning huge lawsuits. People were withholding information for their own causes. State and federal agencies were not held accountable first to the safety and welfare of the American public but to a specific boss with political ties, and I was becoming increasingly disillusioned. Erin's lawyers explained to us that before we could even hope to change laws that were extremely biased toward industry, we would first have to make our legislators change the very laws that protected industry. Suddenly, there were two fights.

2005 had been a terrible year of awakening and reckoning.

The awakening had been just how bad the environment was, yet it was still business as usual.

The reckoning had been with my own husband. While I had been out battling against the world, I had even more battles at home. Robb's conservative roots would not allow him to accept that local industries could really be harming us, that state agencies would allow this for political gain, or that we could, in fact, fight city hall.

And Robb was representative of a definite mindset. He didn't want to make waves. Maybe the problem would fix itself. Rather than say "I love this town. Let's fix what is wrong," people were more inclined to say, "Don't point out the bad stuff." Robb continued to remind us that we had chosen Midlothian because we wanted the quiet life, and I was making too much noise.

By the year's end, we were arguing a lot. He argued that I spent too much time with the DAR folks, that I was more invested in the environment than I was our home life, and that I wasn't going to be able to change anything. Though I was beginning to believe he was right, I still couldn't walk away from the fight. Not yet.

Chapter Twelve

Christmas 2006

For close to a decade now, it's been our mission here at Allred Farms to spread doom and gloom during this annual time of merriment. It is a gift originated by the original grump – Robb – to be sure you don't get the typical, syrupy-sweet holiday letter reporting all the amazing things that happened in the year past.

With that, we hope our year of disasters makes yours seem a little brighter!

Compliments of Lightning, the wild horse, I tore tendons and ligaments in my left shoulder, forcing me to take a hiatus from kickbox instruction. The doctor says I need surgery. Our cat, Suzy, was lured across the street by a little girl who had been specifically told not to lure our cat across the street and the little feline was killed by a car. Then Pete killed our other cat, Seven. Tommy badly burned his feet walking barefooted across a day-old burn-pile. He also got ringworm and liked it so much he decided to share it with all of us. It really is the gift that keeps on giving. Gross and disgusting or, as Tommy likes to say, *disgrossting*. Kerri has begun wearing makeup, much to Robb's dismay; Katie wants to be a rock star, singing "Man, I feel like a woman"; and Tommy wants to be "a hippie." Tommy also has an interest in singing Broadway tunes, although we don't know where he is learning the lyrics.

I got banned from Katie's school and was not allowed to attend her award ceremony for being the only girl in the 5th grade to get the Presidential Award because I took her home after a school field trip when it was 100 degrees outside and the buses were running late. Robb had his truck's tailgate stolen from our own driveway. Worse, the police caught the guy, but he won't give up any information except to say he was selling stolen tailgates for drug money, and the police made a deal with him allowing him to keep the secret. Robb continues his quest, however, to find his tailgate – driving us all crazy in the process. He swears he can identify his own tailgate and will steal it back if he finds it.

Driving to and from the Allred family reunion was a test of my patience. Robb constantly blurts out lyrics from random songs no one has even heard of, many of which, given his passion for heavy metal music, sound like threats. He told Katie in song, "If you cross the Canadian River, I'll cut out your liver." What?! Suddenly, Katie was looking worriedly around for a river outside the window. What did he just say?!

He announced that he wants the *distinction* of being bitten by a rattlesnake. We were driving along in Wyoming when he shared this newest and grandest desire. Personally, I would have just settled for something to eat other than two-day-old bologna sandwiches. To be clear, however, he wants to die at the paws of a bear, but ONLY if there is clear evidence of a struggle. His fear is that local press will get a hold of the story and defame his character: *"Local man, Robb Allred, was killed by a bear. It appears that he simply rolled over and let the bear eat him. Friends say this was his way…."* Should he ever meet his demise by way of bear, there will be signs of a fight! Preferably, the bear will be injured.

Overall, the trip was a great success although there were weird moments. We hiked, trekked, and trudged through more mud, muck, and rain than most Yellowstoners. If anyone ever hopes to "do" Yellowstone with us, they'd better get a doctor's note first. Hey, Robb will suggest, there *MIGHT* be a moose four miles from here, one way, uphill, in a rainstorm. Who wants to go? During one such hike, we suddenly came across an usually tall, skinny man who was really, really tan – George Hamilton scary tan – and wearing nothing but Speedos. I don't think he was wearing shoes. I was distracted by … those itty, bitty Speedos.

I was suddenly thankful Robb was with us. But when I turned to find my tough-guy support system, I found Robb, scowling and recoiling in growing homophobic terror of the moving black Speedos.

Oh, sure. He's ready to meet his doom in the woods against a hairy black bear, but throw just one hairy tan man at him, and it's all "Akk! He's looking at me! Make him go away! Make him go away!"

Other than that, this does seem to be the year of getting or being hurt. Besides my horse hurting me and Tommy burning his feet, I fell down the back stairs of City Hall in Fort Worth, which was made more embarrassing by the fact that this stunning athletic feat was witnessed by two police officers who had to fill out a "promise-not-to-sue-us" report. A brown recluse bit Robb, and Nala unsuccessfully fought a swarm of bees. Twice. And Captain Denial, a.k.a. Robb, got a toothache.

But Robb does not like the dentist. Robb did not want to go to the dentist. So, right off the bat, it was one complaint after another. "A mall dentist? We're going to a mall dentist?" Dr. Daniels is not a mall dentist. He's with our insurance plan, is really good, and, yes, just happens to have one of his offices in a strip mall. Robb's examination determined he would have to have a root canal. The office manager could see that he was distressed and left the room so that we could talk privately. Robb poked his finger at the dental paperwork. The cost. Too expensive. "But you have to have this," I said. "It's not like you're thinking about liposuction." He scowled again and began making excuses about why he could not have the procedure done that day.

"Robb, you can't put this off. Dr. Daniels said your tooth is infected."

"This isn't the shirt I wanted to wear."

Excuse me? "You've got a special going-to-the-dentist shirt?"

"They're going to give me a shot," he went on.

"I know."

"In the mouth!!"

"Well, it's not going to help to get it in your rear end!"

We went back and forth over his wallet. Should he keep it; should I take it? Finally, he decided he should keep it in case he should suddenly be rendered unconscious and the staff didn't know who he was. I said, "I think they already know who you are, Robb."

"What if there's a shift change?"

"This isn't a factory!"

He did get the root canal. Now he needs knee surgery.

At back-to-school physicals, our beloved Dr. Jones walked in and asked, "So, does anyone have poison ivy?" Katie shot up a hand, proudly. "I do." I said, "Wow, is there some kind of outbreak of poison ivy?"

"No, I just ask you because someone always has poison ivy in your house." Ahh. Between the creek, horses, cats, and hay, one of us is always itching. And, once, we were nearly attacked by a zombie possum.

To set up the zombie possum, let me first explain that a few years ago while watching family videos, I pointed out my pregnant self to Tommy. "Look, Tommy. You are in my tummy there." Tommy was horrified. "You ate me?" It was cute, and we all laughed, never really providing a satisfactory answer. This spring, Katie (unbeknownst to me) explained to Tommy that females grow babies in their tummies, and once the baby is big enough, it will just come out. No one really knows when. It just comes out, and there's no stopping it.

Tommy, Katie, and a friend were by the creek when they spotted a neighbor's Labrador, Flower, who was very pregnant. The other child commented that Flower was going to "explode" she was so pregnant. "She's gonna have those babies any minute!"

"Wait! What?! Babies?" Plural? Panic! Run, run, run! She's gonna blow!"

"Local boy, Tommy Allred, was brought down in a hail of puppies. The explosion was fierce and disgrossting. He also has puppy breath. He never had a chance...."

Since then, Tommy has been a little concerned about going to the creek. Never mind the coyotes, snakes, owl, buzzards, our rogue bobcat, and various strays. You can *NEVER* be too careful about exploding Labradors. So, when he wanted to check on a large turtle we'd previously rescued from the highway – and, by the way, you would be amazed by the velocity, veracity, and volume with which a frightened turtle can urinate on you – his sisters had to go. That's when they saw the possum. Lying on the ground, not moving. Playing possum? "Poke it." "No, you poke it." "No, you poke it." "Hey, let's get Tommy. He'll poke anything. Here—" handing stick to Tommy, "Poke it, Tommy." *Poke. Poke.* It moved!

This, in and of itself, could have been very exciting, but when you are a little feller who watches *Scooby Doo and Zombie Island* obsessively, this is waaaaay beyond exciting.

"IT'S A ZOMBIE POSSUM AND ZOMBIES NEVER DIE! ARGHHHH!"

Big surprise, when I went back to check out the zombie possum, it was gone. Try explaining to an imaginative seven-year-old that it's not coming back when, in fact, this is what zombies do.

Katie got into reading the kid-friendly-yet-scary *Goosebumps* series. Her first book was about a pair of ghost hands that play a piano in the attic. She was jumpy for days. For this reason, I guess, it was in bad taste to put Katie to bed, play the piano, and then run out of the room before she could see me. She slept with Robb and me for days.

Finally, while we are now goatless, Robb brought home a new puppy. She appears to be some kind of Rottweiler or Doberman mix. She was starved and half dead. But, he cautioned us all, we are *NOT* keeping her. Still, while we nurse her back to health, he expects us all to call her "Cleave" because (sigh: are you ready for this?) she's a dog "you can cleave to." Her name is Sadie Cleave Sue Allred. She's great friends with Pete, and we've had her for two month, but we're not keeping her.

Love,
Alex

The Unconquerable Marshall Allen
...and his rise to the top

Upon return to their "house" from another run, the company from Station 29 noticed smoke in the distance and called it in. "When we got there, and it was by the grace of God that we did, we saw that the fire was headed toward some houses."

As Marshall described it, a grass fire raced along a half block, headed directly toward the backside of a row of houses, all shielded by dry, wood, privacy fences. In short, the blaze would rapidly get out of control should the fire reach the fence line.

"I told everyone in the truck that our main job was to outrun the fire when we got there. We had to be able to move the water faster than the wind was blowing." It would be the only way to beat it and save the homes. As Marshall, then the acting captain for Station 29, saw it, time was of the essence.

As they pulled up and each man prepared to leap into action, Marshall turned to a young, brawny firefighter named Joey and said, "Your only job is to get the line off the hose reel as fast as I can run with it!"

The hose, a 300-foot hose line, looks like an oversized thick-walled garden hose, but in reality, becomes increasingly heavy as it is dragged from its reel.

"I got in his face, looked him in the eye," Marshall recalled. Because the hose reel was not mechanized and because it would become heavy quickly and because Marshall knew it would be a race against the swiftly moving fire, Joey's role would be critical.

"As long as I didn't have to pull against the reel itself," Marshall explained, he could win that race. "But I really needed someone to jerk the hose off the spindle line."

The siren blaring, each man ready for the truck to come to a stop, it was an adrenaline rush. Once more, for assurances, Marshall yelled to his crew. All nods. Again, he told Joey what he needed.

"Yeah, yeah ... I got it, I got it," Joey said.

In the summer and early autumn months in Texas, grass fires can be treacherous. Deadly fires can spiral out of control within minutes as gusts of wind can change its direction suddenly. Dry conditions, month long droughts, and open fields can prove to be hazardous, and the FWFD's firefighters know the risks.

"I jumped off the truck and took off at a run," Marshall said. "Everything was fine at first." The engineer, Greg "Grizzly" Adams, cranked the water pressure. "I expected to feel some weight on the line, but not so quickly." As he ran, struggling with the increasingly heavy line, he tugged at it, thinking that it was hooked on roots or a tree stump line. It was impossibly heavy, and finally, "I turned around to see what the hell was going on."

The fire roared on, closing in on the fence line just beyond on the row of houses, and then, to his astonishment, "I saw it!"

There at the front of the fire truck was Joey, bent over at the waist, happily patting a Labrador retriever, which happened to belong to an off-duty firefighter nicknamed Pooh Bear. The trio appeared to be very happily engaged in dialogue and had temporarily forgotten the fire.

Marshall dropped the line and broke into a dead run – toward the truck.

As he closed in, Greg Adams revved the giant truck, causing its exhaust and engine to drown out the string of voluminous expletives coming from Captain Allen.

"I called him everything but the child of God," Marshall said.

While the general public gathered around, Greg Adams continued to rev the engine as Marshall's verbal tirade continued. By the time Marshall got to him, Joey realized what was happening. He parted ways with Pooh Bear and ran back to the hose reel and let out the slack. Ultimately, the fire was defeated, and the homes were saved, but Marshall did not speak to Joey for some time.

"When we got back to the station, I was still pissed," he said. "I went back to my room to do some paperwork. Later on that night, he came back to the office, and I thought the guy was going to say something like, 'Hey, I know I screwed up,' but this is what he said. He said, he actually said, 'I really appreciate you getting after me out there. Sometimes I get distracted.' I said, 'Distracted? Son, we're not selling vacuums out there.'"

"I can still see him," Marshall shook his head. "Petting that damned dog." Even as Marshall is quick to point out that he liked Joey, that Joey was one of the nicest guys you could meet, that "he didn't have a malicious bone in his body," they were still in the business of fighting fires. After some time, Joey also came to this realization, deciding that perhaps fire fighting was not for him.

Whenever the fire chief found that he had a difficult fire fighter, one who was easily distracted, or even an officer who had problems with other employees, for whatever reasons, they were typically assigned to Marshall. Two different chiefs on two different occasions apologized to Marshall for sending the more challenging individuals to him, explaining that they did so because Marshall's station seemed to be the only place where those individuals could thrive.

Marshall just had a way of communicating with people.

It was no surprise to Marshall when he received a personal phone call from the chief requesting that Joey be assigned to him. "I just told him, 'Chief, you know, we're all a little different.'"

Several "Marshall laws" were put into effect as a result of his more innovative ideas. Well before classes with his techniques were taught, Marshall learned to use water pressure in various ways not only to fight but to find fire and overhaul the situation.

It is, Marshall said, "a paradigm you can get caught in." He explains how this technique works: "A fire goes up the outside of a house, catching both the roof and gables on fire. Then, as fires are apt to do, it makes its way back toward the house again. Standing protocol on such a house fire is to fight it from the inside out, pushing the flames back and out of the house. But many times, as impossible as it sounds, the fire fighters cannot find the fire. The old saying 'where there's smoke, there's fire' doesn't mean a whole lot if you can never find the damned flames."

Like the snowflake, no two fires are the same. With each fire comes a different approach. "Typically," Marshall says, "the fire fighters climb the outside of the structure, punching holes in the roof trying to find the fire to see how far the fire has extended." And, they hope, to get ahead of the fire. In many cases, the fire fighters must also fight their way through sheet rock and walls, not to mention the heavy black smog, just to find the fire.

It was during such a battle that Marshall took advantage of a big line, that is, a larger, heavier hose. Marshall instructed his men to use full water pressure and aim the line behind "where I was and break the wall with all the pressure so I could see where the fire was."

Marshall had figured out a way to use water pressure to break through sheet rock and "pop a hole" without putting his crew at risk. "It just seemed like the right thing to do," Marshall said. "It was safer than getting closer with tools and a hell of a lot faster."

Not all of his strategies, however, go according to plan, and Marshall is quick to point out what he calls his "failures."

When Marshall and his company arrived at a particular fire, he believed the officers on the scene were not doing enough to find and fight the fire. The firemen were having a difficult time locating the fire. "So I jumped in," he said. "Now, to this day, this one really hurts me. I'm embarrassed."

Marshall and his men went on the attack, determined to find the fire. As he drove his men forward, giving out commands, he climbed into the attic without protective gear. "I just hadn't taken the time," he says apologetically. He followed a young fire fighter up, and together, armed with the hose, they began their search.

"I turned him around in the attic, wanting him to be able to face where I believed the fire to be," Marshall explained. But it wasn't where Marshall thought it was. While the young recruit was hunkered down behind the line, safe from danger, the fire burst through behind Marshall.

Balanced on a ladder, Marshall poked his head and shoulders up into the attic and tapped the young recruit on the leg, directing him where to aim the water line. "When he did," Marshall said, "the water broke through the sheet rock." Instantly, oxygen hit the fire, igniting it. Flames billowed up behind Marshall and seared the back of Marshall's neck, causing him to slip on the rungs and stumble backward and down the ladder.

"I wasn't prepared," Marshall groaned. While he concedes he could not control the fire, "I did have control over being prepared."

"The kid had it under control," Marshall said of the recruit. "But …." Even 12 years later, the memory of it all sickens him. "Goddamn! I left him alone."

Instantly, Marshall caught himself and climbed back up, willing himself to face the fire because he was not absolutely sure that his fire fighter was okay. "It all happened so quickly, maybe two seconds, maybe five seconds," Marshall said. The young fire fighter was safe, but Marshall wasn't. "I had to cut back on the tears," Marshall said. "I was so embarrassed and mad. I'd never panicked before. It upsets me to this day. I'd been in such a hurry to get in the building that I didn't wear my gear, and I failed my men. I was a captain, and I failed my men," he says forlornly. Though no one else thought anything of the incident, it haunted Marshall.

His role of leader was one he never asked for but, once earned, was one he took very seriously. Perhaps this is because he never dreamed of ever having a position of power, and the idea that any of his ideas would become department-wide fire fighting techniques or any kind of Marshall law was unthinkable.

Even more unthinkable was that Marshall, the man who once outran a horse, who scaled buildings and lifted an extraordinary amount of weights, can now be done in by a toe nail injury. No one can prevent some of the day-to-day injuries that happened to Marshall. In part, Marshall's constant movement, his impatient quest to be independent and unrestricted, causes some injury. Others simply cannot be helped.

Because his feet are constantly swelling, Marshall is restricted to shoe wear that leaves his toes exposed. And just as he caught his toes against the door jam, breaking his leg in 2005, he tore a toenail completely off in January 2006.

As he negotiated his chair into his van and behind the wheel, he drove his foot into the brake pedal, tearing the toenail from his toe. This time, he knew instantly what he had done. But there were other complications.

"I had athlete's foot," Marshall said, "and didn't even know it." The open wound allowed the fungus to work its way into Marshall's body. Just as it had happened before, he knew he'd hurt himself by the reflexive responses of his body. Sweating, discomfort, fever. By the week's end, he had flu-like symptoms, but only when bloodwork was performed did they realize his white cell count was off. Almost immediately, from the time that Marshall spoke to an infectious disease expert, did Marshall's true condition show itself. He had cellulites. His fever spiked to nearly 104 degrees, and he was hospitalized for almost two weeks.

As Marshall explains, "The problem is that sometimes I just don't know where it hurts, where I've injured myself." In this case, an unseen ailment triggered a critical response. Something seemingly minor can spell disaster in a matter of hours or days.

By 2006, fire fighters from all over the FWFD voluntarily contribute one or two dollars per paycheck to a Marshall Allen fund to cover his medical and health care costs. Remarkable. It was never anything he asked for or expected. He was a black kid from Salt Lake County, Utah. He'd been given up on countless times, mistreated, misunderstood, and misdiagnosed. He was determined, brilliant, and defiant against how a young black man was *supposed* to behave. Though he proved his critics wrong, he never thought he would be in a wheelchair, and he damned sure never thought he would become one of the most respected officers in a huge fire department.

Protecting God's Green Earth

By the eleventh day into the new year, we were back in Emergency. This time, it was Mary Redding, the school nurse at Mt. Peak Elementary, who called to say that I needed to come get Tommy, "Now!" This, of course, would be the same Mt. Peak that TXI claimed did not need to be factored into general health issues. This would be the same Mt. Peak that *USA Today* would reveal (in 2008) to be in the upper one percentile of worst places for a child to attend school in terms of overall health (because of its exposure to possible harmful emissions). (7)

This would be the same day that Becky Bornhorst called to say that an environmental lobbyist group in Washington D.C. called Earthjustice and wanted to buy both Becky and me airline tickets to go speak at the Environmental Protection Agency headquarters in Durham, N.C.

Specifically, they wanted me to talk about living in a town with cement plants. Since Midlothian is the only place in the U.S. where three cement plants surround a town, I guess I was an easy candidate. In fact, they had wanted Sue Pope, but she can't fly. The last time she flew to testify, she became incredibly ill and needed oxygen. The irony here was that Sue could not even testify against the cement plants because, she believes, the cement plants made her too sick. I readily accepted on Sue's behalf.

After spending yet another day in Emergency with my son, I had a few things I wanted to get off my chest.

Holcim had proposed that they would build plants in Florida and in Missouri so there would also be people from both states to listen to the stories of those living under the plumes of cement stacks. The main topic was actually mercury – which the plants wanted to be able to release into the atmosphere at higher levels.

Initially, I was stunned. More mercury emissions on the heels of the EPA attempting to weaken the Toxic Release Inventory (TRI) information? The entire purpose of the TRI was to gather, inform, and protect us when too many hazardous wastes are put into the atmosphere. Instead, that protection was simply being revised. Who was watching out for us, the general public? Although it had been posed in a mocking manner in the Waxahachie City Hall, attorney Cathy Altman had asked an excellent question. Who was protecting the general public?

Instantly, I began rereading many of the e-mail exchanges between Jim Schermbeck, Becky, and other DAR members. Maybe if I read it 17 times over, I would finally understand. But five days later, on January 16, I was back in Emergency with Tommy at Baylor. Tommy had already missed Wednesday, Thursday, and Friday of the previous week. I had just received a note from the school board stating that Tommy had missed too many days of school and might be held back.

Jared Saylor from Earthjustice was busily setting up interviews with local press, including the *Dallas Morning News, Fort Worth Star*

Telegram, and televised news while Robb was pleading with me to stay low key. With many school teachers and coaches married to employees of the three cement plants, I had to wonder how my nascent crusade might affect my kids at school. I had been repeatedly warned by a mother whose children were active in sports that my children could be judged. But it's hard to be low key and FIGHT at the same time.

The most valuable thing I took from my trip to N.C. to testify before the EPA came not from making any impact on lawmakers but sharing an airplane seat with Becky Bornhorst. An attractive, slender, silvery blonde, Becky is a conundrum. As slight as she is, with very kind eyes and a generous smile, she's supposed to be out somewhere handing out cookies, not pissing off major industries. But in her time with DAR, she and fellow members have put on skits, dressing up as dancing cement stacks, fat cement CEOs, and corrupt politicians. She's attended litigation meetings and taken on politicians, even becoming a stock holder to one of the major cement plants so that she would be advised of business meetings. Well before my time, the DAR members, along with members of Blue Skies Alliance, had rummage sales and bake sales to cover the expenses required to get the word out.

Becky, as near as I could tell, knew all the key players and had an endless knowledge about the environmental issues. But on our flight, she confessed how she'd become involved. She lived in DeSoto, Texas (roughly 15 miles downwind of Midlothian), but when she read an article in the newspaper about the emissions – what kinds and how much – being released into the environment, she became curious. She had no idea what an integral part of this environmental movement she would become. When she first got into it, her kids were still in grade school. She knew she had to move quietly and not make too big a deal about it for the sake of her kids. Even 15 miles from the "company town" of Texas, other Texans frowned upon any kind of environmentalism. It is a cultural issue in Texas; apparently only weirdoes want clean air and water, and she had to tread lightly.

Becky reached a point where she felt like people were shrinking away when they saw her coming – something that seems impossible because she is one of the warmest, most genuine women you could ever meet. You can take whatever Becky says to the bank.

We talked about husbands and how reluctant they can be to get involved in problems they do not perceive to be their own. But when she confessed that she still struggled with the legal mumbo-jumbo, I felt relieved. I had perused the material provided us on mercury and the new rulings and was instantly overwhelmed. I was relieved when Becky read it for about 15 minutes and announced, "Well, I'm done."

Joining us at the EPA hearing was Eric, an angler from Wisconsin, who was outraged that more mercury was being allowed; December, a rancher from Florida who talked about her cows, family, and land but also some of the fights/protests she's been involved with; a woman named Marti Sinclair who was involved with the Sierra Club and had fought against industry when her own son got sick in Oklahoma; and Dr. Neil Carman, a former incinerator inspector and environmentalist. (On another coincidental note, I read an article in *O* magazine that featured Dr. Carman on the airplane trip to N.C. and then met the environmental superstar an hour later).

As I listened to all of their war stories against industry, I was blown away by their level of commitment. This is not a paying job but an exhausting, often disappointing exercise in American politics and business. People who claim that environmentalists are "in it" for the glory and attention have no idea what they're talking about. There is zero glory.

While we were all making the introductions in the lobby of our hotel, Robb called. He had messed up Tommy's medication, complaining that it was confusing and he didn't know what to do, and he wished I was there to help. Never mind that we stood in the kitchen and I gave explicit directions – with visuals! He wasn't listening. So, everyone got to listen while I walked Robb though the next cycle of medications and steroids, and it opened up a new dialogue about all the medications Tommy had been on, including the cycle where Robb and I tag-teamed, waking Tommy every two hours to give different kinds of medication.

Over the course of dinner, I learned that the EPA appointees in the last years all had backgrounds in mining, timber, and cement. No environmental. As I sat wondering, "Why am I here? Is it already a done deal?" we learned that the cement (Portland cement) heads were already there, woo-ing the EPA. I went to bed depressed. In fact, I crumpled up my written notes and watched, *Miss Congeniality II*. I fell asleep with the decision that I would not use my rehearsed speech. Instead, I would just shoot from the hip.

I did. And I did not win Miss Congeniality.

James Cox, an attorney with Earthjustice, discussed the legal dynamics, addressing EPA big shot Keith Barnett and David Cozzie. To their left was the court reporter. The rest of us sat in rows, waiting our turns to speak. Dr. Carman, Becky, Marti, Eric, and the rest all went, reading from their pre-written statements because they had so many numbers, so many reports and findings, it would have been impossible to memorize such staggering data. But in doing so, they did not make eye contact with Barnett, and as I sat watching him, periodically jotting notes to himself, it was clear that he was bored. *Had he already made up his mind in back room meetings with the cement heads?*

By the time it was my turn, I wasn't nervous. I wanted to talk and hoped that someone was listening. I stated my name and where I was from, and I gave a brief description of my background (as required) and then began discussing life in Midlothian. And Tommy.

I'd forgotten to say that he was a perfectly healthy boy when we moved there and then got sick. I wish that I had articulated how an entire neighborhood in Westerville, Ohio, knew to be on the lookout for the wild boy, Tommy, who could not be contained for very long so they could better understand how devastating it was to us all when Tommy sat breathless and weak on the couch because of air quality. Later, Dr. Carman made me promise that I would get those points in because it made it even more powerful. I got wrapped up in what I was about to do and say.

As I talked about Tommy getting sick, I began pulling out all the medications he was taking under the care of Dr. Mandujano, a pediatric pulmonary specialist in Dallas. As I slowly pulled everything out, I could see people stir in their seats. It was a pile of medicine. It was a mini mountain.

The whole time I had been looking right at them, looking back and forth between the two men. For the first time, I looked away and began reading Tommy's medication regiment.

Then I snapped. I just began to bawl and could not control myself. When I reminded them that all the medication that lay before them were routinely being pumped into the body of a 48-pound boy, my baby, rage began to well inside of me.

I was embarrassed and mad that this was happening, and I cursed. I then said, looking back up at Barnett, "I can beat the shit out of anyone, but I can't beat this!" In my bio, I had told them that I was a black belt and taught kickbox, but I think my explosion startled him. When I first began talking, I made a few jokes and even poked some fun at James Cox's legal writing, so I think it really threw everyone off that I should suddenly began crying and raising my voice. Also, threatening violence against EPA guys probably isn't normal behavior.

I told them that I had always loved the EPA, but I was now frustrated because conservatives joked that the EPA was a bunch of damned tree huggers and that environmentalists thought the EPA was "on the take." Bought and sold. I could feel how very, very quiet it got behind me. I told them they had become totally ineffective.

Oh, lordy, what am I saying?

Then I said that I wanted the EPA to do what they were supposed to do. They needed to "snap out of it." I told them they can't imagine what it is like to have a little boy ask if he is going to die. They couldn't know how helpless a feeling that was and how angry it made me because I knew the question ultimately came from the air. The cement plants. A town I had chosen based on a wild assumption that air here was as good as air in Westerville, Ohio.

Then I ended with the story of Tommy spitting on cookies. He had been getting a breathing treatment when yummy cookies came out of the oven. We had a bunch of kids over, and Tommy realized that he would miss out on the cookies because of his breathing treatment, so in desperation, he ran over and spit on the cookies. It was a brilliant if not disgusting strategy, which got him in trouble for being rude.

Everyone chuckled, and I suspect they wondered where I was going with the story. I pointed to Cozzie and Barnett and said that if we were to go out to dinner, and I suddenly spit on their dinner, I could garan-damn-tee that they would not poke around the plate with their fork and say, "Oh, well, she didn't spit over here." I said, "You would be so grossed out you would not touch anything." But that's just spit. We're talking about mercury. We are talking about stuff that we know for a fact causes horrible illnesses and diseases. We're talking about tons of crazy, scary crap that comes out of the stacks and falls down over us. Yet here we sit talking about not IF but HOW MUCH we are going to allow into their environment.

With that, unlike my fellow speakers who would politely ask if there were any more questions, I began throwing lil' Tom's medications back into my Target bag, stood, and said, "That's it. I'm done."

I was mortified.

I slunk back to my chair and cringed, thinking, "Okay, let's take stock of what I just did." I told them they were on the take, told them to snap out of it and that I could beat the shit out of them, *and* that I would spit on their dinner. A good day, over all.

I peeked over at Becky who was smiling at me and gave me a thumbs up. When I realized that she was teary-eyed, I looked around to see that everyone was sniffing. When the rancher, December, went to the podium, she wiped her eyes and sniffed, "Well, thanks a lot, Alex." She was so choked up she could not speak at first and continued to sniff through her testimony.

Later, as we filed out, the clerk who stood outside the hearing room told me that people were peeking in from the lobby. "It was really powerful." And briefly, I thought I had made a difference.

Months later, the EPA gave their ruling. Mercury levels were allowed to be raised. Our testimonies had meant nothing.

TXI forged ahead with their plans for burning six million tires a year, and because it was legally required that they publish a public notice, they put out a notice in a small paper – in an entirely different city. As desired, few Midlothian residents knew about the hearing, so the crowd was small and manageable. But TXI had a very big problem. Members of Downwinders and a persistent former scientist from the CDC named Salvador Mier were in attendance, and they very much wanted answers. A TXI spokesperson explained how tire burning was great and that pollution would actually go *down* long-term. It was his claim that it would reduce NOX, and he talked about how TXI was aware of pollution and wanted to cut down. He talked about how this was "proven technology" and would require minimal maintenance. With the tires burned at 2200 degrees, "creating localized reducing conditions which inhibit NOX formation and context NOX to Nitrogen," the process was declared a win/win.

But as Sal Mier listed the number of birth defects in Midlothian and how we rank in Texas and in the nation, as he pondered the yet unknown long-term ramifications of exposure to these toxins, Wendi Hammond demanded to know how much TXI was being paid for taking and burning the tires. As Wendi asked about how much was the current NOX per pounds/tons of clinker, the industry reps looked unsettled. Rita Beving of the Sierra Club laughed out loud, saying, "I told you they don't know because it changes from day to day." She'd made a friendly bet with Wendi. At the time, I didn't catch the significance of this. It was her contention that TXI couldn't possibly do proper self reporting on anything because their stats, burning, everything changes from day to day, and they do not know what to report. As Wendi hammered them again with a question about which kilns would be burning the tires, the even bigger question was why no one knew about this meeting. Around the room, people complained that they received no letter, no notice in the mail, saw nothing in the local paper.

For more than an hour, residents spoke out, asking questions that were never answered.

At my turn, I confessed that I didn't know a lot about NOX or Nitrogen or SCR or SNCRs, but I knew a lot about magazines, newspapers, and advertising, and we'd all seen firsthand how the cement plants were quick to place their "we're so great with the community" ads, but when it came time to advertising that they were holding a meeting about tire burning, they were suddenly unsure of who to call. Instead of using those same local media outlets, they to put out an ad with the

Waxahachie paper. It was bull, and I let the TCEQ guy know that it was bull. To my surprise, without any prompting from me, they already knew who I was. When I was done and sat down, scowling about the fact that I had spoken out in the first place, thus giving my name, Rita leaned over and smiled. "Welcome to the club, honey. They just put your face with your name."

By the mid-summer of 2006 while the toxic emissions raged on, Loves Musket Corporation quietly began building a fuel terminal in Midlothian without any public hearing, any public consultation or opinion. Amazingly, the public rallied and, with enough phone calls, Loves withdrew its permit. Briefly, we appeared to have won, and for once, it felt great to be on the winning side!

Then Erin called. Were this any other place, she began, things would be very different. However, for Masry & Vititoe to pump millions of dollars into an environment (literally) that was pro-industry with the courts and state agencies very pro-industry, the gamble was too great. There were other environmental cases around the country that they knew they could win, and they needed to use their resources wisely. But before she hung up, she offered this advice, "Fight to reveal the truth."

Chapter Thirteen

On God's Green Earth

The huge irony was that on the day that the permit for the fuel terminal was withdrawn from TCEQ by Musket Corporation, the EPA released the 2004 Toxic Release Inventory report, and Jim Schermbeck said, "Perhaps this is God's way of trying to tell us something."

Many people were celebrating their victory over Musket but could have cared less that it was reported that "nearly 400 tons of various kinds of toxic pollution were released into Midlothian's air, land, and water in 2004, including over 1000 pounds of Mercury, 119,000 pounds of Lead, 58,000 pounds of Benzene, 89,000 pounds of Toluene, and 600 pounds each of Styrene and Naphthalene." Stack releases of Mercury were up by almost 20 percent, and Mercury releases in total up by 30 percent. With increased production and lessening of pollution controls in 2005, we can look forward to even greater tonnage of hazardous pollutants in the next report. (8)

I felt like I was living in the Twilight Zone where reasonably intelligent people could not see through the haze.

Jim Schermbeck had become vigilant in his desire to get Downwinders to work with churches in the Dallas and Fort Worth areas, and, frankly, I wanted nothing to do with the churches. For the longest time, it seemed to me that the biggest hypocrites on earth were those who went to church. The biggest polluters – or proponents of pollution in my own town – wouldn't miss a church service to save their lives. How they could miss the finer point that we were to care for God's green earth was a mystery; didn't they believe this green earth belonged to God? Even that wasn't worth further investigation because I already had the answer. The earth was not God's. All the church-going litter bugs testified to that. They didn't believe. Why should I?

But when Jim was not able to make a meeting with one of the larger church congregations in Fort Worth, he asked me. Me. I said, "Ummm."

I like to be a helpful person and all, but no way did I want to go to this big church and stare at people who I know don't really care about the environment and who look at environmentalists in a negative light. No thanks. When he started to pout, I had to respond because no one tries harder than Jim, so I agreed.

And so it was with great reservation that I attended the massive University Christian Church at the Texas Christian University (TCU) in Fort Worth, Texas. Jim had told me there was a new wave among churches throughout the nation. He said that many churches were finally embracing the correlation between environmentalism, protecting God's green earth, the Bible, and faith.

Yeah, sure they are. I bet they're all just breathlessly waiting to hear what I have to say about air quality and emissions.

To my shock – they were. After opening the meeting with a prayer (in which I was peeking and can tell you they appeared to be rather sincere), the talk went straight to how they could help fight for better air, a cleaner world. Whoa. These people cared. These people were talking about God's green earth and what their obligations to it might mean.

A change, some kind of change, seemed to be just over the horizon. So when Earthjustice called again, we leapt at the opportunity to meet then Sen. Barack Obama. I wasn't quite sure who the guy was, but any senator's interest in our plight was a bonus. The irony here was that as a Texas constituent, I could not get any Texas senator to meet with me or discuss the Midlothian air quality, but I could bend the ear of two Illinois senators.

Both Sen. Richard Durbin and Barack Obama were wonderful, funny, thoughtful, and inspiring, and both senators – independently – spoke to Tommy about having asthma. Sen. Obama told Tommy about his own daughter, who has asthma, and how he blames local pollution for her illness. Sen. Obama was not condescending or awkward in speaking to a child as many adults are, but he got down to Tommy's level, showing him a genuine interest and concern. In turn, Tommy was articulate as he told the senators how it feels to have asthma, and we left on a cloud of hope.

With Earthjustice lawyer Jim Cox by our side, we made our way through the U.S. Senate corridors to find Sen. Kay Bailey Hutchinson. At the last minute, we were able to get an appointment. I had bullied someone in Sen. Hutchinson's office, saying how disappointing it was that I was invited to meet with the senators from Illinois but my own senator was too busy. I was given a small window.

By virtue of her being a Texan politician, I had little hope, but, still, we had an appointment. We were told we would meet her for breakfast and then meet at 10 a.m. with her "environmental advisor." But when we got there, Hutchinson had to be on the floor for some hearing, so there was no "breakfast." Briefly, I caught her arm to tell her where I was from and that I needed her help. She stared at me like a deer in the headlights. She offered us a photo-op and left.

Illinois is a nice state.

Before I left, Jim Schermbeck warned us not to have any great expectations from our own senators and, by golly, he was right.

Back home, we had, however, scored a small victory in that the TCEQ held a public hearing to "listen" to our views on the newest permit for tire burning. This time, the auditorium was full as people who were informed about the upcoming meeting. But as soon as we got in, we were told that this was not a debate but merely an opportunity for people to ask direct questions about the tire burning process and question the TCEQ. The moderator (we'll call her MC) was an unpleasant woman who put everyone on edge because she was clearly pro-industry. By the end of the evening, people throughout the audience were grumbling. Who is she? Does she even care what we have to say?

She opened by explaining what the TCEQ does (puh-leaze) and its functions, and then she let a TXI rep explain what and how the tire burning process would work. He explained that the plant was a great opportunity for Midlothian, blah, blah. But we were instantly confused that if it was not hazardous burning (tires), then why was the process part of the hazardous permit? If they were burning hazardous waste and would be throwing the tires in the incinerator, they had to have an okay from the TCEQ. But wouldn't the increased burning of tires on top of everything else make emissions more dangerous and unhealthy and create more pollution? Sadly, no sufficient answer was ever provided because, alas, the question wasn't deemed significant.

Beyond the regulars, I was surprised to see Dr. Neil Carman in attendance. This was a huge bonus.

TXI had all their pretty little graphs that no one really understood, and, suddenly, we were all very happy that Irv, Jim Schermbeck, Sal Mier, Neil Carman, and the members of Downwinders were there because they could not be snowed.

One resident asked if, during the tire burning process, other emissions from the other plants/kilns and steel mill were considered as part of the pollution. The MC kept asking her to clarify her point, and people in the audience were rolling their eyes. How more clear could she have been? But finally the answer came. No. Only the tire burning was considered and only pollution/emissions from TXI were considered. No one combined the emissions from ALL the plants and the steel mill to see how much worse the combined emissions would make our air.

It was becoming clear there was a real distrust among the public because we'd seen time and again how the plant administrators would use existing studies to save time and money and apply the old data to current issues.

Audra could not contain herself – which still delights me, and I can't believe that once upon a time she would *never* have stood up and talked. But she got up, introduced herself by saying that she doesn't know all the scientific terms and while she feared that her questions might sound "kindergarten-ish," she had a few questions. She was perfect!

She asked why tires weren't considered hazardous. They gave the age-old answer about how much higher temperature burning would eliminate all emissions. They talked about "controlled" and "confined" burnings, but what Joe Public doesn't know is that the burning from the kilns is 1) so dirty that they put out really bad things and that 2) the clinker or ash from the burning either goes into the environment (combined with all the bad things they burn besides tires) or is buried in the ground.

Then the amazing and spectacular Katie Allred went up. At the tender age of 11, she felt compelled to speak. She'd been sitting next to Audra in the question area. When she got up, people began to smile. She tilted the mic down toward her precious face, and the MC said, "State your name, Miss." Katie was so loud and clear, it surprised everyone. She did not appear to have one nervous bone in her body. She spoke her name and said, "So many of my friends at school can't go outside on the playground because they can't breathe, and we already have enough pollution as it is. So, my question is, why can't we send the tires somewhere else?"

The place erupted into applause. As Katie made her way back to me, people were smiling and nodding with great approval. Jim Schermbeck, Rita, Sandra, and Becky were all proud and turned to give enthusiastic thumbs up.

But there were more serious questions to come regarding tests on the dangerous chemicals and burning of heavy metals. The answer: No, there was no new assessment but a "revisiting" test, which means that they used old data. Again. Did they conduct an updated "waste" analysis? No.

The beauty was, the Downwinders already knew the answers but wanted to force TXI to say them out loud, putting both industry and TCEQ on the hot seat.

But anytime someone hammered a hard question, they were shut down; the MC simply rebutted with a "Was that part of your comment?"

If a speaker did not previously write down their "comment," it would not be accepted.

Person after person stood, asking questions that went unanswered until, at long last, Jim Schermbeck stood. Becky Bornhorst had stood, and when she made the remark that it was still more pollution, she was warned to sit or leave.

Jim spoke. He asked about the studies. He asked if the "Was this in your comments?" question could stop being asked when all we want is answers. He asked if the commentary time line could be extended because most people there tonight didn't know about the first meeting.

APPLAUSE.

MC tried to shut him down, and he spoke over her.

He asked how his concerns could be an issue because this was the first time most could have a chance to make comments.

APPLAUSE.

Then he shifted gears and asked if TXI was getting paid to burn tires, how many wet kilns in the country are burning tires with hazardous waste, and what was being burned when the test was conducted? It went on and on without answers. With Dr. Carman at his side, they pointed out failed and incomplete studies, repeatedly asking what we really know, then, about harmful emissions. Facts about birth defects, unusual skin ailments, and upper respiratory diseases were summarily listed. The knights raised their swords, but in the end, TXI got its permit to burn. But for those citizens sitting in attendance for the first time, the serious nature of the questions and the sincerity of the problem was an eye opener!

Jim Schermbeck had already moved on to a much bigger stage: the 2006 Gubernatorial Elections in the great state of Texas. Only Jim could have arranged to have a giant, 30-foot-tall replica of Gov. Rick Perry's head created. And only Jim could have convinced me to use our 16-foot flatbed trailer – one that was registered in the name of my Republican husband – to display the giant head. And only Jim would have then found a truck to drag that trailer and giant head around the state of Texas, trailing Rick Perry's tour bus.

The head, with perfectly coifed hair, had puckered lips, kissing a large cement stack (that also had a dry ice machine attached to a generator to make smoke come from the cement stack) marked TXI, Holcim, and Ash Grove.

The years of 2005 and 2006 had been the most stressful years of my life. Although Tommy was sick well before that, I thought knowing what was wrong would have made things better. Instead, it made things worse. We couldn't afford to move, the entire town was in denial, and I was getting a pretty disturbing lesson in national and state politics. While I had a blast driving the big Rick Perry head with Michelle and Gina, made more great friends, and learned to laugh as often as possible in life, I was getting really tired of stupid. I was beginning to lose that one thing I always had – optimism.

At a soccer game, the daughter of a friend bounced over to me and asked a question that surprised me, "Which is your favorite cement plant?"

Well, gee…let's see. "I guess Holcim," I answered honestly. Holcim had begun to open dialogue about creating "green cement" – cement that does not contain hazardous waste and materials. And I really like – believe it or not – the plant manager. In fact, I really like most of the employees of all three plants.

"Mine, too!" Cassidy said. "We had a field trip there."

That was when I learned that the schools took school board approved field trips to the cement plants and learned about the "harmless steam" that came out of the cement stacks. She was sporting a nifty new Holcim t-shirt!

Chapter Fourteen

All God's Children

The Sunday meetings at Starbucks swelled to a dozen people. There are the usuals: Marshall, Al, Stan, and me. Stan Johnson is a diehard Dallas Cowboy fan who finds it difficult to talk about anything other than the Cowboys (or, in the off-season, the Mavericks), and he is teased relentlessly about this undying devotion. After 30 years as a restaurant program planner for the Army & Air Force Exchange Service, Stan has given his entire life to the service and his country. He is not just an avid Cowboy fan but a rabid, faithful patriot to his country. Stan is also another big guy, easily standing at 6'3" (by his own account), although Al argues with him that he is actually 6'4". Al, after all, reasons that he would know so much better than Stan how tall Stan actually is. Like Marshall and Al, Stan is a large, African-American male who has been entertained by the fact that I have settled so nicely into the group.

I address this with a certain ease because, in fact, the point has been discussed many times. As I had with Al and Marshall, I balked the first time Stan voiced surprise that I would be so at ease with a group of large black men. To explain his surprise, Stan shared a story of his youth in Jonesville, Louisiana.

He recalled how he would often walk to a locally-owned convenience store to buy candy. As was common in Jonesville, many of the family-owned businesses did not have names. "There were just these little 'ol country stores," Stan said. But it was the 1960s, and all the stores were owned by whites. Stan offered a diplomatic and understanding assessment of the times: "We [blacks and whites] were still all trying to understand each other and understand the thing between us." Still, there is one particular memory that stands out for Stan.

He was just a young boy, no more than five- or six-years-old, and he'd walked into one of the nameless country stores in hopes of buying something sweet. As he entered, the white woman behind the register watched him intently. "It wasn't out of meanness," Stan said. "It was just so imbedded in her, that's how it was." The "it" was the suspicion of a little black boy in her store.

But even he could not deny the ugliness of this woman's actions when he attempted to pay for his candy. "She made me place the money down on the counter," he recalled because the woman was unwilling to handle the money as it came from Stan's hands. When he did as ordered, the woman withdrew a cloth handkerchief and began wiping off the money before placing it in the register drawer.

His money was good enough to take, just not to touch.

In fact, Stan has a very interesting theory about money, food, and African Americans. It was, he contends, the African Americans who discovered the drive-thru restaurant through necessity and ingenuity.

It began at a Mom and Pop store deep in the south. "It was a combination restaurant with a gas station. Back in the day, these places would have two gas pumps, you know, where they had a crank on the pump. You had to pump your own gas so you would have to go up to the window to pay because you weren't allowed to go into the restaurant.

"They had a window set up like a movie theater window," he said. "You had to slide your money under the window to pay for the gas."

If you wanted food, however, you would have to drive to the back of the building. "There was a hole cut in the wall with a cash register set by the window. Say you want a hamburger. You stick your head in, order, pay, and wait."

The method was crude but effective. So crude, in fact, that these first-ever drive-thrus could not be called windows. They really were holes. At night, a board dropped down behind to slots braced to the wall served as the only security. During poor weather, board still in place, customers would have to knock on the board.

Born in the early 1950s, Stan vividly recalls how people would stand around, waiting for their orders to be filled. When ready, a brown paper bag would be handed out the window. Thus, the first drive-thru restaurants. But a researcher on the topic won't find any references to African American history or the Deep South. Instead, it is Ray Kroc, founder of McDonald's, who is given the credit. It may have been the African Americans who began the practice, but it Ray Kroc who turned it into a money-making empire.

But all these years later, rather than discuss the nuances of social prejudices, Stan is far happier discussing sports, and he always has a buddy to Monday quarterback with when Cliff walks through the doors.

Cliff Shaw, a city councilman in Cedar Hill, Texas, is a frequent addition to the group. An avid reader and committed councilman, he also works as a system engineer at Lockheed Martin. He is an interesting fellow and blends nicely into the eclectic Starbucks group. An African-American man in his mid-50s, Cliff is a conundrum for any person who holds certain prejudices for or against the African-American culture. He speaks openly about his growing concern about single African-American mothers who want to blame "the system" when their children behave badly. He is quick to point out that many of the growing problems facing the area's high schools and communities are reinforced by the fact that the black community does not hold its youth accountable for bad behavior. These are tough words coming from an elected official. Yet he is also deeply committed to his roots, to black history, and to his community. While Al argues against an incoming, upscale shopping center, saying that gang activity, shoplifting, and petty theft among the black youth will run it into the ground, Cliff counters this with unbridled optimism about the economy and the great citizens of Cedar Hill. Is this just his political shtick, or is he really supporting the youth of his community? Perhaps a little of both, but there is no questioning the warmth and good intentions of this man.

Al Tanner also arrives. By profession, he is a claims adjustor with Allstate. He is also African-American and, by everyday standards, a well-built, athletic, average-sized man. Of the group, he is perhaps the most quiet. He is the most diplomatic of the group, sitting back and listening to what others have to say. One wonders if this is something he learned at claims adjustor school. Just sit back and let people yap away. Most people say too much, and he can learn more by saying less.

Only by virtue of name and body comparison, Al Tanner is sometimes referred to as Little Al when Big Al Jones looms. Vanessa Lewis, a bank examiner with the Treasury Department, also African-American, is vibrant, pretty, and always ready with a huge smile. Like Little Al, she is more apt to sit and listen, but from time to time, when a subject of interest hits, Vanessa is not shy about her thoughts.

Marshall's daughter, Talaya, often shows up after church, flanked by her outrageously funny and beautiful half-sister, Rachel. My own sister, Michelle, has become a regular.

Politics and sports are always the current themes, with race an ever present force.

During the Michael Vick dog fighting scandal, Al insisted that my sister, Michelle, was a bigot because she wanted to see Vick punished for electrocuting, beating, and drowning pit bulls. Never mind that Michelle is a huge animal lover and merely protested Vick's grotesque behavior and blatant disregard for life.

Still, Al argued that this would not have been an issue had Vick been white. Authorities would never have paid attention to dog fighting activities had he been a white athlete. He routinely chastises both Michelle and me for our protests against high-salaried athletes. His point is that we railed against the two occupations that African-Americans tend to excel in

– sports and entertainment. Our point is that we don't care what color you are: manhandling a ball or regurgitating lines someone else wrote should not earn you millions of dollars when social workers can't even pay their electricity bills. A rapper should not make millions for dressing stupidly and spouting bad poetry, not to mention defiling females in both literary and physical terms, when police officers make too few dollars. But this opinion has pitted Al against us on several occasions.

Al is, if nothing else, a man who is unafraid to express his views – however unpopular. He felt compelled to share with a group of black women at a party that it was their fault that black men were so irresponsible, that it was their fault that so many black women were single mothers. It is his opinion that African-American women have bent so far over to "support the black man" that they have essentially given him permission to disrespect fatherhood and familial responsibilities, and black women continue to support bad behavior by making excuses for their men.

Imagine attending that party!

O.J. Simpson was framed. Or so goes the common thought at this table, and Stan breaks into a huge grin when I nearly choke on my coffee over this one.

"Yeah," I say. "He was framed with his passport, crazy man cash, duct tape, and plastic wrap, weeping about what he'd done, refusing to stop for police, and a whole other pile of lies.

"But if it doesn't fit," Stan offered, and I rolled me eyes.

Al then calls me a bigot. But Al was alone as he tried to defend rapper R. Kelly. During the trial in which a video was shown, depicting Kelly urinating on and having sexual relations with a minor, Stan, Cliff, Marshall, and Larry Green, a claims investigator with the Criminal District Attorney's Office in Dallas County, wanted no part of that defense. Even after *Newsweek* did an expose on "why so many black women supported R. Kelly," a social commentary on how African-American women have turned their backs on women in support of men, Al maintained R. Kelly was just a man being persecuted because he was rich and black. At times, his rants are ridiculous attempts to get one's blood pressure up. But from time to time, he is deadly serious, and it is difficult to discern his logic.

Al shares memories of his childhood that include shopping in the downtown Fort Worth department store, Leonard Brothers. Initially, Leonard Brothers specialized in groceries and salvaged merchandised. It was founded by two brothers in 1918, but by the 1930s, they had relocated to a larger building, and during the Great Depression had adopted the practice of check cashing. Even when President Franklin D.

Roosevelt closed banks, the department store continued check cashing with what was called "Leonard Script," a paper currency good to be redeemed exclusively at Leonard Brothers. It was a brilliant business and good neighbor policy that kept customers loyal to the store for decades after the Great Depression. In 1939, the store added air conditioning, and on September 1, 1948, Leonard Brothers became the first store in Fort Worth to install an escalator. Reportedly, more than 40,000 customers rode the escalator one Saturday. It was also the first store to desegregate. In 1960, before the Civil Rights Act of 1964, the brothers had the "whites" and "colored" signs removed from all its restrooms and drinking fountains. The whites-only cafeteria was opened to black patrons as business swelled.

What is astonishing to my own children is that Al lived this.

By 1967, both brothers had sold out of the business, turning the reigns over to the Tandy Corporation, although members of the Leonard family continued to manage the store. Finally, on March 4, 1974, Tandy sold Leonard Brothers to Dillards, and all the remaining Leonard Brothers signs came down permanently, but not before the brothers made a huge impact on the Fort Worth economy.

But what Al remembers is the train at Christmas time.

"There was a train that went around the store," Al said. Indeed, it was an exciting time to be a child. But for the black children, "if I remember right, we could only ride the train on one weekend during the month." In fact, while Leonard Brothers had willingly desegregated itself well before the Civil Rights Act, there was an unspoken, unwritten rule for most shoppers, and one Saturday was the "brown" day.

Things were not so accommodating at the Isis Theater. Built in 1913, near the famous Fort Worth Stockyards, the Isis showed silent movies for whites only. However, the theater burned down in 1935, and when it was rebuilt in 1936, the more progressive thinking of the times allowed the Iris to admit blacks, but they had to use a side entrance and sit in the third balconies.

By 1966, well after the Civil Rights Act, Al has memories of buying a ticket and sitting in the designated area for black patrons. For him, the highlight was to throw popcorn down on other people, "not to make any kind of statement. It was just mischief."

His "eye opening" experience would not come until he went to an integrated high school. For generations, any black student who hoped to get an education higher than the eighth grade was given one place to go: I.M. Terrell High in Fort Worth. Black residents from Fort Worth as well as Arlington, Mansfield, Burleson, Bedford, Lake Como, and neighboring towns as far as 30 miles east were forced to take public transportation if they could not arrange their own. It was the Jim Crow Era, and Al grew up in a time when black children could only attend the Texas State Fair or the Stock Show on "Negro Days." Between 1948 and 1954, the African-American community had outgrown I.M. Terrell, and more black schools were constructed. M.L. Kirkpatrick Elementary and Middle School were two.

Long before Al and Marshall and Stan were born, educators and black communities around the nation were closely watching the U.S. Supreme Court when, in 1896, it decreed in Plessy v. Ferguson that schools could be segregated as long as they offered equal opportunities in the schools. The law became known as the "separate but equal" ruling. In 1954, when the Supreme Court revisited the issue in Brown v. Board of Education of Topeka, Kansas, it rejected "separate but equal." The court handed down a 9-0 decision, which stated "separate educational facilities are inherently unequal." That decision proved to be the beginning of a huge movement in Fort Worth, Texas, and across the United States.

Mansfield, Texas, a small farming community just 20 miles outside of Fort Worth, became the first school district in Texas and one of the first two in the nation to desegregate by order of federal courts. The other school district was Clinton, Tennessee. In fact, many civil right leaders believe those two districts were the launching pads for what was to come in Little Rock, Arkansas, in 1957. Unlike Little Rock, there was no federal intervention in Mansfield; however, Texas Governor Allan Shivers, an ardent segregationist, used the Texas Rangers to enforce segregated schools for another nine years.

The local National Association for the Advancement of Colored People (NAACP) filed a lawsuit in 1955, and angry mobs turned on local black students in Mansfield. While Al was focusing on his studies with fellow students, Deacon T.M. Moody, the president of the Mansfield NAACP, and two other blacks were hanged in effigy in protest at the desegregation demonstration. Downtown stores were closed in support of the protest, and any sympathizers for desegregation were subject to abuse. Only when the school district faced loss of federal funds did city officials consent to integration. (9)

The Fort Worth school district, all too aware of what was happening in neighboring school districts, resisted desegregation. Finally, after an exhausting battle, Fort Worth relented and began to desegregate its schools in 1963. By 1971, a federal court ordered a busing system to enact the integration process.

In 1972, Al Jones, a senior in high school, entered his first integrated school and made a startling discovery. White folks have problems, too.

"I saw white kids who had the same problems as us," Al said. "They were angry at their parents, some got into marijuana." This was a surprise to Al who believed from watching television shows that most white folks lived idyllic lives.

"I thought most white people were rich and thought that most of them were like June and Ward and the Cleaver boys."

To Al's defense, what else could he have thought? He'd been effectively segregated from any insight into the typical American white families living in the 1950s and 60s. He thought most white women, like those on the television, wore pearls and did little to no housework. For one thing, the mothers of his black friends were domestics or in the food service. It was implausible to think white women were cleaning when so many black women were domestics.

"And remember," Al said, "the symbols of authority and all the employers were always white." Like Marshall, Al was looking at the world where an entire group of people, neatly wrapped in a world of whiteness and privilege, seemingly had it all. Even as Al attended an integrated high school with the idea that he would be receiving equal education and opportunities, things were not level. Part-time jobs for teenagers were divided.

Jobs that "were designed to help" and provide opportunities like "a bag boy or parking cars went to the white kids." For Al and his friends, there was heavy labor or the food service.

So when Al leans in to me with a smile on his face that promises to be the beginning of yet another big tease, it is easy to understand why race is so prevalent in his mind.

He wants to know, again and again, why it was that I was not afraid to approach two large black men on October 8, 2006. While my father was going through training as a military intelligence officer, we also sponsored (if that's the right word) a number of African military officers from Ghana and Nigeria. By the time I was six-years-old, these officers were very much a part of my family. I was infatuated with a Ghanaian officer named Major Otang because I loved his accent, and he was the only adult I knew who would sit and listen as I ticked off the names of each of my dozens and dozens of stuffed animals. And, of course, a special little story went with each animal. Yet, Major Otang would listen with respect and (practiced) interest. I adored him, and he called me

"Evergreen." I never got the memo that I was supposed to be cringing in terror from black men.

Instead, I simply explained that I'd been curious about the fire fighter sticker on the back of Marshall's wheelchair and about the muzzle on his dog. But Al is nonplus, still curious about my true motives.

As an adult, Stan traveled the back road of Louisiana, once stopping at a Mom and Pop's restaurant to use the bathroom and get a drink. Years later, as he retold this story to the Sunday Starbucks group, Marshall, Al, and Cliff all shook their heads in unison. "You didn't drink it, did you?" Marshall almost laughed. It wasn't a question.

Michelle and I, the only white people in attendance, did not understand the significance of Marshall's assessment. Even when Stan groaned, "Yeah, I did," and the others laughed sympathetically, we were still ignorant to how Stan's story would end. But when Stan told the story of when he ordered food and actually ate it, the laughs stopped. After eating the food, he became violently ill. Later, rushed to the hospital, on his near deathbed, a doctor would tell him that he'd been poisoned. Mostly like with rat poisoning.

Marshall shook his head again. "Man, you should have known," he began, but Stan waved him off. Yeah. He should have known better than to stop at a white Mom and Pop stand and order food.

I find myself unable to grasp the how or why of these racists' actions, why so many have been so stupid and so cruel and so wrong for so long. Stan is funny, intelligent, friendly, and incredibly kind-hearted. I cannot fathom someone shrinking into the corner of an elevator in fear of him doing harm or, worse, trying to poison him! In the same fashion that I cannot understand such ignorance, Al regards many white people with suspicion. Consequently, over the course of the summer and fall of 2007, this attitude led to many discussions about Barack Obama and Hillary Clinton. Specifically, the men of Starbucks (Cliff, Big Al, Al Tanner, Stan, and Marshall) have discussed whether the U.S. is ready for a woman or a black man as president.

"Coming from Utah [in the 70s], I was already a little apprehensive about being immersed in the old South," Marshall said about his move to Forth Worth. "The few black men and women I grew up around were all from the South." Most, he added, were born just prior to or during the Great Depression. Jim Crow, the Ku Klux Klan, segregation, and rampant discrimination were a way of life for these people. "Growing up, I had heard numerous stories of burnings, lynchings, or the threat of lynchings, and the routine mistreatment of the people closest to me."

Making the move to Fort Worth, though the population of African-Americans was dramatically higher than that of Ogden, Utah, was still an unknown trek to the dreaded South.

Initially, the numbers must have looked good to both Marshall and Al. Of the 20 recruits in their fire fighters class, six were black. But when they officially joined the ranks of the Fort Worth fire department, there were only an estimated 35 African- Americans in the 700-person department.

"From a practical standpoint, this meant that there were not enough black firefighters to have one firefighter assigned to every station and every shift in the city," Marshall said. "Which further meant that when you went to work, you probably wouldn't even see another black firefighter. You were on your own to protect yourself physically, salvage your dignity, and at the same time create an overall environment which would ease the transition of future firefighters into a changed culture.

The harsh reality is this: It was the late 1970s and early 80s. Many of the white "brothers" of the Fort Worth Fire Department were related. They often gained their acceptance to the department because of their family relationships and friendships. Much that was good about the department occurred throughout the 70s, but more was needed. Resentment and resistance were there for any non-whites who dared to take away a position that would otherwise have gone to a brother, son, cousin, or friend. And it is at this point that Marshall and Al took different positions on how to enter the Good 'Ol Boy network.

For that matter, even a white fire chief struggled with how to enter such a network. By the late 1970s, the city of Fort Worth was trying to break free from that "good old boy fire service," and hired a fire chief named Larry McMillan from Phoenix, Arizona in 1980. This was the first time a fire chief was brought in from the outside.

"The Fort Worth fire department was not up to standard," McMillan said, noting that 'ol boy system was more of a "blemish" on the department's record. "I didn't come up in the ranks in Fort Worth so it was a learning experience for me."

Enter Marshall Allen. "Marshall was a big, clean cut, good looking African American fire fighter. He was a natural leader and back in those days, we didn't have too many men like him. Affirmative Action was a big city program and that's probably what attracted me to Marshall. He had the potential to be an all-star! Not because he was African American but because he could compete with anybody."

As Marshall rose through the ranks, he became what McMillan calls the perfect example of a fine fire fighter. "The other thing was the African American community was really challenging the hiring and promotional aspects within the department. Marshall became a real ally for me, making the community understand the restrictions I was under but brought to the table how to recruit more capable minority candidates who could compete effectively and promote."

Very quickly, Marshall understood that his actions were representative of many. "Marshall understood the subtleties of prejudice," Al has explained. "I did not."

Because Al was a product of the South or, rather, because Al grew up in the South's atmosphere of blatant prejudice, he learned how to get along for safety and survival reasons. In Utah, where there was undoubtedly prejudice but it was not so overt, and Marshall learned, also for survival reasons, to read between the lines.

But Al knew what overt prejudice could lead to. When he was nine-years-old, Al was riding his bike less than a block from his house, running an errand for his mother. A white man driving, according to witnesses, more than 50 miles an hour on the narrow and unpaved roads of Al's neighborhood hit Al with his car. Al remembers few details of the accident except that as the car hit his bike and he went up and over the car, he locked eyes with the driver. The bike was thrown some 30 feet, and the driver, knowing he had hit a child, never applied the brakes. When the police did arrive to take a report, "all the old people knew that they [police] would never look for the man because he was a white guy," Al said.

His was a neighborhood where the only white people to travel the streets were either salesmen, creditors, or "white women looking for housekeepers." Looking or stopping for small children was not a priority, nor was it a priority to find the kind of person who would hit a child and run.

Al was lucky. Nothing was broken though he was covered with bumps and bruises and recalls being very sore.

While the group could only shake their heads, cluck their tongues, and make light of the situation, it burned in my brain.

Even then, thanks to Marshall, I was trying to figure out the nuances of religion. I like to say that one of the worst workouts I ever had – i.e. biking to Cedar Hill on an empty stomach only to fry out – was the best workout I ever had.

But my new found interest in religion brought new problems. Questions began to pop up. And to my Starbucks friends, I had to wonder: is it harder to be religious when God is always portrayed as white? Is he white?

Some of the most bigoted, narrow minded, most hateful people I have ever met are seriously devoted to God and church. How can I want to join *that* club?

I asked these questions by way of e-mail to the Starbucks gang but inadvertently sent the questions to a man named Cliff Russell, a man I barely knew, instead of Cliff Shaw.

It was the best mistake I ever made; he sent back this note: "I just have to thank you for asking me to answer your question. I spent about 2 hours pondering how to answer you last night. Then, this morning I got up early and spent another 2 hours re-doing my answer to you. I need to review these feelings and beliefs I have and bring them to the surface again. You gave me that opportunity.

If you travel the world, every group has a GOD that they worship that looks like them. It is our frame of reference, and we naturally think of a GOD in terms of our every day experience. But when I see a painting of Christ with blonde hair and blue eyes, I chuckle. There were no blonde, blue-eyed people living in Jerusalem back then. Nope, not hardly. Darker skin, dark hair, and shorter and stocky builds. But it has never bothered me. I think if all you did was pass around a Bible to people of the world, never having seen a painting of Christ, and ask them to draw him, you would see him in every color size and eye color out there. It is just a cultural thing."

In response to my question about racism and hate, Cliff wrote:

"I get mad, very mad, and sometimes I am not nice to the person or church that does this. I can't stay quiet and let them get away with it. But I have to be careful so I don't become another version of what they are. This isn't just religion, it is race, it is politics, and it is regional. The main group right now that just makes me go LIVID is the churches that hold up the signs at military funerals that read: 'GOD HATES FAGS.' There is NOTHING God-like about these people."

It was one of those rare times in my life that I was alone in the house, working on the book. As I read his words, still believing it was my buddy Clifford Shaw writing to me, I felt myself nodding enthusiastically. Yes. This was how I felt, and the affirmation that a deeply religious soul felt as I did was very empowering. Still, no one has ever been able to answer me the really big questions. Why me? Why was I sent – if in fact I was—to Marshall? Why are some people born black or white, rich, poor? Why are some given the gift of being born in a free society while others suffer at the hands of dictators? And how am I supposed to feel good about a religion where people say if you aren't "saved" you can't go to heaven when we know there are people living in huts who know nothing of Jesus Christ? How is that fair?

      Quite unexpectedly, this beautiful near stranger (now friend) shared stories of how he found his own faith and would ultimately go on a mission. While he had not grown up in a spiritual home, he always felt something in his heart and attended almost every church he could before finding his "home," but not before he felt very discouraged, explaining that different people are looking for different things when it comes to religion. True enough. But how one justifies the atrocities against different groups or races in the name of God is a difficult one and certainly one that has held me back from church. He writes: "I will ask you a similar question that has been with me for all my life. After I got back from the slums of South America, I kept asking myself, 'Why did I get to be born in the USA and not in the slums of India or South America?' I think the answer to both questions is in the same root of the answer. It all comes back to my belief that this life is brief in the whole eternal view of existence. People have very different experiences here on earth, and it is how we handle those experiences as to how we will be judged and how we will be blessed. What isn't a challenge for you can put me on the floor and vice versa. How do you handle it when a major trial comes along? Do you give in or do you fight. Why am I white, why do I get to live in the USA, why do I get to have a nice home, and why do I get to live free? I don't know. But I do know that no one is supposed to feel or be superior to those who are in totally different circumstances. The New Testament is full of commandments about LOVE THY NEIGHBOR, feed the poor, take care of the widow, suffer the little children. Maybe some of us earn more so we can help more people with the money we make. We live in a free country to fight for those who are in servitude. Each time you speculate about it, it opens up other doors. But I do know that there is a purpose for each of us. It wasn't by accident that you are in Midlothian right now. And we do have a responsibility to share and to take care of those around us."

Chapter Fifteen

Christmas 2007
Greeting, friends and family!

    Our septic tank overflowed, the dogs almost killed Little Dude (cat), and we were skunked. Tomato juice does nothing but make you mad. After my big important interview with Homeland Security, I looked down to see that my pants zipper was down. My novel about small-town Texas, **White Trash**, while in the hands of an important someone, has still not panned out. But when Tommy was asked by one of his teachers what his mother writes, he responded, "Oh, some white trash stuff."

    We try to keep things low key for Robb, but it's difficult. Channel 8 contacted us for a story on the environment, and we obliged. Prior to that, I'd been caught by a news crew as I was coming out of City Hall. I was asked if I had an opinion on pedophiles. What could I say? No? So I was on the news, offering my opinion on pedophiles. A week later, another news agency called for yet another story on the environment. Despite Robb's belief that I lurk around film crews for the thrill of being on the news, the truth is that I just feel strongly about doing my part for the environment. So they mic-ed up Tommy in hopes of hearing him wheeze as he ran at soccer practice. The good news is that his asthma has really improved. The bad news – for the crew – was that Tommy had great lung capacity and was talking to the cameraman throughout soccer practice. He kept saying, "*Hey, hey … can you hear me?*" And as he was dribbling the ball down the field, "*Hey, are you getting this?*" When some of his teammates squirted him with water, he warned, "*Hey, don't get me wet. I've got electronics on.*" Then he told his teammates, "*See that guy over there? He can hear every word we're saying. Watch this. Hey, mister, if you can hear me, raise your hand.*" The cameraman obliged.

    During Spring Break, we re-enacted the death of Julius Caesar (class project) with a group of kids in togas, wreaths, and knight's armor. Later, for other class projects, we also re-enacted the Civil War and Napoleon Bonaparte at Waterloo. Tommy has become obsessed with Napoleon, so we've all been subjected to hours of war between our friends, the Brits and the Frogs. During one of our most recent trips to the Cowboy Church (where they also have a rodeo – I mean, if you can praise God, good for you, but if you can praise God AND rope a calf, now we're talkin'), we zipped around to the back parking lot filled with large pick-up trucks and horse trailers. We – in our electric blue van and

Tommy's huge, homemade British flag streaming some five feet above the van. Here come the Allreds who of course only eat freedom fries!

Robb went on his annual elk-hunting trip but did not get anything because of a freak snowstorm. Almost two weeks later, we had another friend go. He didn't get anything because of a freak heat wave. But there isn't any global warming.

Kerri made the high school soccer team despite a pulled hamstring; Katie made the cross country team but kept vomiting during the meets and, at the last one, tripped and fell, knocking out her tooth. She was able to suction the tooth against her tongue and finish out the mile, talking to other competitors all the while. Tommy got thrown out of the Christmas play for turning his "toy soldier" part into his (rather dramatic) take on Napoleon. He was eventually allowed back in. And I rescued two dogs off the highway only to discover once they leapt into my van that one of us had been sprayed in the last 24 hours by a skunk, and I was pretty sure it wasn't me! The front of our house flooded, the cats won't stop killing and bringing home dead bunnies, and Robb still shares my workspace. While I'm studiously working on a piece about water conservation or a POW from WWII, Robb will turn in his chair to face me and say, "Wow, Goldie Hawn was found dead in her bedroom."

"What?" This is shocking news! I'm a Goldie fan.

"Oh, sorry. It says she's redoing her bedroom for the next issue of *Good Housekeeping*!" Or, he'll say, "Barack Obama was just arrested for solicitation."

"What?"

"Oh, no. Sorry. It says here ..."

Truly, it is one of the worst aspects of sharing an office space with an infant.

I asked Robb what it is that he and his brother Pat do while waiting for wild pigs to show themselves at the hunting ground. Frankly, it is difficult for me to envision deep, philosophical conversations between the two. He said, "Well, we have a breath-holding contest." *That's it? You guys sit there and hold your breath?* "Hey, it's pertinent information. We [Pat and Robb] could accidentally drive into a lake. When rescuers come, you [Alex] could say, 'Hey, they've been down there in the water for over a minute! Robb can hold his breath for 1 minute and 47 seconds, but Pat can only hold his for one minute and 13 seconds!" *Ahh.* Note to self: Have them rescue Pat first in the event those two idiots drive into a lake. This *is* pertinent information.

Speaking of pigs, we have neighbors who have named their free-roaming pet hogs Porkchop and Petunia.

Tommy has taken to having "estate sales," only he keeps taking my things and insisting that I buy them back. And, of course, I passed out while getting stitches in my leg, which was highly embarrassing. When I came to, I tried to deny that I'd passed out but couldn't really explain why my doctor was holding my feet up and why there was suddenly a nurse I didn't recognize standing next to me.

Katie began calling me Loverpants. And, somehow, that evolved into "Pantless lover." I tried to embarrass Katie by calling out to her in front of the entire 6th, 7th, and 8th grade UIL team. She beat me to it, screaming, "I love you, pantless lover!" This was just as the assistant principal was walking by. I was stunned into silence as he walked by and mouthed the words, "Pantless lover? Wow." How embarrassing. I had the overwhelming desire to shout, "I do have on pants!" but that didn't seem appropriate.

Knock. Knock.

At 2:40 a.m. – with Robb out of town – there was an officer from the Ellis County sheriff's department at my door. "Do you own a Shetland pony?" Um… no?

As it turns out, the Shetland (named Rebel) had broken free of his corral. Not knowing what else to do, the Sheriff began knocking on doors of people with horses; naturally, he came to my house. It was an early Christmas present for Star: we put Rebel in our corral to be terrorized.

Tommy is taking wrestling ("wrastling") but cares very little about technique. He just wants to wrastle … everyone. This would include Katie who only has about five pounds on the little feller, and I can't get Tommy to understand that this is NOT the time to wrestle the hormonally imbalanced Katie. While Kerri continues with her classical training (violin), Katie has become disturbingly good at Hip Hop dance moves. I do, however, draw the line at my skinny albino baby throwing gang signs.

Sadly, I had to put Star, my 23-year-old quarter horse, to sleep. His knee was blown out, but he had a great life. When he first came to me, he was terrified of lightning and fireworks, but in the last years, confident with us, he actually grazed under an umbrella of fireworks. Suffice to say, it is far easier to bury a small pet than a horse!

I tried to offer fresh cucumbers from my garden to my kickbox class, but they've become so fearful of my "ideas" – no one would accept. They tentatively asked, "What's a cucumber?" *What's a cucumber?* They thought it was some horrible exercise routine. I suspect my Starbucks addiction may have contributed to their growing fear of me first thing in the morning.

One saving grace in all of this has been my new job as the editor of a community magazine (NOW magazine) which I LOVE. I got to meet actor/artist Buck Taylor ('Newly' from "Gunsmoke"), and I'm pretty sure my zipper was down. Dang it! I swear, it's the pants! What other job could or would allow me to step in beefalo poop (cow and buffalo crossbreed), don a dog attack training suit, drag a weighted dummy in a time test, challenge a mounted police officer to a run-off against his horse, fall off a stage, and have an iguana pee-pee on my shoe and then turn around and interview a funeral home director and scale down a ladder into an archeological dig of an 1872 Bismarck saloon?

So, friends, as we close yet another year, there is some information that we want to impart to you – things that we learned the hard way. They are as follows: persistence pays off. The quality of a zipper does matter. Shetland ponies can actually scream in terror when penned in with large, aggressive quarter horses. Karma is real … so be thoughtful. It's really in bad taste to name a pig Porkchop.

It's either laugh or cry. We recommend the former. And remember, screaming as you run away from a skunk does not improve your odds. Apparently, high-pitched noises are upsetting to the little creatures. Oh, and tomato juice won't do a dang thing for you.

Love,

Alex

A Leap of Faith

Although the song "I Can Only Imagine" by MercyMe was released in 2001, I am only now hearing it. This is probably because I would hastily change the radio station anytime a Christian rock song came on. To be blunt, they are nauseating. But this one sneaked up on me. Of late, it seemed like a lot of things were sneaking up on me. As singer Bart Millard ponders what he will feel when he stands before Jesus, my mind wanders to a place it has never previously wandered.

It is startling.

It is unchartered waters.

It is scary.

But I also wonder about Marshall. I know what he believes. But what does he expect when he stands before Jesus? Will he stand? And then, Bart Millard croons, "Will I stand in Your presence? Or to my knees will I fall? Will I sing 'Hallelujah!'? Will I be able to speak at all?" and I am floored. Before I can make sense of anything I am feeling, I realize I am crying.

Later, when I was home and was able to put everything back into check, I called Marshall. I asked him what he thought about Heaven. Would he go there, and if so, who would be there with him and in what way would he appear? Would he be sitting or standing?

Marshall is so practical about things, I'm honestly not sure how he will respond to the question. But he never hesitates.

"I hope I'll be standing," he says, adding how much he'd like to run with his dogs again.

Typically, the only music I ever buy is hard rock or edgy Hip Hop for my boot camp style kickbox classes. We blast the music for an intense workout, but this year I surprised my family when I added MercyMe to my collection and began obsessively playing the song "I Can Only Imagine" over and over and over again.

I don't know what's happening to me. I'm turning into a sappy wreck.

The Unconquerable Marshall Allen
…and his rise to the top

On November 23, 2007, Marshall decided to go to Best Buy to check out the sales following Thanksgiving. The massive after-Thanksgiving sales are dubbed Black Friday and, many times, there are some great deals to be found. Computer geek-freak Marshall cannot pass on any great electronic bargain, and so, bright and early, he was there.

But, of course, there were no handicapped spots open in the parking lot. Undeterred, Marshall drove around the corner and parked on the side of the building, out of sight from anyone, but at least he had plenty of room to lower the ramp to his van.

Using the remote controls on his chair, Marshall eased out of the van, going forward down the ramp. In his haste to exit the van and get to the sale, his rear tire caught the lip of the ramp, and before he knew it, both he and the chair tumbled in slow motion down the ramp. He fell out of his chair and on to the pavement.

This wasn't the first crash Marshall had had in his wheelchair. There had been many. One of the most exciting, however, was shortly after he returned to work on May 14, 2002. Both Al and Marshall, still very much a package deal, were getting off from work when Al needed to run back inside to "finish up some paperwork."

"He specifically told me," Marshall said, "to 'stick right here. Don't move!' So I sat there enjoying the sunshine when I heard a friend of ours start up his '66 Malibu. I knew it was him, so I started to go over there and shoot the breeze."

At that time, Marshall was still in a manual chair. With an initial push, he headed down the sidewalk toward his friend. He noted that the sidewalk dropped off to his right just a tad, but he believed he could handle the slope.

"I was fresh out of the hospital," Marshall recalled, adding that he was still weak. As soon as the chair hit an angle, he knew he was in no condition to wrangle the chair upright. He tried to pivot the chair to his left, but "I knew I was screwed and just didn't have enough strength to stop it or straighten it out."

Time slowed down as both he and the chair rolled down the hill, into a fast approaching curb. As the front wheels dropped off of the edge, "I saw the curb coming up toward me, and my face crashed into the pavement, and I remember thinking, 'I'm going to break my nose.'" But instead, he landed on his forehead. As he slid along the pavement, he could hear his new glasses grinding across the concrete, and "I could see the pavement slide by my eyes just an inch away. Then, all of the sudden, I came to a halt and was just lying there. I couldn't move or roll over, so I just had to lie there until someone found me."

That someone was a female police officer. She had pulled up in her car and had been talking on the phone when the accident occurred. As she moved toward the city building, Marshall said, "She saw me lying upside down, and this is what the trained observer said: 'Oh, my God! Do you need some help?'"

"I said, 'Well, as a matter of fact, I do.'"

Marshall told her to go into the building and say, "Big Al!" He would, Marshall assured the woman, come running. Sure enough, he did. As soon as he heard his name, Al "nearly tore the door from its hinges."(There is yet another story a few years later when Al, driving home, notices Marshall's van on the side of the highway. Marshall had exhausted himself earlier in the day and simply needed to pull over to rest but Al, unsure of the state of his friend, nearly ripped the door from its hinges trying to get to his friend.)

Al was, by Marshall's report, "all excited and he yelled, 'I told you to sit still!'"

Marshall recalls the day so well because it was his birthday. After the crash, after he'd been bandaged and Al had regaled "the girls" with the story of Marshall's accident, a picture came to Marshall's mind.

Picture it: Muhammad Ali vs. Leon Spinks. September 15, 1978, in the Superdome. As Ali sits slumped in his corner with Angelo Dundee yelling in one ear and Drew Brown chewing him out on the other side, the prize fighter can be seen looking across the ring at a card girl as she walks around the ring in a bikini announcing the next round.

Picture it: Marshall Allen vs. the World. May 14, 2002, DeSoto, Texas. As Marshall sits dejectedly in his chair with Mary at one ear and Chase (Mary's niece), Marical (Mary's daughter). and Tayala at the other, all Marshall can do is stare at his caregiver, Richard, for help. Richard, by the way, wanted no part of that action and left Marshall sitting alone, holding a birthday balloon.

"I sure was," Marshall laughed. "I was just sitting there holding my damned balloon while they told me I shouldn't have done this and I shouldn't have done that."

Even when Marshall got his battery-operated chair, there were accidents.

Although he was in his electric chair, the 2007 Black Friday crash at Best Buy was reminiscent of the one in May 2002 outside the fire station (and like his initial horrific bike crash in July 2001) in that he was dumped upside down and could only lie in a heap, waiting for someone to happen by. Just like his initial accident, no one could hear him as he called out.

At some point, a mother and daughter walked by and, thankfully, looked down the side of the building to see a man and an overturned wheelchair sprawled next to a van.

The woman gasped, ran forward, and asked, "Are you all right?"

Almost comically, Marshall retold the story in his typically calm and cool voice. "I said, 'No. No, I'm not.' The woman bent down, 'Do you need help?' As she asked, the daughter ran back into Best Buy to get a manager. "I said, 'Yes. Yes, I do.'"

Because of Marshall's sheer size and position, the manager instantly called for help. Several officers from a local sheriff's department had been on hand, working security. Alone, the manager could not lift Marshall, but with the help of the officers, they repositioned him. It was an agonizing moment for Marshall. To have officers leave their post because of him and his carelessness – never mind the jackasses who caused this by parking in handicapped parking places – was particularly painful for Marshall.

Soon enough, the manager and a couple of sheriff's officers were counting off one-two-three as they lifted Marshall back into his chair.

"Well," I asked him, trying to offer some solace. "Did you at least get a bargain?" He shook his head. Instead, he'd just gone home.

There are many things that happen in Marshall's day-to-day life that are unremarkable. They are tedious, time-consuming events that would mount into volcanic eruptions for the rest of us. Just getting something to eat, trying to get money from his wallet, or manipulating his own computer – things that take mere seconds for another person – are daily, exhaustive exercises in diligence and patience. Marshall shares very little information about these instances. Certainly, he is proud. But more than anything else, he has completely accepted the terms under which he now operates. It is what it is. What will be will be.

He once got stuck in his own lawn. Again, because of his sheer size and weight, the heavy chair/man combination sunk into the lawn, and Marshall found that he could not move. He had to call upon the fire department for help and silently berated himself, fearful that there were more important things for the firefighters to do than push a guy out of the tire ruts he created in his own lawn.

For Marshall, these are not little cute sayings to be placed on a bumper sticker. These are his modus operandi, his life's mottos. When he says "shit happens," that's exactly what he means. It just … does. Sometimes when you don't want it to.

For this reason, I'm sure he would never have told me about this Black Friday incident, but he could not hide the large band-aid on his forehead and, gracelessly, I jabbed a finger at it.

"What happened?"

Thus, the story.

After the police had replaced him back into his chair, they did not know (or perhaps they did) that Marshall had a bowel accident. Mortified, he had simply gone home. He had just wanted to be alone.

In fact, he had tried to stop one of the EMS crew members from inspecting his bleeding forehead, telling the crew that it was nothing and that he was sure they had other far more important things to be worrying about. He refused being taken to the hospital for observation. For Marshall, the injury was not to his bleeding head but to his ego. How many times had he tended to someone in a similar situation? But for Marshall to be the "victim" was worse than any fall he could take.

All of which leaves an important question to ask: how could any self respecting person who could walk – even with a limp – park in a handicap place?

Protecting God's Green Earth

While I was finding my way through another lawsuit, Jim Schermbeck, Becky Bornhorst, Sue Pope, and the Downwinders crew were busily pushing the 'green cement' policy.

Jim sent out a memo to Downwinders: at stake is the nation's first "green cement" procurement policy. The Dallas City Council will be receiving a briefing and then will vote on a comprehensive clean air plan for Dallas. As part of that plan, staff will be giving the Council options about how to purchase cement for city projects. We want the council to choose the option of buying cement only from the cleaner 'dry process' cement kilns rather than the obsolete, dirtier 'wet kilns.'

"For the very first time, the city would be able to vote with its pocketbook to spend money on cement from cleaner plants and steer it away from the most polluting ones."

By the year's end, Jim successfully lobbied in the cities surrounding the Dallas/Fort Worth area to adopt the green cement policy. And for the first time in over a decade, it looked like things had moved in our favor. But for one thing. I wanted out. I was done. I was tired of fighting. I was tired of being the lone voice (it seemed) in Midlothian, and because we couldn't make the mess go away, I just wanted to step away from it.

Through a very aggressive treatment, which pumped Tommy full of far more medications than I would have ever thought possible, he was responding. As he's grown, the severe asthma attacks subsided. At last, we seemed to be winning this one fight.

I joined the ranks of Midlothian and decided that maybe things weren't that bad. My kids were very happy in school. They have many wonderful friends, and our house seemed to be the rallying point for many class projects, sleepovers, and various adventures. Midlothian is mere 30 minutes from great shopping, skating, movies, bowling, bookstores, museums, zoos, and more. In town, we saw friends everywhere we went, and in our own backyard, we had horseback riding, tree climbing, and adventures in the creek. (We have snapping turtles!) But more importantly, my kids and I had become good friends with different families connected to industry. As adamantly as I could tell you there was some pretty bad stuff coming out of the cement stacks, I could also tell you that the people of Midlothian are good folks.

Erin Brokovich once told me, "When you do something for the morally right reason, you can't be wrong." Yeah, but sometimes it really is easier just to walk away. So, I did.

Chapter Sixteen
Swingman

Like clockwork, Marshall can be found in the Starbucks in Fort Worth at Houston and 3rd at 6 a.m. meeting with a group of friends. It's easier to leave the house earlier, beat the traffic, and wait – with friends – for the offices of City Hall top open. By 7:30 a.m., he can be seen rolling into the Bureau of Fire Prevention office.

Never mind all the inconveniences he faces each and every morning to get there … he is there! As no less than a dozen fire fighters have said, "Marshall Allen is a fixture within the department."

One particular day when I was growling at him for driving to work in very bad weather conditions, our conversation drifted into the matter of things that fuel us, that burn so deeply inside of us that while it is now but a memory, it is as fresh and raw as if it had happened only moments before.

It had happened in Utah. Marshall and his buddy, Terrence, had been on the driveway, "messing around," when Marshall had been blindsided by his brother. Morris, Jr., threw a chunk of ice at his brother, knocking Marshall's glasses off and cutting his face.

Marshall charged after Morris, Jr., but before he could exact his revenge, his father appeared. Marshall tried to explain what happened, but "none of that mattered because my father had no intention of fighting me that day. My father was going to teach me a lesson in submission." It had not mattered that Morris Jr. had hit and cut his face with ice with the intent to injure. It never mattered when Morris Jr. lashed out. Marshall was never allowed to exact revenge or even the score. Morris Jr. was special. But this particular day forever cemented that notion.

His father's look of rage frightened both Marshall and his friend. What happened next, Marshall said, was both unexpected and unimaginable.

"I had heard my father describe more than once with utter disdain how, as he was growing up, white men would lash their Negro slaves (which included my grandfather) to trees and whip them until their backs were raw. My father recalled with contempt a time when his father did the same thing to my father's older brother for what he (my father) and obviously my uncle considered completely unjustifiable reasons. But the old man wasn't interested in either my uncle's explanation or my father's pleadings for mercy.

"I knew my father had something different in mind when I noticed he was holding his wide, thick, Western-style, hand-tooled leather strap by its large oval buckle. At this point, my father was standing between Terrence and me, and because my father was only 5'7" or 5'8" and Terrence and I were both around 6 ft. tall, I clearly saw the look on Terrence' face when my father ordered me to strip my jacket and shirt and lay face down in the snow that had piled up against the fence. Terrence attempted to slip away, but my father stopped him.

"And so my little brother and my best friend stood at my feet with my mother just inside the back door and watched my father beat me, in his own terms, 'like a slave.' I remember placing myself mentally in the same situation as a slave and clinching my jaws, squeezing the snow in my fists, and struggling not to scream out loud or urinate on myself every time the damn leather laid across my cold skin.

"I honestly cannot remember how long this went on, but when my father had either satiated his anger or worked himself into frustration, he simply stormed away to the garage. As I arose and tried not to make eye contact with Terrence (who was laughing out of nervousness for having been forced to witness such a spectacle), I slid my T-shirt down my bloodied back as Jim [Terrence] shook his head and said, 'Man I have to go home,' and kind of sauntered off, tossing one last glance in the direction of my father who was backing the car out of the garage.

"By the time I got my coat back on, my father was up in the loft of the garage presently to return with a suitcase, which he flung in my direction. I knew what this meant because so many times as I was growing up, my father and mother threatened to throw me out on the street with 'only a few rags.' I always thought that they fully meant what they said, and all I could do on those occasions was break down out of the unimaginable fear of being a young boy on the streets without a clue where to go or even the option of returning to the orphanage where I was headed when the social worker called my mother. I would beg and cry and plead to stay in the house. And now at 15, the threat was even more plausible, and the fear was even more tangible."

In the next few hours, Marshall felt abandoned. He stood alone by the garage with a suitcase and some clothes that had been thrown out the back door. The prospect of being homeless and alone broke him and, as he described, "I dropped to my knees and sobbed.

"My mind drifted, and I no longer felt the cold. I thought about the times my mother told me about my biological mother not wanting me. How my first set of adoptive parents returned me to the orphanage. How I had been kept in a closet by my foster parents until suspicious neighbors notified the police, and I was rescued by the authorities. I thought about my mother saying that the social worker called her and told her that she had a child that no one else wanted. That I was almost two-years-old and psychologically damaged, and that if she didn't take me no one else would, and I was 'on my way to an orphanage.' I thought about my mother telling me more than once that since they had already adopted my younger brother (at six weeks of age over a year before me) that the only reason she accepted me was that when they were searching and praying for a child, she had promised God that she would take any child He sent her way 'no matter what was wrong with him,' and consequently they had saved me from hell but could send me back anytime."

Only when he heard the click of the back door did he understand that his mother had opened the door to him once again. "I knew it was safe to come inside as long as I kept my head down and my mouth shut." He cried his tears and gathered his belongings and stepped quietly back into his house. "But I understood that I had crossed a certain border in my relationship with my parents. I also understood that if I stayed there long enough I would get hurt."

A quiet rage, one that had already been festering inside of him for years, grew louder. As a young black male in a predominately white world that, by all accounts, appeared to scrutinize and judge him, he was getting really pissed off. He was tired of the double standard he'd both seen and felt in grade school. He was tired of the preferential treatment given to his brother. He was tired of classmates having and flaunting nice clothing and toys and gadgets that he could never own. He wanted to lash out and, at very early age, Marshall decided to mug someone.

At the time, had he been asked why he attempted to mug someone, his answer would have been simplistic. He wanted money. He wanted stuff. But it was more than that. He wanted vindication. He wanted power – the kind of power that would allow him to take something from someone else and put him in a position over another person. He was looking to be top dog. But first, he would have to bring his little brother along.

"Otherwise," Marshall almost laughed, "he would tell." Marshall was off to wreak havoc among the good citizens of Ogden, Utah, but he faced a couple of challenges. Morris, Jr., had to come, and "they roll up the streets by 10 p.m. in Ogden. We were the only fools out there."

At this, Marshall cannot help but laugh. But the non-event, Marshall later realized, marked a turning point in his life. "I was not an exception. I was the rule." That is, he had begun to follow the path of so many young and frustrated black youth.

He had been so angry and so primed for violence, it was only luck that prevented another human being from crossing his path that night. How differently his life might have turned out had some unfortunate person been outside walking a dog or having just missed a bus. How lucky for both the Allen boys that they had not been able to test their mettle and unleash their frustrations. Only later, after Marshall had decided he had to leave home, did the luck run out for Morris.

But not even Marshall could protect Morris, Jr., from the legal system. By his senior year in high school, Morris, Jr., was experimenting with drugs and some of the illegal activities that are often associated with drugs. Just how much he did or how far he went, Marshall cannot be sure. But by the early 1980s, when Morris, Jr., was caught trying to steal tires, he took a wild swing at the police officer with a tire iron. He was charged with and convicted of assault on a police officer and was sent to his first stint at the Utah State Prison.

In the years that followed, Marshall and Morris, Jr., had little contact with each other. There were a few exchanges of letters and post cards, the last one being a Christmas card from prison. This was Morris, Jr's., second stay in prison.

As the story goes, Morris, Jr., had taken in a buddy who was down on his luck, allowing the friend to sleep in the basement of his home. But when the friend was arrested for making and distributing methamphetamines, Morris was swept up in the bust for a parole violation. While he swore he had no knowledge of the illegal activities, he was convicted and sent away a second time.

By this time, Morris, Jr., was married and had a son, and, briefly, Marshall stayed in contact with Morris and his family. But time and patience eroded the already tumultuous relationship.

But once more, Marshall would have to test himself as top dog when he was accepted into the fire academy in Fort Worth, and he would leave Utah forever, but not before one of the greatest gifts was bestowed upon Marshall. Technically, the material item awarded was not a gift as Marshall paid money back. It was the sentiment that forever stayed with Marshall and invited him to "the family."

Even before Marshall's career as a firefighter officially took off, when he was still a recruit with the Salt Lake County fire department, the brotherhood stepped in. Marshall could not yet afford a pair of required black shoes. "I did not get my first paycheck for about six weeks." So, one day after some water rescue training, the battalion chief, Harry Ballard, ordered the truck to pull over to the curb in downtown Salt Lake City. Without another word, the chief had arranged for Marshall to go into the shoe store they parked next to and purchase a pair of shoes with Ballard's credit card. "All the other guys knew beforehand," Marshall said, still clearly humbled by that experience. Though he worked hard to repay the good battalion chief, he never forgot that moment.

He was more than ready to begin his new life as a swingman in Texas.

"It's a willingness to serve and save other people," Marshall said, "the moment the rookie receives his or her first assignment as swingman."

In fire service parlance, a swingman is someone (usually a new person) affectionately also known as Boot, Rookie, Squid, Newbie, Jr., Kid, Worthless Pile of .... "Well, you get the idea," Marshall explained. "These are the guys who show up to work, usually ahead of schedule and ready to go, bright eyed and bushy tailed." The swingman goes wherever he or she is needed.

"These people fill the holes rather like the little Dutch boy with his finger in the dike. If someone calls in sick or goes on vacation or goes down at a fire or goes to the hospital to see their baby being born, the Battalion chief picks up the 'big phone' and moves the remaining firefighters around in their battalions or throughout the city like pawns on a chessboard. It is not unusual for a 'swinger' in a city the size of Fort Worth, Texas, to go to several stations in one day. I've done it myself."

"Most rookies are anxious to forsake their nomadic lifestyle for a permanent assignment (as permanent as can be expected) in a process known as 'going regular.' A few, like myself, enjoy the change of pace and scenery and characters associated with traveling all over a large city or county. I intentionally stayed on the swing list until I promoted to the rank of engineer."

In fact, he stayed on the swing list until it was time to move up the ranks. It was a time when he had finally felt secure in the department and knew he was there to stay. For all the firehouse pranks, Marshall is certain that it was the more tragic events that bonded him to his brothers and sisters.

One day we were going through old pictures when Marshall came up on old newspaper clipping. He pointed to a picture that had been captured by Ft. Worth Star Telegram photographer Glenn Ellman. A group of the Ft. Worth fire fighters were huddled around the body of a 12-year-old girl, trying to resuscitate the child. It was late in the summer, and Marshall had been serving as an engineer at Station 26 when the call came in. A woman, driving southbound on Hulen Street, had turned into the path of a young driver, hoping to beat him and make it into the parking lot. It was the kind of foolish and chancy move that many of us have made more times than we care to admit. The woman was on a mission to buy her daughter back-to-school clothes, and rather than wait for the on-coming car to pass, she gunned her engine and sped ahead. She caused the collision and killed her daughter.

In that same picture, Marshall pointed to Captain David Polson (the same guy who years earlier dragged an innocent man back through a burning house to "safety") as he crouched down, arm partially wrapped around a large African-American woman. The woman appears inconsolable, and Marshall verifies, "She was."

On another call, Marshall and his crew arrived at the scene of a drunk driving accident in which the drunk driver had apparently decided to commit suicide on the highway by driving his car into on-coming traffic. He was fine, but the passenger of the other car involved was instantly killed.

Upon impact, the Volvo hood buckled, as it was designed to do, but the metal then became a projectile as it broke away from the body, crushing the 17-year-old's skull.

Later, the firefighters would learn that the 17-year-old was a model having just returned from Europe – her first successful overseas job. It had been her boyfriend who picked her up from the airport and was delivering her back home where she could, no doubt, regale her family with the exciting tales of her European experience.

On both occasions, Marshall said, the fire fighters returned to their stations with nary a word exchanged between them. What was there to say? Together, as a collective group, they battle fire and respond to accidents from mild fender-benders to horrific car crashes. They laugh over the ridiculous calls they receive regarding little boys getting their heads stuck in iron fences or snakes, often already dead, lying in public view. They shake their heads, sometimes in disgust and sometimes from sadness, when they are called to deal with citizens who are unable to care for themselves or simply want a human hand to reach out to them. How, they wonder, have we allowed ourselves to so greatly neglect our family members and neighbors?

These men and women of the fire department show up to private homes and wade through thigh-high trash, waste, and feces. They deal with drunks and drug addicts, victims and abusers, brawlers and the homeless. Each is treated equally, and though it can often be incredibly difficult, the firefighters try to remain understanding and patient. How does one learn to show the same professionalism toward an obnoxious college student, drunk from too much tequila, as would be offered to the bloodied victim of a beating? How does one weigh the euphoric, supercharged glory of saving a child from a burning building, having narrowly escaped death, only to learn there was another child in the same room, accidentally left behind to die? And how does one digest this and remain politely if not stoically silent while the parent, the very one who started the fire by way of burning cigarette, dismisses any heroism as negligence?

How frustrating it must be to work for what seems a lifetime on a small body or a grandfather as his family looks on only to have that soul slip away. How helpless it must make the rescuers feel to put the victim on a gurney and send him or her in an ambulance and never know what happened to life they tried to save. Then, as they are trying to work their way through these complex emotions, another 911 call takes them to yet another crisis.

For this reason – for the unresolved, the unknowable - every station house needs a Rocky.

"He was so full of it," Marshall laughed. "You never knew when he was telling the truth or not." Although he could spin a yarn, Marshall is quick to point out that he was still a "hero among heroes" when the work needed to be done. "We heard stories about Rocky while we were still in the academy," Marshall laughed. But his persona in the firehouse was legend. As his stories grew in proportion and the firefighters laughed, he would insist, "This aint' no lie!" which only made his stories all the more entertaining as it most certainly was.

There was the story of when he, Rocky Ardoyno and fellow firefighter, Willie Cole, another known storyteller, were horseback riding across the wooden bridge. Suddenly, the board of the bridge gave out and, as Rocky's horse (or Willie's horse depending on who was telling the story) fell through, Rocky (or Willie) was able to grab a hold of the beams of the bridge with one hand. Still holding the horn of his saddle with the other hand; it was a struggle, he later told his listeners, to hold both himself and the dangling horse, but, as he explained, "I just got that saddle."

But perhaps one of the more legendary stories among the firefighters was when Rocky squared off against Chris Bowers, yet another legendary storyteller. The day's topic had been poisonous snakes, and the mamba, an African species of snake said to be so swift that it can overtake people on horseback and so venomous that its bite can kill a person within minutes, was properly identified by Bowers as the most lethal. But Rocky argued this.

There was, Rocky told the roomful of fire fighters, a new species of snake recently identified by scientists. It was the dreaded Artic Snow

Adder. When Chris Bowers chimed in that he had heard about this snake and its particularly toxic venom, Rocky corrected him by saying the snake wasn't poisonous at all. As it happened, this adder was so sneaky, so vile, "that is waits for you to fall asleep, sneaks into your sleeping bag, crawls up your ass, and freezes you to death from the inside out."

The expression on Rocky's face was pure satisfaction. Everyone at the table knew that the purpose of the entire story was to trap Chris and had little to do with snakes or reptiles factoids.

The swingman has no home. He or she is assigned to different stations while learning the ropes -- discovering the stench of a decomposing human body or watching a co-worker (in this case Al Jones) oh-so-gingerly lift a diabetic victim from the floor to her couch, using special tenderness not to hurt the lovely lady in her Victoria Secret undies, then learning that this "lady" was a well-known transvestite. In the not-that-it-matters category, you can well imagine the great delight this brought fellow fire fighters when Al returned to the station house. These experiences, however funny, however awful, are forever bonding.

It is another reason for the swingman to *find* a home. Once a permanent station is assigned, there is ownership – of the streets, of the equipment, of the city, and of the station. But for Marshall, the Blue Indian of the Utah Mountains, he wanted none of it, and he wanted all of it.

When Marshall first came to Fort Worth, he wasn't interested in making best friends. He didn't care to claim a home with a group of men he had not yet connected with. He was not the guy who pulled silly pranks and was certainly not the man anyone else would try to short sheet. But he wanted to take in every street and corner of the city. He wanted to learn every rule and regulation of the fire department. He wanted to be in a position where he could make the executive decisions because he was the one person he could always rely upon. Where others wanted to find a permanent station, Marshall reveled in the swingman position. And by the time he was assigned his first station, he had learned the names of everyone in the FWFD and the layout of his city. For Marshall, the uncertainty and instability of the swing shift offered just what he needed. It was about control. And he desperately needed control.

But it's a funny thing about life. And coincidences.

All these years later, he is not only living these sentiments, but inspiring others. From where he sits, it is all so clear.

"I hope that everyone will take stock of some of their own concerns. We, as people, become mired in trivial things sometimes.

About my second week in the hospital, I started thinking about things that I had not really thought about. Things that were so important and consuming to me on July 1$^{st.}$ Now, I don't even give them a second thought. Everyone needs to take the time to rearrange priorities. I believe we all would be better off.

"I think that there was a reason this happened to me. God did choose me. If people can see someone as large and healthy as me stricken by a truly bizarre incident, then maybe it will make them take a second to look at their own mortality and the fragile nature of their existence. If it takes them seeing me in a wheelchair to do that, then that's fine with me. You need to tell your wife or husband everyday that you love them. Tell them how important they are to you. Tell your children you love them and give them your time. Do the things that you want to do today. Tomorrow is not promised to anyone."

Marshall still dreams that he can walk. "In my dreams, not only am I still able-bodied, but I'm still a firefighter. I don't mean just a member of the Fort Worth fire department, which is a privilege in itself, but an active participant in the daily adventure that is fire operations."

Though there are no specific recurring dreams, Marshall does have a recurring theme in which he is assigned to a fire station but is unable to find his "turnout" gear. "Sometimes the alarm goes off signaling a run, and I am left scrambling through locker after locker looking for my gear so that I can mount the apparatus and respond to the incident. Sometimes, I climb on without my gear, taking a chance that I will be able to get by with just my gloves or whatever I was able to grab. Then immediately upon return, I begin my search endlessly through every locker and every nook and cranny in the station for my missing gear. Needless to say, I never find it."

When asked what he makes of this, his unprofessional analysis of the recurring dream/theme indicates that while his mind is able, "I'm missing a critical aspect of what makes a firefighter. I miss being a firefighter in the operations sense, but realize that I will never find that magic locker holding my gear."

Firefighting, being the swingman, is in his blood.

Chapter Seventeen

Christmas 2008

Dear Friends and Family: you should know, Santa Claus is not who you think he is.

As you know by now, every year we send out our annual holiday letter, spelling out all the things that have gone wrong so that you – our dear readers – might find just a wee bit more sunshine in your own lives. For nearly a decade, we've dished the dirt, but nothing could have prepared even us for our own BAD SANTA story.

As many of you may know, I am the editor of a community magazine, and for an article, I interviewed a guy who plays Santa. He's super into it and wanted only to be photographed as 'ol St. Nick. But when the format changed, and he was asked to pose for a picture as his normal self, Santa flipped out. He ranted and raved, threatened a lawsuit, rambled incoherently, and hung up on me (twice)! Later, Santa sent me a viral worm in the way of an e-greeting card. So clever is this diabolical Santa that he has a 'Naughty and Nice' book where parents provide personal information about their child, such as names of pets, teachers, and what sports they play. To a child, these are bits of information that only Santa could know, right? Ah, but to my new friends at the Sex Crime Unit and local FBI office, these are also things that identify a bad man who is overly interested in little kids.

The other kicker to this story is I had to convince a very nice retired couple to let me come into their home and decorate it in the beginning of November (within 48 hours) as a replacement feature for my December issue!

But the fat man of the North Pole can't rattle the Allreds easily. We laugh at disaster; we chortle at chaos and scoff at surprises. We've had pulled hamstrings, broken toes, poison ivy, and dead animal bodies presented to us. Tommy got eight staples in his head then demanded to be called Ironhead Allred. He also recently asked for a flamethrower (Ummm, no). Robb recently got a root canal. Anyone recall the last time he was at the dentist and was certain they were going to steal his wallet? Katie has a serious hair straightening addiction. The rest of us are exposed to the lovely aroma of fried hair as it wafts down the hallway each morning.

Kerri is now driving (we're working on her learner's permit), and Katie is already practicing how to look cool in the front seat next to her drivin' big sis. What they do not know is Robb is already looking on eBay for a camera to be installed in the car, and I'm working on my large "Hello! I'm a new driver. Please do not look at me, get too close to me, or honk at me. I am a giant insurance liability" sign to be affixed to the back window.

Our septic tank had to be replaced, but it was during the rainy season, so we had to wait to "dry out" before it could be replaced, which meant that I had to go to the Laundromat to take care of personal matters. For two months! It got to the point where I would arrive at the Laundromat, and my good friends would say, "Hola, Alex. Cómo estás hoy?" To which I would respond, "Estoy bien. Hey, gracias por preguntar. ¿Y tú?" Fun though this was, I eventually began to wonder, *what is wrong with that septic tank guy? Why can't he just come here and fix my septic tank?* So I asked him. He told me that Robb had expressed enough concern that our lawn and trees not be damaged by the line installation that the guy said, "I ain't going there until the ground is completely dry." Hijo de una perra!

The irony here is that while I was busily learning Spanish at the Laundromat so that our precious trees wouldn't be disturbed by the septic tank guys, we had what can only be described as a mini-tornado touch down, and it destroyed many of the aforementioned trees.

As spring arrived, Calvin and Little Dude (cats) continued their slaughter of all living creatures outside. All mutilated creatures are then displayed proudly next to my car. The girls and I work hard to rescue what creatures we can, but there are too many creatures, too little time. One particular day while running errands (including a little visit to the Laundromat), I saw something poking out of my tire. A lizard! On further inspection, I could see a trickle of blood coming from its mouth. Words cannot describe how disgusting it looked with its little stiff arms and head poking out of the wheel well of my front tire.

You know those ridiculous stories you hear on the news when some idiot is pulled over and the police officer asks, "Is there a reason you were driving so fast?" and the person says, "Yes, officer. I was trying to make the dead lizard shoot out from my wheel." Really, when you think about it, it's not so ridiculous, and after some very hard, very fast driving, I saw that I made it stick out another couple of inches. Finally, I got a nice man to take out the lizard, and he said, "This lizard is alive!" I felt horrible for days. That poor, poor, brain-damaged lizard! Stupid cats.

Robb signed the feller (Tommy) up for wrestling and Cub Scouts and proceeded never to be home because of work. He became an assistant cub master – a role that a now very uncertain Aunt Mimi

(Michelle) has picked up. Boy, you haven't seen funny until you see Michelle in her scout master's outfit!

When gas prices were soaring, we bought a little white Corolla to jet around in. The cats like to vomit on it. But not before Katie popped the hood, in search of the latch to open up the trunk. Let me repeat that statement to you: Katie released the latch that holds down the hood … while cruising down the road at an nifty 50 MPH. there was a loud "WHAP!" noise and sudden, blinding whiteness. The hood flung backward, cracking the windshield and rendering us blind. After making it safely to the side of the road, I berated Kerri for popping the hood when I heard Katie's small voice. "Soooo, what exactly happens when you pull that one lever?" Sometimes I still beat Katie just for the heck of it.

Did you know that if you and, oh, say, your sister get locked inside a stadium (to run bleachers) and the police are called that you could actually be handcuffed because "trespassers will be prosecuted"?

We took two family trips: one to Jamestown with my parents to revisit this great nation's beginnings. It was fitting then that we had no electronics for the 22-hour drive – no movies, no DVDs, no Gameboys. But we did have plenty of bologna sandwiches. Papa (aka Marc Powe) self-appointed himself keeper of Tommy. I'm not sure why. (During one visit to an art gallery after Tommy was explicitly directed not to touch anything, he hand-carried a $575 painting for me to see. Akkk!) Robb and I have worked hard to keep electronics to a minimum in our house -- no t.v. or computers in bedrooms, little exposure to video games ... Then, Robb went out and bought Rock Band. Tommy can hardly focus on anything except playing drums and belting out "Black Hole Sun" while Katie sings "Are You Gonna Be My Girl!" at the top of her lungs. But when Robb was exposed to the song "The Bird is the Word," a 1960's beach song, his tourettes kicked in, and there has been NO PEACE in the house. *Hey, kids! Have you heard?* No, what? *Have you heard the word?* What word? *That the Bird is the word!!*

We took another trip to Colorado and stayed in a cabin at an elevation of 29,000 feet. Okay, maybe it was actually only about 12,000 feet, but it felt like 29,000! The mountain was called Mt. Terrible, an old miner's claim, after almost 30 people died at the turn of the 19th Century. It was all fun and games until both Katie and Tommy got "terrible" and very scary altitude sickness. With no phone, no mode of transportation, and a hailstorm, it made for a rough night. That and we were not allowed the amenities that one becomes so comfortable with ... So when you hear the old question, does a bear poop in the woods? know this: yes, and he's not alone. We went on to have a blast, four-wheeling all over the terrifying but sensational Alpine Pass.

On our way to said Mt. Terrible, we were delayed in leaving home, but Robb refused to stop in any hotel in the state of Texas, saying we had to make it out of the state before stopping or we would be "defeated." Defeated? By whom? Still, ever determined to save money, Robb found us this hole-in-the-wall motel in Clayton, New Mexico. We were suspect. What can you expect for a two-queen-bed suite for $49.95? Surprisingly, it was pretty neat until morning. Around daybreak, we suddenly understood why it was so cheap. We covered our mouths, gagging and packing things as quickly as possible to get away. Only Robb Allred could lead his family to a motel directly across the street from a stockyard/slaughterhouse.

For Halloween, I made Katie and her friend Katie Bates (who always comes over and breaks things) giant Starbucks cups and friend Macy Dunegan a large Starbucks pumpkin loaf. And what, you ask, is so scary about a Starbuck coffee on Halloween? Answer: What's scarier than a $4 cup of coffee? But even more frightening than inflated prices is the not-so-subtle whines of young teenagers. *I can't walk. I'm losing circulation in my arms. The giant straw is poking into my thigh. Birds are swooping down and pecking at the real bread crumbs you used to authenticate my pumpkin loafness.* Babies!

When Tommy went to the emergency room to get staples in his head, Robb and Michelle (Aunt Mimi) had to take him because I had pneumonia. This was an internal struggle for Robb because 1) the Broncos were currently playing a game and 2) Robb does not like going to medical professionals because one might be inclined to touch him. Robb is searching for a good doctor who can treat him without actually ever touching his person.

My pneumonia lasted so long I was on a constant cycle of oral steroids, steroid injections, super strong antibiotics, and breathing treatments. I had many steroids surging through my body – made worse because I was not allowed to exercise for an entire month! – I've never been so jumpy in my life. Also, the word hemorrhoid is funny only when you never have to write it down as "reason for your visit today." During the time I was sick, my children attempted to "help" me by washing my cell phone, breaking the garbage disposal, and allowing a full container of Hershey syrup to open/ooze down the back of the fridge ... all in two days. And my doc said, "Get some rest. Let your family help you out." Right. That kind of help, I don't need.

We had a baby rattler (snake) in our garage that I had to bash with the shovel, and Katie's re-enactment of Paul Revere's ride for a social studies assignment was an embarrassing display of dispassion by Snow, the horse. (Let us all be thankful that it was not Snow who was asked to charge through the early hours of April 18/April 19, 1775, or we'd be a British Colony right now.) Nala, our 12-year-old Shep/Boxer mix, has begun to lose control of her facilities, and, amazingly, where she decides to walk and poop is always exactly where Robb decides to walk in the dark. It's really quite remarkable – though Robb does not find this connection nearly as interesting as I do.

Indeed, there are many things to be grateful for. But finding a Santa on every corner is not one of them. The girls and Tommy have become a little concerned, if not embarrassed, by my new hostility toward the bell ringing, velvet covered, bearded men in red who all say things like, "Ho, ho, ho! Happy Holidays." I'm quick to turn. "You talkin' to me, Fat Man?" You have to watch that guy.

So let me give you a little piece of advice this holiday season. Love one another, be safe, be the best person you can be, and watch your back. Santa Claus is coming to town!

Love,

Alex

The Unconquerable Marshall Allen
...and his rise to the top

Before Marshall's accident, Marshall was known to step down from the fire truck, "pretending not to hear what a person was asking just so he could step off the truck," said firefighter Darrin Partridge. The look was always the same. "This look of amazement would come over 'em. Marshall was just so big."

It was something that Marshall secretly enjoyed: the way a jaw would go slack or a person would unconsciously take a step back as Marshall moved closer. Marshall Allen impressed people with his impeccable manners, baritone voice, and powerfully built body. Whatever he did and wherever he went, people stared. Since his early years as a "Huron Indian," running up and down the mountains in Park City, Utah, he relied on his strength and size. Years before his accident, he had made the conscious decision to shave down his size from 340 pounds of rock solid muscle to a mere 275 pounds.

With his power lifting days behind him, even Marshall was not comfortable with how large he'd become, noting that it took a lot of work to fuel his body. Between the protein shakes, the constant mini-meals scheduled around the large meals, it was too much work.

Oddly enough, just before his accident, he'd cut red meat from his diet and had begun eating only sparse amounts of poultry, telling his wife and kids that no one really needed to eat such heavy, hard-to-digest meals. That Marshall would go from an eating machine to a budding vegetarian just before his accident was coincidental, but important. The fact is that introducing meat into the colon of a quadriplegic is not a good idea as it is extremely difficult for the already stressed digestive system.

For anyone who believes in destiny or the idea of divine intervention, if they believe in God, any God, Marshall's story strikes a chord.

Why did he suddenly decide to learn how to use voice activated computers or stop eating red meat before his accident? Why did I, a former national athlete, suddenly decide to go on an early 28-mile bike ride without eating only to run out of fuel near the Starbucks in a neighboring town and stop only to place my bike in the path of Marshall so that he would come talk to me? Had I not, what were the chances that I would meet Marshall and his dog, Caesar? Almost instantly, I began to ask *why* I met Marshall.

Before his accident, the people in Marshall's world viewed him as a giant of a man who was in control of everything around him. He was master of his domain. After the accident … well, he was the victim of a freak accident and was now viewed, by many, as a victim of terrible circumstances.

Poor Marshall.

Poor, poor Marshall.

He would prove them wrong.

But there is a quiet riot burning inside of Marshall. This is not to be confused with the rage that reared its head from depression and frustration. No. Today, he is a "happy" and "content" man with much more to accomplish. The riot – the quiet riot – is the rebel in him who refuses to be silenced and is determined to change the way we view our neighbors and look at ourselves.

How odd that I stopped at Starbucks only to have Big Al, simply making conversation, tell me that they were just "waiting" for the right person to tell his story to. Why did the McDowells drive down that road that day, which enabled them to find Marshall, and why did Talaya's mother wait for 15 years to tell Talaya about Marshall, only to die that very night?

A quiet riot began to grow inside of me as well. As a result of Marshall and my affections for him, I was moved to think about so many things – things that had previously been taboo for me.

Was there really such a thing as divine intervention?

But while I was wrestling with very new, very foreign concepts of religion, Marshall was battling some very old demons of racism. While I had decided to step back from the environmental fight in Midlothian that had been so important to my family, Marshall was stepping up to a new one. For me, backing away was the only logical thing to do. You can only beat your head against the wall for so long. You can only say the same things over and over so many times. And, seriously, WHY should I fight for someone else's kid when they obviously aren't that concerned?

When Marshall was standing, it was easy for him to fight. Whether it was a racial slur or a derogatory comment about another person, all he had to do was turn and look at the offenders, and they would typically back up, apologizing all the way.

In his chair, with the quiet riot growing, Marshall learned to temper his anger. He learned to pick and choose his battles carefully.

"One of the things my father taught me was that standing up for oneself was not only normal but expected and, consequently, no indicator of a man's character. A more accurate indicator of a man's character lies in his willingness to stand up for someone else who, because of absence or inadequacy, is unable to do so for himself.

"By the time I was the first black firefighter hired by the Salt Lake County Fire Department, I was already accustomed to the idea of my obligation to clear a path for those who might come behind me. That was far more important than clearing my own path and making my own life easier by negating, correcting, or ignoring abusive, insulting, ignorant, arrogant behavior imposed upon members of one group by the thoughtless and insensitive members of another group. And I still feel this obligation today."

It's the quiet riot. It is the unconquerable Marshall Allen, refusing to take bullshit sitting down.

Some twenty years later, in the beginning of 2008, Marshall decided that he could and would no longer tolerate inexcusable behavior. After months and months of enduring racist statements, the quiet riot came to a roar, and Marshall filed charges with the grievance department. When a white civilian employee with the department remarked that Mexicans should be put on birth control before they "take over L.A." to another white contractor, Marshall had to wonder, "Can this guy really treat a Hispanic contractor fairly?"

There is no reason to name names; while this happened in Fort Worth, Texas, this kind of sentiment exists all over the United States. So when this employee said that he could not tell one black football player apart from another, made derogatory comments about Asian women, and/or told obesity jokes, Marshall could not ignore it. He had tolerated as much as he could.

When Marshall confronted this person to let him know how distasteful he found the remarks, the man was always extremely apologetic. Then, when he was away from Marshall, though always within earshot, the jokes continued.

"In the 22 years before I broke my neck, I had rescued numerous firefighters and civilians alike. I had saved lives and brought lives into this world. On two separate occasions, approximately five years apart, I had total strangers walk up to me in public and thank me for saving their lives. I have fought racism and discrimination and even sexism within the department and outside." Yet, almost daily, Marshall was forced to share an office space with and be congenial to an outspoken racist.

In his grievance, Marshall wrote:

"Baylor Hospital upgraded my room three times in order to accommodate the large number of visitors. Black, white. Male, female. Jew, Gentile. Rookies and retirees, they all came.

"But they didn't come because I was some sort of fire-breathing captain or omniscient paramedic. They didn't come only because they respected me. They came because they knew I respected them, whether they were in my presence or not. And they knew that if the need arose, I would defend them whether they were in the room or not.

"They came because after all of the debates or arguments or exchanges of ideas, I did not insult them or embarrass them or alienate them in order to make my point or win an argument. And some of them came because I was able to show them something they had not seen before even though it was all around them. And we could work side-by-side for as long as necessary to get the job done."

Marshall's distaste for disrespecting human beings was not only known to this coworker but to every other firefighter or civilian who worked alongside Captain Allen. Yet, this other person insisted that he felt stressed that he could not freely express his distaste for Hispanics, African-Americans, and the obese. The man needed to be able to (loudly) rank Asian women against whites, African Americans, and Hispanics. Almost daily, the job and the people Marshall loved so much were routinely disrespected by this individual, and for the first time in 28 years, Marshall said, "I did not like my job."

What he wanted was for all firefighters to be held to the same standard that we should all be held to. Instead, office politics became overwhelming. Marshall leveled charges of "conduct prejudicial to good order," which is a terminable offense. He was quickly warned that, should he carry through, "lines would be drawn."

He is a man of action and always has been. The lines are very clear to him: unacceptable behavior is just that – unacceptable.

There are those who might have argued that Marshall was playing the race card, that he was *just another* disgruntled African-American, or that he was hyper sensitive about "a joke." I knew better. For Al, almost everything is about race. While I don't usually agree with Al, I understand how his upbringing has made him suspicious, even angry with white people. I don't like it, but I try to understand it.

But Marshall rarely discusses race unless it is absolutely relevant to the topic – a historical reference or needed description. Never was this made more clear to me than when I rifled through old photo albums. After a two-year friendship, discussing all aspects of his personal and professional life, I made a stunning discovery. Marshall's brother, Morris, Jr., is white.

He's white ... and Marshall never thought to mention this.

As he described feelings that his brother was somehow *different* and that he knew even as a young boy that his brother was given preferential treatment by his parents, he never once mentioned the small fact that his brother was white.

As I stood – stupefied – studying the picture of Morris, Jr., Marshall appeared puzzled by my response.

Oh, hadn't I mentioned that?

Suddenly, my mind was racing. Was Morris favored by his African-American parents because he was white? I recalled a story in which Obelia, while tending to two young toddlers, openly doted on the light-skinned little girl. It was during a visit Al and Marshall made back to Ogden, and the friends were angered by Obelia's bias. Was this a replay of Marshall's life as a child?

To Marshall's credit, he just hadn't thought it relevant in his description of his brother. It is the character of a man that matters most to Marshall. No one could ever accuse this man of reverse prejudice, a supposed backlash against whites. He doesn't have any!

It had been a painfully difficult decision to file a grievance with the FWFD. As much as he loves the fire department, as much as he loves being with the department, however, he knew what he had to do.

"It's over," he called after the hearing. And for Marshall, it was not about victory, embarrassing another person, or having him lose a job. It was simply about doing what was right. It was about Marshall's law. And he did what he set out to do. The other party was forced to apologize "for the record," and now understands that he is being watched. But the complaint also reminded the FWFD the value of proper education and training.

As the room cleared out, Marshall simply slumped in his chair. Those involved in the hearing – the grievance officers, the fire chief, and those who stood accused of bad behavior—could never know how physically taxing doing the right thing was for Marshall. As his heart rate and stress level rose, his body was unable to regulate the pressure changes, and he was left weakened.

But the irony is, he was stronger than ever.

And so was I. My heart swelled with pride because of what Marshall had done and how strong he'd been, and suddenly, I knew what I was supposed to be doing as well. It's the quiet riot. What might have once been noise in my head was now a single, clear voice telling me that protecting God's green earth was not to be taken lightly, that it would sometimes hurt, but it was my journey to take. It's Marshall's law.

On Faith and Hope

I was head cheerleader for the "life is a series of coincidences" chant. And for those who wondered how my fight for clean air could have anything to do with Marshall, or more precisely, how I could blend the two, my answer was simple. I didn't have to. Marshall was doing that for me.

I had begun to feel sorry for myself. After fighting the environmental fight for just a fraction of the time other DAR members had, I wanted out. I was tired of standing up for others. Then, just when I was ready to call it quits, Marshall showed me he could stand up for everyone even when he couldn't stand.

Keeping the Faith

But for all of his acts of bravery, both in and out of the chair, Marshall's marriage was falling apart. For Mary, the strain was not what she had bargained for. Though she did fight to take possession of a house that was literally redesigned by firefighters for Marshall's wheelchair, no one can argue that she was not there for him when Marshall was injured.

Briefly, the act of her leaving, though he knew he was better off without her, was truly heartbreaking, and we worried desperately over him. Only briefly. Because he is also a warrior.

Protecting God's Green Earth

A critic of the local industry, diagnosed with cancer, had moved away but continued to blog about Midlothian. Exactly six parents in the area were diagnosed with cancer, the father of a friend of mine had such aggressive cancer that he was dead before he could ever really get treatment, and e-mails continued to pour in from people questioning why their face was swollen or suddenly reddened as though they were sunburned or why they were constantly coughing. On the day that I learned a former kickboxing student of mine was diagnosed with leukemia, I learned that a school teacher had also been diagnosed with that same disease. A physician at Waxahachie Baylor voiced concern over the disproportionately high cases of people with kidney stones. And a brave soul name Jeff Millet railed against the school board and city council after the *USA Today* report revealed the dire health conditions of our schools and our children downwind from the cement plants.

The tide had turned on the small town of Midlothian. Through aggressive building, almost tripling the population in less than a decade, more and more outsiders were moving in and hearing the rumors (or getting sick), and they began asking questions. The good ol' boy network was crumbling.

I had no interest – zip, zero, nada – in making trouble. In fact, few will ever know how many interviews I walked away from because I did not want to highlight Midlothian as some toxic cesspool. Much to Jim Schermbeck's frustrations and to those of the Earthjustice and Downwinders organizations, I passed on speaking opportunities. I would tell them again and again how difficult this was because, believe it or not, I love Midlothian and its residents. I didn't want anyone to lose jobs. I just wanted cleaner air, and when I knew that the technology to make this happen is out there and that other places are doing it and that people are getting sick around you … well, anyone with a damned brain in his or her head wants to explore the options of better air quality and not bury her head in the sand.

Green cement seemed to be such a solution. It is a win/win for everyone. Local industry can keep jobs, America shows the world that quality cement can be produced while protecting God's green earth, and we can all breath a little bit better!

But as Jim Schermbeck, Sue Pope, and the good people of Downwinders aggressively sold the concept of "green cement" to surrounding cities, Ash Grove Cement plant filed a lawsuit against every entity that passed Green Cement resolutions for future building. Like a growing number of cities, Dallas city officials could not justify hospitals, school, homes, churches, and public buildings being built with cement that contained hazardous or toxic waste, but Ash Grove claimed that Dallas was, in effect, shutting down free enterprise by only buying green cement, and, for the first time in a very long time, I heard Jim Schermbeck laugh out loud.

Oh, what a difference a decade makes. How much had changed.

Chapter Eighteen
Hell Freezes Over

In the days and weeks that followed meeting Marshall Allen, I was a wreck. For four decades, I had it all figured out. Then, after just one bike ride, everything I thought I knew started to unravel. As an adult, to lose my seemingly solid belief system is frightening. Suddenly, I'm not just asking "what does this mean?" but "what does everything mean?"

In desperation, I found my way into a local church. I had no reason to choose the Midlothian Bible Church other than its location. There, I found Tim Wallace, a kind-looking, handsome, athletic, 40-something youth pastor. As it turns out, he's a bit of a ham, loves intense exercise, and tries, whenever possible, to sneak away to a bookstore where he can sip coffee and peruse new fiction. He was the ideal person to answer my questions.

When I wandered into the church in search of a pastor, I found Tim, who was talking to a group of teenagers. When he asked if I needed something, I thought I was going to burst into tears.

When I initially decided to write about Marshall and his amazing life, I needed to talk to his friends, family, and co-workers for background information. What I found was a kind of devotion and admiration people expressed to me about Marshall that was much bigger than Marshall, his life, or his chair. And I was completely unprepared to digest, much less accept, the crazy set of circumstances that led me to him, so it was a very big and emotional deal for me to come to a church in search of answers.

I picture angels up in heaven having a rousing game of ping pong when one looks down to see me reaching for the door to the church.

Oh, oh ... she's reaching. Look at that! She's opening the door!

She's stepping inside. Easy does it …. She's in!

When I learned that Tim Wallace, the son of a preacher, had once rebelled against the church and organized religion, I felt a little more comfortable. Maybe he would understand me better and not pass judgment. Maybe he could give me some answers. Maybe he could explain why I just suddenly woke up and peeled out of my own house for a long bike ride without eating or getting anything to drink. Instead, he gave me a book, *Traveling Mercies* by Ann Lamott.

The author, the daughter of hippies, writes: "My coming to faith did not start with a leap but rather a series of staggers from what seemed like one safe place to another." The book grabbed me. I liked it. I pondered about the things Lamott wrote. I wondered and worried over it because this was exactly what had happened to me. It was not a single bike ride, but a series of events that had led me to Marshall and Big Al.

Somehow, Tim knew this and believed the book would be perfect for me. Ann Lamott is this earthy, crunchy chick with crazy hair who occasionally enjoys dropping the "f"-bomb and, despite her most ardent attempts, cannot seem to contain herself within the confines of what society deems normal for any self-respecting female.

I asked my friend Audra, "Why do you suppose, of all the books in this guy's library, he had me read this one?" She replied something along the lines of, "You're kidding me, right?"

Lamott writes an amusing story about how a cat led her to a better understanding to God. I hate cats. Or, at least, I used to hate cats. I am a former dog trainer who didn't see any purpose or appeal for owning a cat. Then one day when I was with Audra, we discovered she had a stowaway in the undercarriage of her car. A kitten. A half-starved, dehydrated, injured, terrified kitten who would come home with me and made me fall in love with him. Sooner, as he was named, was a great cat. He slept on our goat's back (but that is another long, complicated story) until an owl killed him. Then, we had another cat, but Benson, who came to us when we got our crazy horse, Lightning, was also killed by the owl, and then Pete, our Labrador, killed two of our cats. That, I assure you, was devastating to us all. Except Pete. If God was trying to get my attention …

"Holy, crap, Audra! What if God's been trying to send me a message by way of cat, but Pete keeps killing them? What else could God do but try to get my attention with something that Pete or the owl can't kill? Like a giant Rottweiller?"

Specifically, a large, massive, scary-looking Rottweiler named Caesar. Caesar, who just happened to belong to Marshall Allen. Caesar, the same beautiful dog that I noticed on the day that I parked my bike in the path of Marshall. Caesar, who because he was wearing a muzzle, made me ask if he did so because he was mean or just to make a person on a bike feel better.

No owl or overweight Labrador was going to take Caesar down.

Audra, while amused, asked, "Why are you fighting this?" *Do you need a brick to land on your head?*

Audra, like Tim, had left the church at one point in her life. She left the church when she realized that her participation in the services was for social, not religious, reasons.

It is one of the things I dearly love and admire about Audra. Even as a young person, fighting her own demons, she saw the hypocrisy of using church for a social outlet. But in her 30s, after the birth of her son, she rediscovered her faith. To her, my experience appeared to be a gift, but to me, it was nothing short of torture.

"Did God get your attention in order to tell Marshall's story?" she would ask me again. "Or did He get your attention to get you?"

Argh! Audra! Knock it off!

(By 2008, Audra received her Masters degree in counseling and can be very annoying.)

Still, her voice resonated in my ears. What an ego I had. I thought I had been sent to tell Marshall's story. One of the perks of working for *NOW* magazine (a community magazine outside Dallas/Fort Worth) was how good we make people feel, telling feel good stories about artists and athletes, volunteers and valedictorians.

All the editors and I would get 'thank you' letters from people who loved having a pat-on-the-back story written about them. We – the editors – take the matter of writing such stories very seriously, so it was easy to convince myself I was doing the same with Marshall.

But that feeling faded pretty quickly. And before I knew it, things had suddenly flipped on me. The idea that I was being used by some greater force or a higher power creeped me out. If you never believed there is anything there and suddenly there is, it's a little daunting. Or worse: if you never believed there is anything out there and then suddenly think there *might* be but are uncertain, it's downright upsetting.

Compound this with the fact that I had secretly mocked people for going to church. They were weak or scared or both because they had to look for a higher power to give them the strength to deal with everyday life.

If there was a higher power, He heard me calling his flock a bunch of babies and scaredycats, and that is just embarrassing. What constitutes being smitten? Or smote? Is name calling churchgoers a smitable offense?

I tried to stop writing the book. I tried just to write about firefighter facts and Marshall's life in Ogden, Utah, but that was impossible. For even as Marshall continues to question the Bible, he prays every night. Even though he admits he prayed in the ditch, he questioned His existence. I was getting even more confused by Marshall – the one person who could have probably set me straight one way or the other. He baffled me so much that I tried to walk away from the book project.

"But he can't *give* you the answers," Audra would say. "You will figure this out on your own."

Argh! Audra. Knock it off!

Each time I put the book aside, something miraculous or, certainly, unusual would occur. Many years ago, I interviewed a professional female boxer named Sumya Anani after an ESPN Friday Night Fight bout in Waco, Texas. I liked her, thought she was cool, and we kind of, sort of, stayed in touch. Her legacy in the boxing world is nothing short of amazing. Four time world champion and pound for pound the toughest female fighter out there. But it was a match between Sumya and newcomer Katie Dallam that would become the basis for the Hollywood blockbuster, *Million Dollar Baby*. (On a side note, it totally sucks that the producers, including Clint Eastwood, changed enough facts about the movie so that they didn't have to pay one penny to either Sumya or Katie, who is alive but still struggles physically.)

On December 11, 1996 in St. Joseph, Missouri, Katie Dallam stepped into the ring with Sumya, a relative newcomer to the sport of boxing herself. But despite Sumya's lack over experience, the women were terribly mismatched. Katie suffered a broken nose in the first round but was allowed to continue to fight. What no one knew then was that Katie and her manager had been in a car accident the day before the fight. While members of Dallam's family describe the accident as a mere fender bender, others have speculated that it could have contributed to the final outcome.

In the fourth round, after Sumya delivered another 140 blows to Katie's head, Katie's manager finally threw in the towel as Katie hung helplessly on the ropes. After the match was called and Sumya was declared the winner, Katie said that her head hurt. Then, she passed out and slipped into a coma, literally fighting for her life.

There were no medical supplies available and no EMS crews on hand so Katie did not receive any real medical assistance until she arrived at the local hospital. The diagnosis: A major vein in her brain had ruptured and was beyond repair. It would be some time before Katie, a once well educated woman, would learn to walk and talk again, eventually learning how to paint. And suddenly, Sumya, an extremely likeable woman, was the most hated woman in boxing. People incorrectly assumed that Sumya's character in the movie, Blue Bear, was based on Sumya. Wrong! And for that reason, she called me. She wanted the truth to be told about who she really is. She had been publicly vilified and was devastated. I put her in touch with some contacts I had, including some possible radio gigs but, beyond that, I hadn't a clue as to how to help her. The most compelling part of this story was that while Sumya was undoubtedly one of the fiercest fighters in the world, hers was a story about recovery. Ultimately, Sumya walked away from boxing and now operates a highly successful yoga practice and hosts her own radio show.

None of this, of course, is to diminish the achievements of Katie Dallam, who brought herself back from near death and paralysis to be a (partially) walking and talking artist. But Sumya's sudden phone call got me back to thinking about paralysis and spirituality.

Another time when I tried to walk away from the book, there was a ring at my front door. Brian Bates knew of my struggles and felt compelled to come by to share a story. I'd been struggling with the whole man's free will thing – you know, the staged answer as to how God could allow little girls to be murdered when ding dong! Here comes Brian … He had been the first police officer to arrive at the murder scene of Amber Hagerman (the murder case that would ultimately result in Amber Alert messages). He explained to me the circumstances of how that moment both tested and renewed his faith in God.

Alone, he stood in a freezing creek bed holding Amber's naked, nearly decapitated body so that he could secure the crime scene. Her head was so nearly severed that he had to hold her head with one hand and her body with the other. He had to focus on the one little pink sock she was still wearing and ignore the tiny, naked, broken body in his hands and ignore the painfully freezing water as it bit at his flesh and bones. Only nine-years-old, and the child has been abducted, raped, brutally murdered, and cast away like trash for Brian to hold together until a crime scene photographer could come.

His explanation to me, in regards to God and faith, was that Amber was not the victim of a vengeful God but one of man's will. As his voice cracked and I heard him choke on some of his own words, his conviction was steady. God granted us free will, and as a horrible result, terrible things happen. And in those horribly agonizing moments alone in Amber's deathbed, he prayed for her. For this officer, his role in finding Amber made him stronger in his faith and made him realize why he needed to pray to God. As he explained it to me, his faith is unwavering not in spite of, but because of man's free will.

But what was even more compelling was that his wife, my friend, had not known he was coming by to share that story – a story that he had never really shared with her. When I teasingly accused Gina of "turning

Brian loose on me," she said, "What are you talking about?" Brian revealed things to me that he had not shared with Gina. To say I was touched is a vast understatement.

Unanswered questions continued to pound in my brain – day and night. Why had Talaya's mother so suddenly told her about Marshall after years of secrecy only to die hours later? Why had the McDowell's had their children with them the day they found Marshall? Why had Marshall decided to become a vegetarian just prior to his accident? Why would a guy as physical as Marshall suddenly decide that voice activated computer software was the way of the future? Why had I awakened so suddenly only to take a bike ride that I couldn't finish?

Audra would occasionally ask, "So, how's it going with Marshall?" But I knew what she really meant. *Did the other brick land on your head yet?*

When my horse, Star, died, this was yet another reason to delay the writing process. More people were asking me how the writing was going, and I would simply say I had writer's block. I didn't have writer's block. I had God block.

Then a woman literally jogged into our driveway and asked if we were looking for a new horse. Her friend, Debbie Baker, had cancer. It was irreversible and ravaging, and all Debbie wanted was a really good home for Sammy, a six-year-old Paint. (I have to be careful I don't drool on him I love him so much!) As it would turn out, Sammy was previously registered to a family named Browning, the same name of Dorothy Browning who sponsored Marshall in school in Ogden, Utah. And it would turn out that Sammy's line was from, in fact, Ogden, Utah. And he was registered on my birthday.

I was stunned.

Sammy's …. Mormon? I called Audra. "Holy crap! Sammy's Mormon!"

"Why are you fighting this so much?" Audra laughed.

I was hanging over the front gate of the corral, looking at the horses and lost in thought when a voice rang out in the early morning air. I looked up toward the street to find Tim Wallace, the always entertaining pastor, jogging by my house. He waved, and I waved back then looked up to the sky and said, "You win."

When I told Jim Schermbeck that I hoped to fold the stories of Marshall Allen and his friends in with those of the Midlothian citizens, he said, "You must be one hell of a writer." It seemed implausible to mix such an unlikely batch, but Marshall is, if nothing else, a man about messages and a man who brings people together.

To Jim, I said, "Honey, I once wrote an 850 word article about a funeral director who only gave me 36 words to go on. I am one hell of a writer!"

The truth is I'm just a writer presented with one hell of a story. Or stories.

(Sorry, God. There's a lot of 'hell' talk here, but because I always said I would only go to church when hell froze over, and I've now been kind of going without any word of hell freezing, I think I should be allowed some liberties with the use of the word hell.)

Hell.

The mind blowing truth, at least from my perspective, is that Marshall was sent to me. A man in a wheelchair was sent to save me. And just to be sure, He sent another. For an article for my magazine, I met, befriended, and wound up training with another quadriplegic named Jonathan Merchant, who blew away the medical community by not only swimming but competing in full triathlons!

While Marshall will intellectualize the existence of Adam and Eve or the physical creation of an ark (but, I mean, really ... can we actually believe that two of *everything* was loaded up into Noah's Ark?), Jonathan is unwavering in his faith.

Then in 2008, when we decided to put our house on the market, our real estate agent shared with us that her son was also a quadriplegic. Robb approached me with a stony expression. I secretly suspect he knows about the giant Rick Perry head on his flatbed trailer. He knows about a lot of the things I've done, but we're one a don't-ask-don't-tell policy regarding my environmental escapades; he looks the other way. But this latest bit of information was even too much for him to ignore.

"What's with you and all these quadriplegics?" he uttered in whispered tones. "It makes you wonder if something is going to happen to us." And I had to admit I had wondered the same thing.

What was the reasoning here? The idea of coincidences had long faded from my mind.

In fact, I dragged out the meetings and the book writing, allowing my time with Marshall to become more social than anything else. However unconsciously, I was afraid to finish my "work" with him, fearing that with the final chapter, there would be a horrible reason that I suddenly understood about catheters, severed spines, poop management, and all the daily inconveniences and frustrations that a wheelchair bound person suffers.

At the finish of the book, with the writing of a final chapter, I could very well be setting the wheels of some other intervention in motion. Was my acceptance of God also the acceptance that everything was in His hands and I no longer had control? Was something going to happen to someone I love? Or would all my questions about God and faith become nothing more than a nostalgic memory?

But there was something else at play. These three quadriplegics are not ordinary men, so it was no surprise to learn that Eric Wycliffe, a 23-year-old who was paralyzed at the age of 19 while diving into shallow water, had also become privy to the use of voice-activated computers *before* his accident because of a learning disability. Today, though almost wholly paralyzed, he drives a truck, manages 200 head of cattle, and runs his own business. Astonishing!

Jonathan had returned from Bosnia with the U.S. Army when a freak auto accident left him paralyzed. But like Marshall, he would not be kept down. When a friend literally threw him into a pool to see if he could swim, Jonathan made the decision to train for Ironman.

These "quads," or as Eric's mother and real estate agent Jamie Wycliffe would say, "the quad squad," were a testament to strength, courage, tenacity, and dogged perseverance.

Both Marshall and Jonathan were suddenly starting their lives over after divorce. There seemed to be far greater things in life than writing a book or fighting for clean air.

In truth, I struggled with the book because I wasn't able to tell the full story of Marshall and how I came to meet him. Through my tremendous admiration of an extraordinary man, I tried to tell Marshall's story from his perspective but failed. I was having an identity crisis.

I'm a smart-aleck, wild girl who was practically foaming at the mouth over local politics and was utterly confused over the sudden emergence of God in my life. Me bequeathing my allegiance to God was like Rush Limbaugh turning into Miss Manners. The thought of either one makes me feel a little ookey.

But there was also something else.

It wasn't just God or the idea of God that kept me from writing. I was held back because my subject, my superman, my warrior in a wheelchair is human after all. In the time that I've known him, I have seen him cry three times. He didn't boo hoo or anything, but he was visibly upset. One time was after Mary left him. That's a given. But the two other times occurred while we were discussing his father.

While Marshall has been fairly candid about his depression, how medication and, yes, the accident, helped him with proper diagnosis, he is loathe to talk about why he was depressed.

He was given up for adoption and abused in the foster care system. He was adopted by a family that showed preferential treatment to the white son, and he was reared in white Mormon Utah in the 60s and 70s. There wasn't a lot of money, but there was plenty of prejudice. Certainly, these are all reasons for frustrations and depression. But what he won't talk about is the abuse. His devotion and loyalty to his parents, particularly his father, will not allow him to articulate those things that most haunt him. So, instead, he suppressed the feelings.

Before he found the fire department, he was looking for trouble. He was looking for a way to vent his frustrations and growing anger. While Marshall will talk about how he learned to keep his anger and depression buried inside of him, he is slow to talk about why he had these feelings.

As I spent more time with him and listened to him tell stories about various relationships with different women, his children, friends, and co-workers, I knew. There is a beast that dwells within him, and I had mistakenly believed this flawed him. So much so that I'd become territorial of him or, more accurately, his story. He was the unconquerable Marshall Allen, and I wasn't about to tell a story in which he was depicted as weak or vulnerable or unlikeable.

But he is a man about truth. He wants me to tell this story because it has everything to do with dignity and honor and truth.

He sees things for what they are. While the old Marshall would not have wanted to ask for help, this new Marshall is unafraid.

So, one day when we were sitting together and he suddenly looked funny and I asked, "Is there anything I can do," he did not hesitate. He said, "Yes, if you don't mind," and I followed him back to the van. The tubing to his catheter had kinked, making things terribly uncomfortable for him.

I had to run my hand under his leg and buttocks, trying to determine where the tubing was kinked. I couldn't, and he was forced to go back home so that his aid, Richard, could help him.

There were also times when he couldn't seem to get the front door to lock and, out of frustration, would simply give up. "Sometimes, it's easier just to stay home."

I recalled a time when he had decided he wanted a sandwich from Subway. Although he now has a relatively small appetite, it was a craving powerful enough that he went out to get it. As the shop was only five minutes from the house, most people would never give the trip a second thought. By the time he'd returned, he was so frustrated, the sandwich wasn't worth the effort.

Marshall remains steadfast in his claims that he is more content now than he's ever been. But, there are times when his patience is certainly tested. What we consider to be the most mundane chores – so simple, in fact, we give them no thought – can be nightmares for Marshall. Just getting out to his car can be a 20 to 30 minute venture, never mind the effort and number of people involved in getting him up and dressed.

His accident humbled him and helped him. While many of us are given to exaggerating such expressions as "life or death" and "life altering," Marshall's accident brought about both experiences. Suddenly, unwittingly, Marshall was a role model. To friends, family, and co-workers, he redefined courage. Through Marshall, I'd found new strength in fighting for what I believed in and a faith that was buried so deep inside me I didn't even know it existed. To consider that Marshall still had a beast inside him was unthinkable. He was Superman, not the werewolf.

While I continued to see Marshall, I shelved the book and did not pick it up again until 2009. Not until the U.S. House of Representatives called and asked if I might be willing to talk about what was going on in Midlothian.

The beast had to be drawn out.

Chapter Nineteen

Christmas 2009

Dear Friends and Family –

It's that time of year again. If you've never received a holiday letter from us before, the rules are this: in the spirit of giving, we won't tell you how amazing and perfect our lives are (as this would be a complete work of fiction), but we will make you feel so much better about your lives by relaying the bad, the ugly, the disturbing.

We decided to wait until the U.S. housing market hit an all time low before trying to sell our house. Next, we set up a schedule so that with our own insane schedule we would have to be out of the house at a moment's notice or when the house was always in chaos. About this same time, Robb began growing out some weird beard that made him look like a Puritan because, I later found out from a friend, he knew it was driving me crazy. And he never quite got the concept of selling a house. It was very annoying to him that people would call and actually want to *see* the house ... without him skulking about with his brooding manner and strange beard. After six months of driving dogs around in the car when people came to look at the house (I was starting to cough up hairballs) and Kerri's senior year of high school approaching, we pulled the For Sale sign. In hindsight, we probably should have removed Tommy's arsenal of hand grenades and world domination maps *before* putting the house on the market.

Tommy was attacked by a pit bull. An infection set in, and he had to be transported by ambulance to Children's Hospital where Tommy was given a bed with its own television remote attached to the bed! By Tommy's standards, the attack was almost worth it. Another cool offshoot of the dog attack is that when Lego found out that while a pit bull was busily tearing open Tommy's arm, he refused to set down his Lego helicopter he'd just completed; Lego sent Tommy the super deluxe Star Wars Battleship model. Lego – you rock!

On the downside, while we were in the Emergency Room for the second time, Tommy and I were on a gurney awaiting the ambulance. The place was packed, so we'd been left in the hallway when an enormously large, hairy man in a bathing suit was brought in. He was parked just in front of us. There was some story about him falling into a pool and having to be fished out. Tommy and I stared – transfixed by Sasquatch. I'd never seen so much hair on a human body, and as I sat pondering his exact DNA, Tommy spoke. "When I grow up," he said. "I am *never* going to shave." Um …Huh?

We went paintballing, and it turned violent. Michelle got shot in the mouth by Tommy and could not fully formulate the words, "I'm hit," so I shot her in the ribs. Tommy shot me at very close range in the ear, so I shot him in the ribcage. Tommy is 10. I feel no remorse. Katie and Tommy like to pretend they're vomiting, but because that is insufficiently disgusting and disturbing, Katie also likes to pretend she is a dog and hikes her leg on things. She is 14. We're not worried about Katie acquiring a boyfriend any time soon. Meanwhile, Kerri had her first boyfriend – which was troublesome to her because he actually wanted to hold her hand.

I woke Katie early one morning, and she said, "Show thyself the door, ye wench." When I walked into the kitchen, I found Tommy's head in his bowl. No spoon. "Buddy! Use a spoon!" To which he replied, "We don't have those where I come from!" *When did we become pirates?*

I helpfully suggested to Robb that he might want to trim his eyebrows, so he decided to shave them himself. It was pretty hard to keep a straight face when he came in the room and asked if I noticed anything different. *Other than not having any eyebrows?* Mostly, he just looked really surprised for a couple of weeks.

I tried to help Robb with buying new shirts, which was very difficult as – apparently – all the shirts are "gay," making it a challenge to find a shirt that will not result in him accusing me of trying to emasculate him. I know it's not PC to use words such as "gay," but with Robb it really is okay as he is equally prejudiced against all groups of all people everywhere. He now includes anyone who sits in a coffee shop, reads the *New York Times,* or likes to dance. No one *likes* to dance, he says.

Kerri finally got her driver's license and was never nervous until it was time to sign her license and she promptly messed up her own name. Yes, her official license has a scribble on it. I followed her to school for almost two months. One time I was driving Kerri and lecturing her on the importance of keeping "eyes on the road!" – okay, so technically I was not watching the road when WHAP! this oversized raccoon committed racoonacide. I never saw him! Kerri threw her hands up to her face and screamed, unable to speak for some time. It was horrible, but I rallied. "You see what happens when you don't pay attention, Kerri!? Raccoons die!"

Katie has entered a new phase where she pretends to be dead – eyes open, sprawled out. So each time I enter a room, there she is. I don't mean 3 or 4 or 40 times. *Every* time I come through a room, she is there – sprawled out on the island in the kitchen, across my bed, on the floor in the hallway.

Elbows out, hunched over her plate, Katie eats like a crazed hockey player. This, combined with the strange blend of a Southern/French accent she now affects all the time (when she's not dead on the floor) has led me to the conclusion that she really does need to go to charm school. At the same time she is trying to convince me that she *can* act ladylike, she's been repeating French phrases to me. So after hearing the same one over and over again, I asked what "J'aime beaucour a la pét!" means. Katie smiled, "Doesn't that sound so elegant? It means, 'I like to toot.'" Oh, yeah… charm school, here we come.

Tommy keeps taking my stuff and tries to sell it back to me. How does he think it fair that I buy back a skillet??

I've complained of this before, but this year, I really mean it … our 'vacations by Robb' need a serious overhaul. If we're not experiencing altitude sickness, sleeping outside slaughter houses, or having to rotate shower days for everyone, we're enduring long-term kidney damage. Our last trip to Wyoming had me heading into town so I could find a toilet. Kerri ran at me. "Where are you going?" When she learned that she could use a gas station bathroom, she was elated! "I've been holding it for two days! Please! Take me with you!" When an Exxon potty looks good to you, you need to reprioritize.

Recently, a bunch of us entered the Muddy Buddy race, which was a 6 mile race with an obstacle course and a mud bath that you have to crawl through at the end. Extreme muddiness is guaranteed. Kerri and her buddy, Cheyenne, won 1st in their division while Michelle and I (with a combined age of 90) beat out Katie and her buddy, Macy (c.a. 28), and you better know we are not letting Katie live that down! All the mud broke my washing machine.

While Kerri continues her passion for music, playing the fiddle, classical violin, piano, mandolin, and viola, we have desperately tried to garner that same interest in Tommy and Katie. Finally, we enrolled them in violin lessons together during which they spend much of their time giggling, but at least they are having fun. Still, we worry about their poor instructor. What kind of headaches must he have??

One day we drove by a neighbor's house who had tied a donkey and a cow together. There is a Future Farmers of America reason for this, but at the time, I asked Katie, "Geez, what kind of conversations do you think those two are having?" Katie didn't miss a beat. "You're such a cow…Well, you don't have to be an ass." She may not have a career in music, but she is definitely headed for the stage. While making their

Christmas lists, I heard Kerri and Katie berating their little brother. I came into the kitchen. "Whoa. He can write whatever he wants… he may not get it but that's the fun of Christmas." Kerri rolled her eyes. "Momma, he's asking for a better banking interest!"

Tommy decided to relieve himself outside at boy scouts behind some bushes and right IN FRONT of a church window. A rattlesnake fell at my feet when I opened the barn door, the cats have taken to hacking up giant hairballs on the vent of Kerri's new little car, and we're pretty sure it was the dead/reincarnated raccoon that came back and mixed a can of paint with bird seed on the back porch. It looks like he was trying to spell out "You're next."

Finally, an ode to our Shep/Boxer mix, Nala. After 12+ years, her hips gave out on her, and before the pain was too much, we put her down. After Tommy was born, she became his watchdog, and when I would not immediately respond to his cries, she would punish me by not allowing me to touch her for a day or so. She will forever be remembered as the softest-furred, sweetest-natured, thumpingest-tailed pup in the world! Heaven just got a little bit softer!

Agnes Pharo once said, "What is Christmas? It is the tenderness of the past, courage for the present, hope for the future. It is a fervent wish that every cup may overflow with blessings rich and eternal, and that every path may lead to peace."

Yeah, well, look. I just want people to use indoor plumbing and preferably not the Exxon station. Body hair should be kept to a minimum, and I don't think livestock should be tied together. Never try to play "freeze tag" on ice skates and just know that the term "hairball" is misleading. It's not just hair. But in the spirit of the season, let us say this to you: "Pouvoir Paix est sur vous et n'a jamais laissé un jeu de accoon avec la peinture rouge."

Happy Holidays,

Love,
Alex

The Unconquerable Marshall Allen

In May, on a mercifully cool day by Texas standards, Marshall could have died. He'd been having problems with the battery in his chair and had been using his old backup chair, which was also having some battery difficulties, when I met with him earlier in the day.

On this day, our meeting had been important because an award-winning documentary filmmaker named Mark Birnbaum met with us to discuss Marshall's story. Mark and I long ago worked out a deal to tell the story of Marshall and his triumph over tragedy. Mark was instantly intrigued and asked to meet with Marshall.

Dignity, Marshall had said, was the most important issue he wanted to cover in the documentary. If people could truly see what Marshall goes through each day while performing the most basic everyday chores – brushing his teeth, getting out of bed, getting out and turning a key—they would better appreciate the circumstances of their own lives.

After the meeting, Mark had to help push the very heavy combination of Marshall and chair back into Marshall's van. Later, Mark would call to say he was excited about doing the project. Everything I'd promised Mark about Marshall had been delivered. Marshall is stoic and almost regal in the manner he speaks to people. He is extremely intelligent, intuitive, and proud. It is easy to forget he is in the chair until something happens to remind you. That Mark, an award winning documentary filmmaker, had to push Marshall into the van made the difficulties all real for Mark.

When Marshall got home, he unlocked the wheels of the chair from behind the steering wheel, but it stuck. With limited arm motion and strength, there was little he could do. After sitting in front of his house, van engine still running and faithful companion Caesar by his side, Marshall decided to drive around back and pull into his garage for more shade. But as he drove up the slight incline to his garage, the wheelchair rolled backward away from the steering controls. In fact, the chair had unlocked. The van then slipped into neutral and rolled backward, crashing into the alley fence. Marshall's phone fell to the floor, and after over an hour, the car went dead. No AC. No power. Sitting in the direct sun, he said he began to sweat (and as a quad, he says he can't remember the last time he actually felt sweat), and he began to get scared.

By the second or third hour, drifting in and out, he used his own urine bag to rehydrate himself. Again, as a quad, his body goes into shock far more quickly than ours, and he knew that things were getting bad. He also poured some of his urine over his head to cool himself. Not only did he drink it, but at one point, as the bag slipped out of his hands, Marshall fumbled frantically to keep it from falling to the floor, from losing the "precious liquid."

Before he cooled himself, however, he could only watch in frustration as a teenager wearing an iPod and another man in a car saw Marshall's van blocking the alley, paused, and, not hearing Marshall's cries, turned and walked away.

Eventually, a neighbor wondered why the van was back against the fence line and came out to explore. As soon as he opened the door, Caesar jumped out, ran to some shade, and flung himself down. Though fully aware of what was happening, Marshall said he could no longer keep his eyes open, but he talked his neighbor through what to do next.

It was about this time I called Marshall only to have a stranger's voice answer. It was hard to understand what was happening. Something happened to Marshall. I hung up and called Big Al.

In the end, Marshall would be okay, but it was a sobering moment for a lot of us. We forget. He's Marshall. Superman. Yet all of this happened just feet from his own house. This time, he confessed, "I was actually scared for my life."

With a phone just inches from his body and his house only a few feet away, there was nothing he could do to save himself but drink his own urine.

A few months later, as Richard was getting Marshall into bed after a shower, they slipped. Richard would beat himself up for what happened next, but Marshall is quick to point out, "I was there, too!"

Falling at an angle, Marshall broke his femur and required surgery. After five days of being cooped up in the hospital, he was like a giant kid, antagonizing us as he pretended to run his newly casted leg into a wall.

"Marshall!" I yelled at him when he steered his foot toward another wall, swerving the chair at the last minute, causing me to gasp. "Knock it off!"

For Marshall, who was once again in his chair, fully mobile and going home, life was good and nothing else mattered. I was reminded of something Dr. Bruce Lance once said. "Marshall Allen is the only man I know who could get stronger after being paralyzed."

Even better, he has made those around him stronger.

Marshall has redefined me and my family. Daily, he unconsciously makes people reprioritize those things that are most important. This does not occur because people feel sorry for him or somehow view his chair as a sign. It's that Marshall thing – Marshall's Law – where his dignity, authoritative manner, and ever optimistic outlook make those around him take stock of how they are living their own lives.

Years ago, when I was so overwhelmed by Marshall, his story, the circumstances of our chance meeting, I asked my buddy, Audra, Why me? "I feel like I was led to him," I'd confided, certain I was supposed to tell his story. When Audra suggested I needed him as much as he needed me, I had dismissed her. There was no question that Talaya needed Marshall as much as he needed her when they, at last, met. But me?

I didn't need anyone, thank you very much.

At least, that is what I thought. Marshall helped me redefine 'happy' and 'healthy' and 'thankful,' not to mention 'zest for life!'

To say that Marshall was thrilled to get out of the hospital is an understatement. For good measure, he aimed at a wall one last time as we exited the hospital.

"I'm not kidding, Marshall! Stop it!"

Have A Little Faith

Well, there's a fine how-do-you-do. I finally show up to the party just when everyone else seems to be leaving. I'd read that religion is on the decline in America, and fewer people are attending church – of any kind. Today, I find myself engaged with more and more people who use science and skepticism to question God – you know, all those things I did and said my entire life. I understand all the arguments about the impracticality of God and religion, how there is no real hard evidence to support the Bible in the face of our evolutionary discoveries and how conveniently people twist religion to suit their own needs.

Every time yet another religious leader is caught cheating on his wife or wearing women's clothing, its proof positive to the agnostic that religion may be more hype than hope. Every time the super religious make outlandish statements about someone or something they don't believe in based on their own beliefs, the intellectual sect run screaming. I give you Pat Robertson's rant on feminism. He said, "The feminist agenda is not about equal rights for women. It is about a socialist, anti-family, political movement that encourages women to leave their husbands, kill their children, practice witchcraft, destroy capitalism, and become lesbians."

Jeepers. I just thought I was being a pioneer in women's sports and being a strong role model for my family.

Positiveatheism.org has an entire page devoted to outrageous and radical quotes by Pat Robertson. He alone makes great fodder for why one shouldn't believe in God. When religious leaders, such as Steven Anderson of the Faithful World Baptist Church in Temple, Arizona, and former vice president of the Southern Baptist Convention Rev. Wiley Drake publically prayed for President Obama's death, Christianity feels dirty.

So, where does that leave a person like me? After four decades of snickering at people who worshipped an unknown and unseen force, how do I just suddenly *believe*?

Hell, I don't even know how to pray. (*Sorry, God*). But I don't. Everyone says it is easy. "You just pray. Just talk to God."

Talk to the guy I've always questioned? Talk to a force that kind of scares me? My whole life I lived on the edge with a simple motto: be fearless but be kind. That was working pretty great for me. I don't make enemies (except maybe a few anti-environmentalists and a bad Santa…and might I say, how does one – in good conscience or in good relations to God – *oppose* clean air?) and I have no worries. But here lately, I'll think a thought and then worry that He might not have approved of that thought. It's very stressful.

All I really do know is this: I woke up for no apparent reason only to take the most ill-prepared 30 mile bike ride of my life so that I could meet the unconquerable Marshall Allen. Sammy, the paint horse, is probably Mormon (which might explain his sweet tooth. Mormons are serious sugar addicts) and comes from the same territory Marshall grew up in, possibly even sharing the same Browning connection. And Pastor Tim Wallace always seems to jog by my house right when – I swear – I'm having these deep what-is-the-meaning-of-life thoughts.

Again, I would like to emphasize that Tim Wallace isn't the pastor type that I've spent a lifetime avoiding. He's not some prim and proper goody-goody who hunts me down for some "you must be saved!" moment.

His favorite movie is "Cool Hand Luke," and he loves his dog, enjoys jogging, and says he likes to "sneak away" to read at Starbucks. Me, too! He uses the word "grooving" and has the greatest self-deprecating humor ("People *often* say I remind them of a bald Brad Pitt"), hangs out at the gym, and cracks up at my outlandish statements. But it was also he who taught me, finally, how to pray.

In truth, it wasn't anything he said. In fact, it was what he didn't say. He didn't pester me or pressure me, call me up and ask if I was going to come back to his church. He didn't do any of that. He was just kind of around, being low-key and cool in his own spiritual way, and I was 'grooving' to that.

But to pray? What if while I'm praying and my mind wanders, as it is apt to do, I get a thought in my head like, "I wonder if He is really there?" Will He become offended and leave? Or, what if He was listening to someone else pray and then comes in right in the middle of me thinking a perverted thought? Not that I'm given to perverse thoughts, but, you know, sometimes my mind goes weird for a second before I can get back under control. What if God tuned in at that very second I was wondering if George Clooney is wearing a thong? I only had such a thought because Gina was joking about George wearing a thong, but now I'm the one with this picture in my head just as God tunes in. That would just be my luck! So I'm a little dodgy on the praying thing because I open myself up to some serious, eternal scrutiny, and THAT, my friends, is a little more than I'm prepared for.

Two things happened. First, we took a trip. It was during our annual insane family vacation – this one sending us to the top of a 13,000 feet elevation cabin without any mode of transportation, any cell phone coverage, or even a gosh damn map to find our way back down the mountain. Out of habit, I gave Tommy his asthma medicine, which sent his heart rate up. At such high elevation, his heart began pounding and hurting so desperately, he was clutching his chest and crying. I was certain he would die. He and I curled up on the floor of the cabin – the lowest point – and as hard sleet fell against the cabin, I did it. I prayed and …. not too long after that the sleet/rain stopped, and Tommy fell asleep.

Holy guacamole.

Then, the next summer, Tommy was attacked by a pit bull. While I made light of the incident in the holiday letter, the truth was a terrible infection followed. Briefly, there was a real fear that if the infection settled in the bone, amputation could be a reality. But surgery seemed imminent. Prior to his trip to Children's, Tommy received a blessing from Robb's church, and while I didn't see how it could hurt, it wasn't going to help. It was, I reasoned, one of those things that just made Robb feel better. But it wasn't going to save Tommy's arm.

Throughout the day, three different surgeons came in the room to look at Tommy's arm and consult with one another. While they stood talking about, I guess, strategy, a thick, disgusting glob of black goo literally fell out of his arm. Then, as simply as that, the head surgeon kind of smiled at me and said, "Well, we're not going to have to do surgery." The "infection" miraculously fell out of his arm.

Just like that.

Just like that.

Just like when Marshall changed his mind and said he didn't want to die and the car stopped.

Insanity.

Then, this summer, I was jogging with a running buddy, Jill, and we were talking about a variety of things, including Marshall, when I saw a logo on a parked truck that caught my attention. Tom's Lawn Care.

I wonder.

So, the next time I saw that guy, I asked him, "By any chance, do you know a guy named Marshall Allen?" At first, he just stared at me. Then, there was a slow smile.

"Big, huge black guy?"

I had recalled Marshall telling me a story about a man named Tom Cearley who owned his own lawn service. After Marshall's accident, Tom had come to visit him in the hospital and offered him a year of lawn service, telling him, "It's just one less thing you'll have to worry about."

Eight years later, Tom clearly remembers the day they met. Or, rather, passed each other. It was the day of Marshall's crash. Tom had been running in one direction as Marshall passed by on his bicycle in the other. They had waved to each other, and Tom had been struck by how large of a man Marshall was, perched on a tiny bike. As he doubled back on his route, Tom saw that the road was filled with emergency vehicles, and when he saw Marshall's bike, he knew something had happened to Marshall.

I gave Tom an update on Marshall with the promise to send him Marshall's e-mail address. Just like that, eight years later, running with the Midlothian high school cross country team in the city park of Waxahachie, Texas, I met the guy who briefly encountered Marshall in the city of Ovilla.

"I don't ever get too far from Marshall," I told Jill later.

To anyone else, it was a rather unimpressive meeting, but for Jill, privy to the Marshall Allen story and my journey, it was anything but. "I'm so glad I just saw that," she smiled. There was a strangely wonderful *feeling* in the air.

I poked my foot in the door of church again.

I do not want anyone to get the wrong idea here. My entrance into church has been slow. I don't want anyone getting too excited and rush me, crushing me in a religious stampede. My plan has been to slink around unobserved in the back of the church, but they're so danged friendly; they all keep seeking me out. I'm bringing out my old football moves. There is a lot of ducking and weaving involved, which Audra has termed classic "avoidance."

I was sitting in church no less than six months ago when I made a discovery. Right there on the first page of the Holy Bible was something I did not know exists. I've heard it before, but I guess I thought it was more of an expression, you know, something someone pulled off a t-shirt.

I was embarrassed and startled. How could I be in my 40s and not know how the Bible begins?

Let there be light.

Man, what a great beginning, and it makes so much sense. That's an even better beginning than the all famous, "Where's Daddy going with the ax?" from E.B White's *Charlotte's Web*. Let there be light.

Two adorably nice (and knowledgeable) missionaries, Michael Rowley and Landin Hagge, had taken to jogging with me while we talked God and life. They were smart. They figured out if they wanted to get anywhere with me, they needed to run along with me (although I am keenly aware of the fact that these two strong young men had to harness themselves to match my turtle-like speed). They once made an allegory for me, likening my entrance to religion to that of running a marathon. Genius. Believe me, there is a kind of spiritual experience to be had in order to train for and run 26.2 miles without stopping or walking.

It really all does come down to having faith, doesn't it? You just have to have a little faith.

Surprisingly, a brick landing on your head doesn't hurt as much as you would think. *(Don't tell Audra I said that).*

And later, Sue Pope would have a little giggle over that, telling me, "God is light and life. Not a brick! The brick didn't hit you. You opened the door and let the light in."

Well, imagine that. And imagine a woman like Sue Pope, with everything she has been through, still believing in light and life. It is a curious and glorious thing. Let there be light.

(Don't tell Audra I said that either).

Protecting God's Green Earth

Salvador Meir gave an impassioned speech before US Senate, compliments of the US House of Representatives subcommittee on Investigations and Oversight. Few people in Midlothian knew about it as there was little press coverage, but it was and is quite telling that our little town garnered so much federal attention.

The national attention was an embarrassment to the ATSDR (Agency for Toxic Substance and Disease Registry), which was already being investigated by the US House of Representatives for its blunders with the Hurricane Katrina trailers and the asbestos problems. That Midlothian was red-flagged meant that the ATSDR needed to reevaluate what was going on. During the summer, agents came into town and interviewed many citizens. While many were afraid to speak to them, Nancy Ingram, from the Environmental & Injury Epidemiology & Toxicology Branch of the Department of State Health Services, was the lead coordinator, putting together a panel of citizens, school and city officials, and industry folks to reevaluate previous data.

While I had no delusions that people were suddenly going to see the light and change industry overnight to be more environmentally friendly, I hoped it was a beginning to a more open and respectful dialogue between citizens and industry. But as quickly as the panel was formed, it was disbanded. After just one meeting, a "very well placed call," Nancy said, was made, complaining that the whole affair was just going to be a waste of time. Reviewing outdated and inaccurate data would get us nowhere.

Certainly, there is validity in that complaint. Still, I wanted the opportunity to meet and get to know the industry folks. I wanted to have open and frank dialogue in a small, more comfortable setting without any finger pointing, shouting, or accusations. For one thing, I think Michele Moser, the plant manager at Holcim, is an intrinsically nice guy, and I welcomed the chance to get to know him a little better. So, when I found out that panel was scrapped and done so from my own side, I was pissed. That is until I learned that the data that would be analyzed to determine if there any ill effects to the emissions from the cement plants was, in fact, the same data provided by the cement plants and previously ineffective TCEQ, a state agency widely ridiculed for being in the pocket of local industry.

Meantime, some long time environmentalists hit an all time low. They were tired. Specifically, one woman who had been a dogged activist for clean air, never weakening, never backing off, simply walked away. After almost 20 years of fighting, she was exhausted. "With all the documentation, photos, and video that I have," she said, "I cannot get any of the industry or government to see what is happening in Midlothian. Not only did they get the environmental laws changed in their favor, but they also got the civil laws changed in their favor so that NOBODY can sue them."

The *cause* had taken a toll on this activist. "It is a no win situation. I've lived here since 1988 ... the damage caused to my health cannot be turned back. So, the time that I do have, I want to just enjoy life."

So do I. We had resolved to sell our home and move out of state. I decided that while I got into fighting for better air quality for all the right reasons – the health of all children – I could not obsess over it anymore.

But this is hard because I see it every day. Every morning when I get up to take my kids to school, no matter which way I drive, I see one of the cement stacks cranking out the very crap I know is dangerous to our lungs, hearts, and health. While others can pretend not to see it or convince themselves that it is "just steam," I know better.

Findings from the Children's Health Assessment and Planning Survey, a project led by Cook Children's in Dallas, found that asthmatic children in the Dallas/Ft. Worth area are three times higher than the state average. And, according to Dr. Nancy Dambro, medical director for pulmonary medicine at Cook Children's Medical Center, the numbers are only getting worse. (10)

Additionally, a new study released concluded that "Children in Texas are more likely to miss school when certain types of air pollution increase — even when the levels are below the limit set by the federal government." (11)

Before I know it, I start in again until one of my little lovelies says, "Momma! Please! Stop!"

What I learned is that while I must never give up on what I know to be morally correct, I should never lose sight of who I am. I have always been a happy person, but stress was creeping up on me.

Once again, it was Marshall who put things in perspective for me. Shortly after Marshall was released from the hospital, a bunch of us went over to his house. Somehow, his urine bag had slipped to the side and fell to the floor whereupon he immediately ran over it. Urine sprayed all over the kitchen floor. By the time I walked into the kitchen, I could see that he'd tried to drop some paper towels on the floor to soak it up, but there was just too much.

Marshall was frustrated about it, but did all that he could do – he thanked me for cleaning up. And, honestly, it was no big deal. While I dragged out the mop, I could hear him in the other room talking to my daughters, Kerri and Katie, and my sister, Michelle. They were joking about something, and I suddenly remembered the dead mouse analogy.

We'd been sitting at Starbucks, and I got up to get Marshall a refill. When I turned around, I saw a man and woman, hands laid upon Marshall's head and shoulders, praying over him.

Marshall bowed his head as well, and the trio were lost in prayer with me standing perfectly still, coffee in hand. When the prayer was over, they said 'goodbye' and left.

"Who were they?" I asked. Marshall knows EVERYONE in the world, so I figured they were friends. He shrugged. "You don't know who they were?" I asked. He smiled.

Man, if I had had two strangers come lay hands on me to pray, I would have either run screaming or side kicked them into a wall. There's a huge ookey factor to strangers laying hands on me for prayer. But Marshall said, "I just figure it's like a dead mouse."

Excuse me?

It goes like this. I have two cats – Little Dude (who is actually quite large and fuzzy) and Calvin. They both love, love, love to bring me dead squirrels, birds, half-eaten bunnies, and lizards. I, in turn, have learned not to vomit at the sight of these magnificent trophies they have bestowed upon me as symbols of their undying devotion.

As Marshall put it, he is secure and happy with who he is in life. A public prayer is not necessary. Still, he recognizes how happy the act of praying makes other people. It gives them hope and purpose, and if Marshall is the vehicle through which these people find happiness, so be it.

It is not the gift but the intent of its delivery that matters most.

It is not the prayer but the motivation behind it that He will most hear.

Soooooo, if you're wondering if George Clooney wears thongs, well, probably you shouldn't be, but if the thought does creep into your head, you probably won't be eternally judged for a millisecond lapse of perversion. That's all I'm saying.

That dead mouse helped me with two things.

First, I got a dead mouse. So, trying not to see what horrific mutilation took place, I told the little mouse I was sorry and disposed of his body and then pet Little Dude who was looming large on the hood of the car. He was so proud.

Second, when the call came for us to travel to Washington, D.C., once again to testify before the EPA and individual members of the US House of Representatives, I went armed not with anger but humor.

From the get go, we were beset with problems. While every other normal person flew through the security desk at the EPA building, they were not so sure about allowing two giant walking cement stacks in the building. Katie Allred and Katie Bates were severely limited in mobility; only their little arms (from the elbows down) and heads poked out of the large white cylinder costumes. Because of the design of the costume, they were also forced to take teeny tiny steps as they walked, and with the cotton (a.k.a. "the steam") falling in Katie B.'s eyes, they bumped into each other, other people, the walls, and the security guard who was desperately trying not to look amused while his supervisor looked on.

When we made it to the 4th floor, with a security escort, my father – Mr. Straight-and-Narrow – was more amused than I'd seen him in years. Suddenly, people were coming out of their offices to take pictures, asking the girls to pose; everyone just cracked up. When the EPA's mediator laid eyes on the girls, she immediately 1) took a picture, 2) called a friend and took a picture with her cell phone, then 3) explained to me that she wanted to put us in the slot just before lunch. "This is too funny," she said.

The morning testimonies had dragged on. There were plenty of speeches filled with scientific data, personal pleas, and all the other typical things one would expect to hear at an EPA hearing regarding mercury emissions. My parents slipped into the room to secure a place, landing right next to industry folks from the west coast. While I hovered near the door, next to speak, I listened in disgust while an industry cement head basically threatened the EPA. He told them that if we force industry to use modern technology to reduce harmful emissions to the citizens of this great nation, those costs would force them to buy cement overseas where there were even less pollution restrictions than we have here.

I could feel my blood boiling. I was tired of the bully tactics. Green cement is an awesome solution for everyone. But I have to remind myself about the dead mouse. I have to remember that I am no longer in this fight for the reasons I once joined. Tommy is getting healthier. He's on some super sonic medications, and, I hope, as his lungs continue to develop, he will be weaned so that he can one day be med free. As he has gotten stronger, I could have walked a long time ago, but I now know that this is something I am supposed to do. I know that I am here to help protect something special and precious – a gift that was given to all of us. By virtue of living on this planet, by simply being alive, we need to appreciate and respect this gift AND the intent in which it was given.

So, when I hear my name called and begin to walk down the aisle to take my place before the EPA heads and speak from my heart, I know I'm in a really good place for the first time in a long time.

"Next, from Midlothian, Texas," the voice says to a full room, "is Alexandra Allred and the two walking cement stacks."

There is a rustle as everyone turns to watch the two cement stacks waddle down the aisle. There is laughter and light and humor. And the cement head sitting next to my mother slaps his hand against his forehead and mutters, "Oh, shit."

Chapter Twenty
The Revolution
What a Difference A Decade Makes

Many years ago, Jim Schermbeck warned me environmentalism is not for the faint hearted. Indeed. In the five years I have been with DAR, I have seen many well-intended, once motivated people simply fade away. When people are passionate about something and believe they are right, when they devote hours upon hours to a cause that then seems to go nowhere, where is their payback?

I'll be honest. Had Tommy not gotten sick, I don't know that I would have become active in my community. But that seems to be the way it always is. It isn't until it hits home that I become aware and, believe me, I'm not proud of that. And how many times have I heard, "Well, no one in my family is sick ..." Ah, well, gee, then I guess there's no problem, is there?

Some years ago, a local business owner practically rolled her eyes at me saying there was pollution everywhere. She didn't see why everyone was getting all sideways about Midlothian's air. But just months ago, she found me again and excitedly (though not happily) asked me if I knew what benzene was and what it did to a body? As her husband, a remarkably kind and well-liked man in Midlothian, began the fight for his life, she had become educated about what comes out of the cement stacks. Sadly, in November, 2009, he passed away.

She told me that even while her husband was lying in the hospital, they had law firms contacting her about possible lawsuits against the cement companies in our area. While I was (and am) sorry for her family, I was struck by how much has changed. A decade ago, no Texas law firm was interested in such cases. In 2005, Erin Brokovich's arrival, while exciting, was still preemptive to what was to come, legally speaking. A website was erected by the city, calling Midlothian "one of the most monitored areas in the state of Texas," but as the EPA and the US House of Representatives continued to take a harder look at those monitoring systems and the data, local agencies were being forced to answer hard questions; and now, new systems are being put in place.

As for Downwinders at Risk, they suffered their first major loss in 1999. It was a permit fight. It was TXI's official request to burn hazardous waste, even though they'd been doing that since 1987. They had to get what's called a federal RCRA permit to do so - Resource Conservation and Recovery Act. "It was the longest, most expensive permit fight in Texas history up to that point, and I think since, concerning the largest single hazardous waste incineration permit in the country," Jim said. Since its founding in 1994, DAR's primary mission had been to defeat this permit request through the state's administrative permitting process.

TXI's decision to build storage and mixing tanks for its incoming hazardous waste rather than just off-loading it from trucks as they came through the gate required "official notice" of TXI's decision to build tanks. "The company had not yet wised up about how to play that notice and made the mistake of running it in the Midlothian papers. Publication of that notice was the first time most Midlothian residents had seen TXI associated with "hazardous waste" - the words had to be used in the RCRA permit description. It was that notice that set off the initial public outcry over the practice that continues up to now. Before then, the term "Resource Recovery" was used by both TXI and then Gifford Hill to describe their hazardous waste burning.

"Nobody really believed we could beat TXI in the Texas administrative hearing process, but we thought the fight itself leading up to the hearing might frustrate TXI and we could win in the court of public opinion. Once the hearing started I thought we could at least win an important concession - scrubbers on TXI's kilns. Scrubbers would mean the effective end of waste burning because of a federal law known as the "derived from" rule. The substantial amount of waste collected/generated by the scrubbers would have to be classified as a hazardous waste if hazardous waste was being burned in the kilns. This in turn meant TXI would have to send the waste to an official RCRA hazardous waste disposal site, an expensive proposition. This would nullify the profits from waste burning and make it unlikely that TXI would continue to burn waste."

"In the end, we lost on every other issue, and TXI got its permit."

Disillusioned and depressed, Jim said the group wanted to crawl away and lick their wounds. Instead, they successfully linked the smog/ozone problems to the cement kilns. "1999 marks the turning point where the group's focus quit being the waste burning at TXI and instead incorporated all of the plants' impact on DFW air quality. That's what the last decade of work has been about."

In the last decade, the once little known group called Downwinders at Risk has popped up on the radar of most big environmental groups, the U.S. House of Representatives, federal health agencies, the medical community, and a growing number of U.S. Senators. Still, one of the group's biggest problems has always been industry friendly officials. But a decade later, after exhaustive, tireless campaigning, the new EPA Regional Administrator of Region 6 was named. Dr. Al

Armendariz, research associate professor from the Department of Environmental and Civil Engineering at Southern Methodist University in Dallas, Texas, is a choice that has environmental groups applauding. Unlike so many appointees in the past, Dr. Al, as he is affectionately known, will oversee Arkansas, Louisiana, New Mexico, Oklahoma, and Texas.

What is even more important to note is this region – Region 6 – has more permits and more industry than any other region in the United States. As Jim pointed out, "It's the home of most of the US petrochemical industry, the Texas Gulf Coast, and Louisiana's Cancer Alley."

When I called Sue, who had been laid up for some time, she was breathless. Literally. "He could change the world," she beamed. And for the first time, it felt like we had someone in place who had no ulterior motives, no political aspirations, and no business connections that would prevent him from actually doing his job. Rather, Dr. Al truly cares about the environment.

A few days after the Dr. Al announcement, Jim sent out a note to the Downwinders group, an on-again, off-again bunch who have always been small in numbers and severely limited in funds but big and full of heart. He said, "You can say without equivocation that had it not been for us, today's news would be very different. We all should take a moment and understand how often we box above our weight."

I feel as though I only came in on the last round. For Jim, Becky, Irv, Debbie, Sue, Sandy, Reecea, MerleAnn, and Cynthia, the battles have been long, exhaustive, and bloody. But they did it. They boxed above their weight and, at least for this battle, won.

In the last year, our group got a major shot of enthusiastic adrenaline when Stephen Smith, Nelda Mills, Margaret DeMoss, Caroline Bell, Diane Castillo, and Cynthia Fava joined the board to Downwinders. Cynthia rejoined the group after a few years of hiatus from the exhaustive job of activism. For her, this really was the *Rocky* story. (You know, Rocky didn't win in the first movie! He won in the second.)

As for the former Golden Gloves boxer, Marshall, he is eyeing retirement, which scares the crud out of most of us because we can't imagine what this energizer bunny would do except, we hope, promote this book and mentor those in need. If ever Marshall was meant to do anything, it is to help others.

It was about a decade ago that Talaya received the life altering news that a man named Marshall Allen was her father. It would take her a few years but she would find him. And while he was worried that he was "broken" when she found him, Talaya concedes, "I was a mess."

Marshall saw to it she stayed in school, earned her college degree, and figured out what it was she wanted to do with her life. The apple doesn't fall far from the tree, as they say, so it was no surprise when Talaya announced she wanted to go into civil service. She wanted to become a Dallas Police officer.

So as the year 2009 drew to an end, Talaya was officially a rookie police officer with the Dallas Police Department and ready to live out a fantasy to write her first ticket for someone illegally parked in a handicap parking spot.

There is a reason for everything. I know that now. I know now that mothers tell their daughters about lost fathers and I take bike rides without water for a purpose. I know in a crazy, hectic, insane world where governments complicate simple rules, where wheelchairs get toppled, and where cancer can take neighbors and friends, we can find a few rules to live by. It is not the gift but the intent that matters most and it is not the prayer but the motivation behind it that He will most hear.

Once upon a time, before the brick landed on my head (or I simply opened the door), my life felt pretty jammed up. I wasn't always receiving the messages that were being sent. To engage fully in the writing of *Swingman*, I hesitatingly left my post as editor at the *NOW* magazines, agreeing to freelance from time to time.

Once upon a time, I was afraid to write a book about faith. I was afraid that once I finished it, something terrible would happen to someone in my family. But as the writing draws to a conclusion, I see now what journey I've been set upon, and I really am groovin' to the lessons about standing up for what I believe in and openly discussing faith! A recent freelance assignment from my freelance editor, Sandra Skoda Strong, was a reminder of this. She wrote, "I believe this one was made just FOR you!" A main feature was to be written about a man named Rod Kaufman. My lead? He is a quadriplegic with an outstanding attitude, energizer bunny stamina, and a drive to help others.

Well, imagine that.

I had also been afraid of hurting the feelings of a few very special people to me who happen to work at the local cement plants. One, in particular, is the nicest, kindest man you could ever hope to meet. What would he think once I laid it all out? Would he be mad at me? Stop speaking to me? As the book drew to a close, I had no choice but to confront these fears head on. I sent him an e-mail, outlining the book but reassuring him how very fond I was/am of him.

His response? I should never apologize for standing up for my beliefs and while we had differing opinions about exactly what is happening in Midlothian, he believes my efforts for better air quality control has pushed his company to be a better business and neighbor.

Well, imagine that.

As the year and our remarkable decade came to a close, Tommy came running up to me with pen and paper in hand. "We have to write our New Year Revolutions," he said. Leave it to the Master of Cute to call it what it really is. Our new thinking IS a revolution.

Revolution. Noun. Meaning a major change. A dramatic change in ideas or practice.

Yup. We're in the middle of a revolution over here. The citizens of Midlothian are, on the whole, talking about needed changes, and most want cleaner air. Most citizens are willing to talk about previous problems and how we, as a whole, can make things better.

What a difference a decade makes.

My buddy, Audra, once told me Marshall would one day help me figure all this out, but that I couldn't expect Marshall to tell me what or how or if to believe in God. It would just happen.

Indeed. Here's what happened. This is it. The conclusion to all this madness. So prepare yourselves. Marshall Allen is NOT perfect. Shocking, I know. He's handsome, charming, brave, brilliant, stoic, and true. He's the unconquerable Marshall Allen. He's changed policies and confronted racism and injustices. But he's not perfect. And as I slowly got to know him and understand those demons that haunt him yet still see him as the loving, loyal, amazing man that he is, I began to understand this "free will" thing with humans. The once empty words of police officer Brian Bates as he described how he held sweet little Amber's broken body in a freezing creek suddenly made sense. The once seemingly random, chaotic series of coincidences that brought Talaya and Marshall crashing together had purpose. And once I came to terms with the fact that Marshall Allen is not a perfect being but perfect at who he is, I could accept the idea of a God.

I didn't get into environmentalism for kicks. I became active for the love of those around me and for what was right after Tommy got so sick. Nor did I jump on my bike to go find religion. I've had this wild, amazing, fun life filled with even better friends and family. On the flip side, I'd lost faith in my fellow neighbors, mistaking their complacency about the air quality for stupidity. While I'd felt a certain invincibility about my own athletic abilities, I'd had very little faith in my fellow man (or woman).

But things are different now.

I see how things have changed.

I got a dead mouse.

I'm walking on faith.

And I've seen the writing: "Let there be light!" And I can't wait to see what the next decade brings. Research could end paralysis (please, God, let Marshall stand one day!) and cure cancer. Politicians should be bound to the people, not corporations. Prejudice and intolerance would be something only for the history books. It would be a public humiliation to park illegally in a handicap parking space. One day Marshall would get to ride a fire truck again – just once more! Protecting God's green earth would not only be a duty but an honor. And that very special thing that so many of us seem to have lost would return – faith.

It's a revolution, baby.

Christmas 2010

Dear Friends and family –

For more than a decade, we have made it our mission not to report the happy happenings of our lives but to spread misery. It was something that Robb demanded after Tommy was born, letting me know that people don't want to know that we have cute kids who do cute things. But what the original Grinch could not know was how much more people wanted to laugh at us … and so began the letters.

Robb started out this new year by walking into the study with a strange expression on his face. "This egg nog isn't right." I had no idea what he was talking about. In the 18 years we've been married, I've never purchased egg nog, but there was much finger waving toward the refrigerator. Upon investigation, it appears he chugged Egg Beaters. However coincidentally, he was sick a few days later and regretfully and violently ended his nearly 19-year-no-vomiting streak. We are all so sorry. No … really.

No sooner did he recover from this that he needed to buy new slacks and a jacket for a funeral but was so determined not to spend more than $25 on the pants that he opted for larger pants when they didn't have his size. He went up two waist sizes and one length shorter but, by golly, he got his sale. Later, he would say (as though truly perplexed by this new condition), "I feel like I got shorter and fatter." He thinks that because he periodically makes pancakes (yet never cleans up) this makes him "the best damned pancake maker in the world." Most recently, because he has no clue how to look for a kitchen appliance he screwed one of my beaters into his Black and Decker drills and made pancakes.

Katie has some new obsession with expiration dates on food and responds to questions to which she doesn't know the answer, "What am I? Abe Lincoln?" This can also be effectively used when she doesn't want to do something. Sammy, our large, sometimes frisky paint horse burst out of the gate and ran across the driveway. "Katie!" I yell. "Run over here and keep Snow [other less adventurous horse] from escaping so I can get Sammy!" Katie: "What am I? Abe Lincoln?"

Kerri continues to ask for more patience, saying no other sister has to deal with Katie, who periodically pretends to be a T-Rex, drawing up her scrawny little arms toward her chest and leaping out at people at the most unexpected times and screeching at us. Katie also says one of the reasons she likes <u>not</u> shaving her legs is that then she can pet her own hairy legs. "It's like having a little pet cat and I never get lonely." The girl is insane. But she has created her own jingle for a dog food company she wants to create one day – Kibble My Bowl – so maybe all of this will be worth it one day.

After yet another doctor appointment – Kerri was on crutches, Tommy's ankle was messed up, Katie and Tommy were busily taking turns converting my new cell phone into Spanish and taking pictures of their armpits. This time, Katie had to see Dr. Jones because her eyes have been crossing when she tries to sleep and she's had some heartburn issues. She was only half listening while we talked about the retinal issues and seeing an ophthalmologist. As we were walking out, Katie said, "Okay, let's make sure I got this right. I have esophagus spasms and my eyes have something to do with my rectum?" Dr. Jones has asked that we never leave him as we provide far too much entertainment.

A stray rooster has suddenly taken up residence at Michelle's house. We wonder if the rooster knows she's a vegetarian. Across the country, Robb's cousin, Tami, rescued and nursed back to health an abandoned rooster who now lives with her and rides along with her in the truck when she goes into town. His name is Chester.

Kerri got a new job at the gym where I get to get on the elliptical at night and watch her vacuum! I loudly cheer her on and welcome other gym members to rank her cleaning abilities yet she does not appear to appreciate this.

Katie has announced that she wants to be Buddhist. I bite. Why is that? She said, "Because they're very peaceful people and I like that." Are you aware of the fact that they don't eat beef so you'd have to say goodbye to your beef lasagna? She and her buddy, Macy, an equally skinny little kid, eat entire family sized lasagnas for breakfast when allowed. She also listed "eating" as one of her hobbies in school. She said, "I didn't say I would be a perfect Buddhist."

Tommy, who loves school, begged to stay home from school one day. There had been a big build up to the film for boys on puberty and Tommy really didn't want to go see the "poo-berty movie" for fear that upon sight, unspeakable things would happen to him. They didn't. Now, in the 6th grade, boys are expected to change into their pre-athletic clothes. It took us about a month of convincing Tommy not to sleep in and then put school clothes on top of his gym wear. But unspeakable things could happen at any moment.

Katie has taken to having picnic dinners in her room in which we are to sit on a blanket on her floor every Sunday to enjoy different exotic sandwiches and dips she discovered in "Cooking Light" magazine. She's a chef in the making and we are her guinea pigs. But we can only enter her room by way of invitation. If we do not have our invitation in hand, we are not allowed to go into her room. Twice, Robb had stolen other people's invites so that he could stand first in line at Katie's door. It's gotten ugly a few times, what with his insincere protests that the invitation clearly marked "Tommy" is his. Always centered in the middle of the picnic is a jar marked "Ford Focus Foundation." Katie wants a Ford Focus as her first car and requires tips for her services only I've ceased offering tips because she is slowly destroying the little Corolla we have. Some of you may recall after only owning the car for one week, Katie unlatched the hood, thinking it the trunk, causing the hood to slam backwards at 55 miles per hour, cracking the windshield, denting the hood and giving me a heart attack. Just after getting her permit, she had an accident with an old woman. Fortunately, because the other driver was 90-years-old and Katie had the reflexes of a 102-year-old, allowing me to compose this letter while the accident was occurring, little damage was sustained. She stained the seat with upside down fruit juice, cracked part of the interior and broke the inside door handle so that now whenever I want to get out of the car, I have to roll down the window, open the car from the outside to let myself out. Oh, yeah … her first car will be a doorless, dented Corolla.

  Our world is changing as we are preparing college applications for Kerri. She's got an impressive resume with all her classical music and fiddling and artwork but apparently she thinks her job is done as she likes to tell me that all the other parents in the world fill out college applications for their kids. What am I? Abe Lincoln?

  We are told, by Kerri and Katie, that Kerri is the only 17-year-old in the world with an 11 p.m. curfew and is not allowed to watch R rated movies and Katie is the only 15-year-old (and 8 months) in the land without a cell phone. This last one is made worse by the fact that Robb likes to call out to Katie as she is leaving, "Okay, Katie, just text me when you get there!" which only enrages Katie. These social constraints do not affect Tommy who mostly runs around in his drawers, twisted sideways at the waist, with some sort of weapon in his hand.

  For Kerri's birthday, she wanted a cello. Tommy wanted an Uzi. Katie asked for a vacuum. She is a serious neat freak. To counter Katie's extreme neat-ism, Kerri is a slob. How does a beautiful girl live like a disgusting little hog in her own room? I can't run a vacuum in her room for fear of destroying it. Kerri has a mentor, Ms. Worley, whom she adores and I must wonder … is she, too, a slob? (Hmmm, Ms. Worley?) Not to be outdone, the little feller and his obsession with Lego's continue to cause bodily damage to all. Stockpiles of army and Star Wars warfare are everywhere. And you can never know what will happen with Tommy and his laundry. Any idea of what a Tootsie roll looks like after it's been through the wash. People will say, "Imagine if you had two or three more boys!" I don't have to. Tsunami Tommy = four normal boys. And with Katie and Macy's obsession with "Buffy the Vampire Slayer" (something I turned them on to after getting a glimpse of the *Twilight* craze and I pointed out how obviously the author copies the Buffy series), Tommy has taken to whittling (with his trusty little Boy Scout pocket knife) wooden stakes – just in case. So, I don't question while making beds and I stumble upon a wooden stake by Katie's dresser, on Kerri's desk, under my bed …

Robb has decided that he needs to do the grocery shopping now because I waste too much money on fruits and vegetables and healthy foods. On one such trip, he coerced Katie to go with him and they argued over Swiss cheese – which she loves. Later, I would ask, "Why? We can afford cheese, Robb." "Yeah," he says, "but we don't have to be extravagant! We don't need to pay an extra 35 cents for Swiss!" Finally, he relented but bought the block kind and told Katie she would have to slice the cheese herself because he would be damned if he was going to go as extravagant as getting SLICED Swiss cheese!!

He literally triples the time I take in the grocery store and comes home with Shrek – green crème filled Twinkies, which, by the way, no human in my house is allowed to consume. We could not wait until he went elk hunting only because he was walking around the house blowing his elk horn – which the rest of us agree is poor sportsmanship to call a little friend over to you just so you can kill him. He says he's "providing" for his family. Ahhh, because clearly he has no idea how to navigate an actual grocery store.

Hunting also gives him the excuse to wear clothing that we otherwise will not allow him to wear. [Please see our BONUS page in this year's letter because sometimes you just have to see it …]

We went camping – sort of. Kerri, Katie and I kept crawling into the Yukon for heat and drained the battery. When we went white water rafting, Katie tried to pull Tommy into the water as she was falling out of the boat. And much to Robb's dismay, Kerri has a new adorably cute and sweet boyfriend named Kyle. Robb, who is still refusing at admit that Kerri is going away to college, calls the kid "Lyle," "Tyler" or "Skyler," but these are vast improvements from what he was calling him. He does NOT like the idea of ANYONE dating his baby. And speaking of babies … When Robb and I both had an ear ache, I tried to share my medication with him but he refused saying, "I don't know what girl things are in those ear drops." He won't see doctors as they might actually touch him and he doesn't trust vitamins ever since he found out certain ones are beneficial to women – something unspeakable might happen to him. He said he thinks he's going through "mental pause."

In just one day, the dogs escaped while I was mending from pneumonia. The A/C was out, the cable out, I couldn't stop coughing and a book deal I thought I had locked up went south, when I called Dish Network about our cable. I was told because I'm not Robb – I don't have "permission" to have a tech come out to the house. What? Am I Abe Lincoln? So, I said, "What do you think the probability is that I've broken into this house to watch TV and upon discovering that it is out have decided to call to have it fixed?" Nothing. Grrr. I tried to call Robb who was on a conference call in Virginia, hung up and called back. This time when they asked my name I said, "I'm Robb." A thick Indian accent asked in surprise, "You're Rrrrobb?" "Yes, my name is Robb. My parents named me Robb." Pause. "Rrrrreeally? I am Rob, too." And the reality that this outsourced Indian and I were both named Robb hung over us both for a moment. I said, "Hi Rob." He said, "Hi Rrrrobb."

Our horse tried walking into our house, we had not one but two Copperheads in our garage and Katie is going to have to have surgery on her head. She asked if they could use a tazer gun on her to knock her out. Later, we found out that they will have to do some liposuction on her to use the fat to fill the cavity in her skull. While there are some issues about where they are actually going to find fat on her skinny little body, Robb is delighting in the fact that he will forever now be able to call her "fat head."

The only family that could possibly rival us is the Dunegans. Their son Sam, while under anesthesia for neck surgery, asked the doctors if they could make his scar a big "S" on his neck. One week later, daughter Macy had a 7 ml kidney stone blasted with sonar. Macy wanted to name the stone "Earl" and when it passed, she wanted to play the Dixie Chick's "Goodbye Earl" in tribute.

Some really wonderful buddies (and one sister) and I have trained for the White Rock Marathon. In that time of bonding, Linda's been stung in the face, we've run through spider webs in the dark, screaming through cemeteries, faced attacking squirrels, a rogue bobcat, leapt a snake and Jill had a skunk actually run over her foot. She still contends that it was a possum. Because of the extreme heat, we were forced to run in the early hours and often had no idea what we were running into. But after enduring dehydration, road raging drivers, pneumonia, various injuries, delirium and more, we are set to run December 5th.

Meantime, Robb's very busy schedule limits our time together. He suggested we travel together. As of this reading, he will discover that I have entered us into the Amazing Race show. My pitch is this: an active, social butterfly marries a social misfit who dislikes most people. With my uncanny ability to get lost and his unfathomable ability to dicker with the cost of everything on earth while scowling at anyone with a beard – though he has one – we could make an entertaining couple AND we could spend time together. Meantime, I've been contacted to do a "Sister Reality" show with my very camera-shy sister. You can't make us up! We're stranger than fiction.

    Finally, after years of horrible school pictures, my children have decided, "Why bother?" and have opted to have a contest for who can have the worst pictures possible. And this is how it goes at the Allred household.

Christmas 2011

Dear Friends and Family -
It's that time again when letters of holiday cheer travel the world to friends and family with tidbits of good news and morsels of triumphs and jubilation. Yeah ... well... not here. We could tell you all the wonderful and cool things that happened but why? What's the point? The economy is in the toilet, we're all getting older (or fatter) and no one really wants to hear how great another person's kid is doing. At least, this has always been Robb's contention and so, in honor of his holy grumpiness, we submit the anti-holiday letter.

Following last year's marathon that we ran, in which a man urinated on Kerri during the race but I didn't believe that a man would actually urinate upon another runner and had her sit in really strong-man urine for longer than I'd care to admit, Katie had her face removed in a complicated surgery that involved a plastic surgeon, a neurologist and Ear/Nose/Throat specialist to remove a tumor that left her with staples that literally went ear to ear across her skull but she stoically rallied (although she didn't have eyebrow control for six months) which is better than how Robb handled smacking his shinbone into a trunk at the foot of our bed. His version of the story that I purposefully "hid" his pillow and then placed a trunk in his way so that he could maim himself is true when I fiendishly placed the trunk there EIGHT years ago! While flipping channels (something he does so often that he even forgets what he was originally watching), just a 30 second viewing of Sylvestor Stallone spells doom for the family. For the next 24 hours he walks around in his best slack-jawed, droopy-eyed Rocky Balboa, mumbling. NO ONE CAN UNDERSTAND HIM! And if he happens upon Patrick Swayze or Steven Seagall movie, it is all over! There is no peace for days! I think the voices in his head are what prevent him from being a fully functioning person. We are coming on 20 years of marriage and I think I would make an excellent hostage negotiator.

Phone rings and Robb asks who it is and I say its Kerri, that she needs something to be dropped off to school and as I leave I say, "Okay, see ya in a little bit." Robb says, "Okay, then." But after I left he walked around the entire house calling my name, having no idea that I'd left. Later, I expressed concern over this ... how many times can we go through this? He says, "Welcome to my early senility. I'm not going to suffer alone!"

I have to smell everything for him. He will pull out some dirty jeans from the dirty clothes. "Smell these. I just want to know if they stink." They stink! I don't have to smell them ... yet, he will insist that I smell his sweaty hat, his pants, things from the fridge that look suspect. We went to lunch and he saw some guys who looked like they just got off the oilrig and Robb said, "I wish I had that kind of job but instead, I sit at my computer like a girl!" So, he counters this by trying to see how long he can go without taking a shower and ... I'm supposed to be thrilled that he works from home so we can have "we" time.

In preparation of Katie getting a phone, we got unlimited texting. This may have been a mistake.

Katie: Do we have binoculars? **Alex**: Yes. Why? **Katie**: Just wondering. Do we also have a ski mask, walkie talkies, some rope and duck tape? **Alex**: Ummm

I'm at lunch with friends when Robb sends a text:

Robb: If you don't come home without a Diet Dr. Pepper, you better bring some friends as back up.

That same day from Katie:

Katie: After track today I want to come home to a steamy delicious meal. That means you have 3 hours. Make it good.

I don't respond and get:

Katie: You did not respond to my first text about food. Since you're not replying back we can only assume that you're too busy making our delectable welcome home lunch. Carry on.

Still later, and this really is my fault because I left Robb alone with his own thoughts:

Robb: Cup – be on the lookout for a sister-wife. Don't be too quick to poo-poo it. Think of all the advantages. I'll send you my requirements later.

Robb: I'll assume since you've not yet responded that you've already taken up the search. Please send pictures of any likely candidates.

Alex: That is so funny because I did find a brother/husband. He actually picks up after himself, fixed the toilet and the light in the closet and cleans the kitchen.

I did not hear back.

Katie didn't click over when the phone beeped despite the fact I was supposed to be on a radio station in L.A. for a book promotion, we hit an owl (who hits an owl?), Tommy charges me a quarter every time I swear, dammit, and despite Robb's warnings about feeding a stray we fed her and now we have three cats in the garage and three more lingering around the house. It was kind of eerie for a while there. After a six mile run, Michelle and I were poisoned at Schlotzsky's – the tip off should have been all the dying (legs still kicking) crickets all over the floor (they'd obviously sprayed that morning) but we were starved and decided to order a pesticide sandwich anyway. Robb and I got a call from the **Amazing Race** folks and they actually wanted to see a videotape of us. Our application was "funny" and "exciting" but he was incredibly difficult to film. NO ONE COULD UNDERSTAND HIM! But then I was invited on to a reality show in New Jersey about dresses based on the fact that I never wear dresses. This would mean I, along with Kerri, Michelle and Jill Dunegan, would be caught in a freak blizzard, spend the night with a stranger in a hotel and eat popcorn that came from her suitcase before going on national tv in a big purple dress (check listings for the new season of **Jersey Couture** on the Oxygen Channel in January '12!) and flew to New York to do a commercial for clean air. In a moment of weakness, I ate a tiny $18 bag of baked chips from my $600/night room. How do I explain THAT to the sponsor picking up the tab?!?

In preparation of Katie getting her license, Robb set out to find the worst car he could find her. He would actually sit at his desk, perusing Craig's List and chuckle at the thought of putting "princess" in some of the heaps of junk of sale! While learning she took out a sign, drove into oncoming traffic and horrified countless other drivers yet still proclaimed, "I drive like a boss!" Finally, I said, "I don't think "boss" means what you think it means." I ask Tommy to take a shower and somehow this translated into 'go in your room and padlock a Nerf gun to your pants.' His assault on my washing machine continues. Kerri secretly replaced her contact name in a friend's phone so when it rang it showed that DEATH was calling. I found myself saying things I never thought I would say like, "Katie, don't sit on your brother's chest, he has asthma! Sit on his legs." OR "Kerri, don't spray the Windex bottle in your brother's mouth. It's a brand new bottle." OR "Boy, our donkey sure is loud!"

Robb said the word "swag" and Katie was horrified. As she was explaining to him why he must never use that word again, I laid it out more simply. "You're not cool anymore." What? Since when? "Since you got teenage daughters." But this was unacceptable to Robb. He is, he insists, the coolest man alive. Nope – Katie said only cool people can say that word and when Robb asked who was cool enough to say "Swag," she said her friend because he once got chased by the police. Robb said, "That's it? He got chased by the police so now he can say swag?!" He couldn't let it drop and later that night he said, "If being chased by the police qualifies you as cool then I'm the coolest sonofabitch she'll ever meet!" (Quarter!) He's really cool since he once hid from the po-po when they were looking for him but she doesn't need to know that level of coolness.

Sadie escaped and mauled a neighbor's cat and once again we couldn't sell our house but the good news is that there was a huge chemical fire to compound our already bad air and despite the fact that the EPA said everyone was "okay", we have since learned that fish dying in local ponds and streams have opened up a criminal investigation. We went on our infamous Allred vacation, this time going more exotic. People were very excited for us when they learned we were going to Belize. The beautiful beaches, the sand and sunshine... yeah. No. We went into the jungles and Katie declared this was it. She's "done" going on our "vacations." They are not vacation they are adventures! Okay sure, Tommy ran across the border without military escorts and went into Guatemala, Kerri fell off the edge of a waterfall, we were eaten alive in the jungle, Tommy managed to tick off particularly vicious military ants, there no AC, treacherous rocks nearly killed our rental car, we kept the kids close due to all the child trafficking billboards, we may have eaten cat and we're very confident we ate dog but ... Katie is such a baby!

Sammy did something to his leg – no one knows what – managed to colic in the middle of the night so that Robb and I could only watch him roll in agony at 3 a.m. while the equine vet on call had her fax line on. When Sammy rolled head-first into our little pond, I got to sit on the ground in the freezing cold, half in mud with Sam's head on my lap to keep him from drowning. The upshot was meeting Dr. Tony Ellis, an amazing equine vet and Sammy eventually went to live with him. Now when the Ellises travel, I go to their house and care for their mini-farm. Once when Corky, one of their dogs, escaped and de-feathered Lory's prize rooster, Rubin, she brought him in the house to cool down and she made him scrambled eggs. She says it makes Rubin feel better but I'm pretty sure that's avian cannibalism. I also read to their chickens and 100 baby chicks that the Ellis boys had for an FFA project. There was no de-feathering involved. They would gather around me while I read/edited my book and occasionally pecked at my chair. Everyone's a critic. Life is good if you're going to be an Ellis chicken, unless, of course, you're a "burner" chicken. Apparently, this means you get cooked right before thanksgiving. I'm pretty sure I ate one of the chickens I read to. Sometimes Kerri likes to go over to the Ellises and get knocked unconscious by Sammy. It's okay though because when we fracture our bodies, Dr. Ellis has agreed to let us stand next to Sammy and the x-ray machine for a two-for-one deal. Next time he x-ray's Sam' leg, I'm going to stick in my broken toe.

Let us now ponder the wisdom behind purchasing a semi-automatic air soft weapon that has now made Tommy's antics legendary in the halls of Frank Seale Middle School. It has a sniper scope! When he comes home from school, he runs through the house, out the back door and begins furiously digging his foxholes in the back yard. Apparently, I've been in his cross-hairs more than I ever want to know. It took me exactly one day to destroy Kerri's laptop after I destroyed my own – I think I have a kind of electricity that comes out of me and ruins appliances. Katie has some new obsession with expiration dates on food. While eating his elk summer sausage, she mistakenly asked Robb what the expiration date was and he said, "Pretty fresh! As of two weeks ago it was frolicking on the open plains!" *Daddeeeeee!*

Still writing for almost no money. When I do phone interviews, the kids have taken to writing me notes. I'm talking to a US Representative and get a note: "Nod your head if you want him to go or shake your head if you don't mind." What?? Who is he? And what am I supposed to mind? When I went to D.C. to be an Air Ambassador and cornered a White House representative at the elevator (I really did …and it got Tommy's book on the White House website), I later found a note in my bag. "I will destroy you." Oh, dear.

After great teenage angst, Kerri decided upon Texas A&M, made the university's orchestra and I drove her up for student conference and to look around. While there, I got a parking ticket on campus, then got towed away by a lying, fat-cow, had to pay almost $200 and went into a mild rage in which I flipped off the lyin' cow-lady's co-worker because I always try to be an excellent role model for my children. Kerri clapped her hands with glee. "Can I do that, too?" Sigh. Pretty sure I owe another quarter. Pretty sure I owe a LOT of quarters.

Christmas 2012

Dear Family and Friends -
Indeed, it is that time again. For those of you new to this letter, please see www.allredgreetings.blogspot.com. For Robb's benefit, letters from 1999 to present are being offered… But the premise is this: Robb hates happy letters in which great times are highlighted. This is our anti-happy and to borrow from Tommy, there have been many burnages this year!

[A burnage, as in a burn, as in "oooooh, burnage" is when someone burns you with a witty comeback or something just goes wrong, was coined by Tommy!]

Here goes: Got a new car and 10 days later was hit by an uninsured, illegal. An owl ate our cat. Tommy has some kind of unidentified rash on his leg and Kerri has now been diagnosed with asthma. Katie's eyes are crossing again and we're back to more CAT scans. And for reasons we do not understand, Tommy's hair grows **up**. He wears a Panda hat to flatten his hair but it's not working. He's totally missed the point of when to put deodorant on and has an obsession with his pocket knife. Ex: Robb to Tommy: "Buddy, I don't think we need a knife to throw the football!"

The publishing house that discovered/first printed **Fifty Shades of Grey** is now my publishing house. I got invited to a really cool book convention but it was for romance/erotica writers and I was put on a panel, "Save the horse, Ride the cowboy." What? *Um, hello. My name is Alex. I write about funny ladies and air quality.* Oh, and speaking of .. the feds finally came in and determined that maybe looking at air quality data provided BY the cement plants isn't such a great idea. Ya think? This just in: Our air appears to be bad.

Tommy talks in code: JK. LOL. IDK. But the thing is, he doesn't even own a cell phone so why is he abbreviating everything? He says because he's the only 8th grader in the ENTIRE WORLD who doesn't have a cell phone, he needs to keep up with the times. Katie's cell phone is dead and we've decided not to replace it right away because … she actually looks at us now. Kerri made the huge mistake of backing up in front of Robb. When she went off the driveway, Robb was aghast. He's so good at driving in reverse, he says, he once got a ticket for speeding – backwards. The police didn't even know how to issue the ticket so they wrote him up for accelerated exhibitionism. Kerri isn't much better forward on a bike and flipped over her handlebars at A&M at a busy intersection. Embarrassed, she played dead, facedown and spread eagle when she heard someone snicker until the light turned green and traffic moved on. *Move along! Move along!*

After two years of dating, Kyle is still referred to (by Robb) as "Kerri's friend." This is a certain step up from being called Lyle. Katie almost died in the donut shop. Not because of the chocolate sprinkle donut she choked on but by the "Heimlich help" she received by a group of high school boys who "rescued" her. We have requested the security video tape for a good laugh! She is in a cooking feature in a magazine, the same person who only recently discovered the light in the fridge goes out when the door is shut, following an article in **Girl's Life** magazine for a dog-jogging business she and friend, Macy, started. But let's be honest. After running with just two dogs for ¼ mile in the heat and the business was over!

At the dentist, when Robb was having a crown replaced (he called this major surgery), the hygienist commented on Robb's red beard. When I went to check on his "surgery," Robb was heavily denying his reddish tints. On the upside, he haggled a price for his tooth. Who haggles with a dentist? This was after a great production of what going-to-the-dentist shirt he should wear.

We were watching the show, "What Would You Do?" on racism that took place in a deli. Suddenly, Robb stopped the show and scrolled it back. "Waiiiiit a minute," he said. I was so proud of him. I, too, caught the subtle nuances of another man's body posture. The drama unfolding was very intense. Robb paused the show at two men coming at each other. Behind them was the deli's menu. He pointed! "Do you see the prices on that roast beef sandwich?"

Robb: Oh. What's that? I see you want to Walgreens. Glad to see we're the Rockefellers.
Me: Um, yes, for medicine.   Robb: Oh, I see it had to be prescription, couldn't just have over the counter.   Me: It's steroids! It has to be prescribed.   Robb: Oh, glad to see you can afford all those co-pays for a doctor visit.   Me: I have pneumonia.   Robb: Oh, well, aren't you fancy.

He went hunting up in the mountains with his cousin, Duane and they honestly think being in a tent at 13,000 ft in 9 degree F weather is fun. Even the elk headed back down the mountain. He carries his knife into church, peels off fingernails and places them upon us. It's escalated to the point where he'll show us his nails and "let us" decide which nail will be put upon us.

In the beginning of the year, he watched the show, "Gold Rush" and walked around mumbling like the old codger, Jack. Now, his new fav show is "Duck Dynasty" which highlights the lives of millionaire hillbillies and Robb has chosen to emulate Si. If you know the show … well, I need not explain my pain. When he got home from his mighty hunter trip, he came in and dropped all his crap all over the kitchen floor. Two days later, when I asked about the status of said crap, he said, "I'm the hunter, you're the gatherer. You need to gather all this up." It was suggested that he could start <u>hunting</u> for a hotel.

Robb thinks speed limit signs are just suggestions.

At the romance/erotica convention, there were all these women with the romantic notion of what it must be like to live with a cowboy, a mountain man, some rugged, hunter who is not big on words or heavy thought. I was looking at these women and thinking, 'Wow, you people have not thought this through! Trust me. It ain't romantic! It's annoying!"

Someone wrote me a sweet note, saying how much she enjoyed watching our family and what a quiet and calm influence Robb is on our family. Wait. What?

He's calm like the flu. I just signed a new contract with <u>The Writer's Coffee Shop</u>, the Allie Lindell series (woohoo!) but am very challenged because I share workspace with a giant child. Robb constantly makes up false news headlines. Also, we play, "Am I Chinese, Korean or Japanese," where Robb reads all kinds of names, butchers them and I have to guess nationalities. I must watch all sports highlights. I must also watch movies I have seen before but when I point this out, he denies it as he has NO MEMORY of anything. *We've seen this before.* No, we haven't! *Yes, we have. That guy dies in the end.* What? How do you know this? *Because we've ALREADY SEEN IT!*

A friend suggested that Robb be tested for low thyroid as it is linked to poor memory but Robb says he doesn't *have* thyroids. "Only women have thyroids."

Katie loaned her car to some kid and we got to play "What did that kid run into" when it was returned damaged and without explanation. Very classy. It's also fun when you receive a text picture from your violin playing/artist daughter (who needs her hands!), muddy and wearing a mouth guard with the caption: *Playing Women's Rugby at A&M*.

Tommy called me at work, breathlessly asked for Mimi's cell phone number. I asked why and he says, "Nothing. I can handle it." Click. Tommy was a guest on CNN's The Clark Howard Show and was tagged as a "future millionaire." The next day, he found pretty blue flag all up and down our street (that the electric company had carefully measured out the day before).

Knock. Knock: *Have you seen our flags*? Ummmm. And how many times must I wash tootsie rolls or Leggos? Speaking of washing machines, my new publishers made a YouTube of me doing laundry. It's in production but involves a lot of screaming. By Christmas, try looking up **Damaged Washer on YouTube** – the idea being to have a series of "damaged" spooks. Okay, sure… I destroyed my own washer after a mud run competition but Robb's view is why buy a new one when that one works perfectly fine. Please see video! Besides, all the running got me, Michelle and some really great friends featured in **Real Simple** magazine (July 2012), profiling our running club. Then Katie got a job at a donut shop so Michelle and I jog 4 miles to the donut shop, stuff ourselves and then jog home. It's a win/win except for when people ask, "Didn't I see you in **Real Simple**?" *Move along, move along!*

The show *Jersey Couture* finally aired and the producers labeled me the "Dress Virgin." Really?? I got a chance to go to London and testify before the International Olympic Committee and Tommy decided to have an emergency appendectomy. Turns out he's highly sensitive to anesthesia. Following surgery, he stood up on the gurney and tried to fight a nurse. They called it "not unusual." We call it too much Call of Duty. He also decided to have pneumonia right before his Boy Scout camping trip. When we traveled to California, because Katie was going to appear on a talk show that shall remain nameless (but let's just say that it's a comeback for a person who says she wants to be classy this time [hint: she was on Dancing with the Stars] but when we got on stage the producer said, "Okay, Katie, you're like, 'Mom, I want to be a reality tv star no matter what,' and Mom, you're like, 'Oh, no, you're going to college' and Katie, you're like, 'Mom, it's my life.' The producer walked off and Katie and I were in shock. When we sat on the couch, the host mugged the camera: "Coming up next – meet the teenager who says she wants to be the next Snookie!" What?! We went there on the premise of getting into acting with values!!), we stopped to go hiking in St. George, Utah – a balmy 105 degrees F. When we asked what shoes to wear, Robb said, "Think stubbed toes, water and lots of rocks." He was NOT kidding. For 3 hours we were submerged in water, fighting rocks and sometimes scary current. A family from Denmark passed us and Kerri suddenly felt a warm spot in the freezing water. This would mark her second consecutive year of someone urinating on her. Robb came up with our new family motto and he's super proud of it. It really does say everything about EVERY family trip we have EVER taken. It goes like this: <u>We're the Allreds! We do things the hard way!</u> On the same trip, he drove us crazy clearing his throat so I put an allergy pill in his drink, thinking it would dissolve. He took a swig, spewed it all over our rental car, now refers to this as the time I "tried to poison" him and, to show me, refuses to take allergy medicine.

This year has marked 20 years with Robb and I may have kidney damage. We play this stupid who-calls-the-holiday-first game. "Happy Fourth of July," "Happy Memorial Day," and "Merry Christmas." He is so unbelievably competitive that clocks get turned back, people hide in closets or just disappear. It's so stupid! I lie in bed, writhing in agony because I have to go to the bathroom but it's after midnight and the holiday – whatever it is – has arrived. Is he asleep? Is he just faking? As the hours creep by, I am in pain. Did you know if you hold it too long, fluid can back into the kidneys! I roll quietly out of the bed and… argh! "Yeah, yeah, happy freaking Valentine's Day! Jerk!"

I got conjunctivitis, flew to D.C., was searched b/c they thought I was high. Also, please visit my new **facebook page**: **<u>How to Board an Airplane</u>**. I paid for my freaking seat … I should have a place to put my luggage!! WHO'S WITH ME????? (Please LIKE the page and add to it!)

Kerri came home from college and I was telling her to do something. She looked at me, "Momma! Why are you repeating everything five times?" *"I have to becau….wait! Did you just hear me? You were listening?"* Wow! She learned! One of them made it out! No one else listens. All Katie likes to do now is get in trouble and Tommy wants to be a bodyguard. And let's be clear: A knife-wielding bodyguard. A knife-wielding bodyguard who likes to take his purple unicorn camping. My 70+ year old parents decided to get a Labor-Dane (yes, Great Dane) mix who has no social skills, pulls on the lead, doesn't understand personal space and may have worms. I think Kerri is lactose intolerant. The cats like to hack up hairballs on my new car.

Katie told Robb that he's not allowed to use the word "swag." Robb wondered why and was told he's not cool enough. Who, then, he wondered was cool enough to use the word "swag" and when Katie named a person at her school, Robb asked, "Well, what makes him so cool." She thought. "Well, for one thing, he was arrested once." In a super mature parental move, Robb replied, "Well, if that's the case, I'm the coolest S.O.B. you've ever met."

Later, when I yelled at him about this, he denied it. He denies everything. Much later, we read something about a celebrity who was denying something. I explained to Robb the premise of press releases. This leaves the option to later deny whatever truths are needed. "That's why they have their people." He pondered this. "I'm gonna start doing that. I'm going to start denying things." You're going *to start* … denying things. But he was still going… "Will you be my person who says stuff and then I can later deny it?" Will I be your *person* who says stuff you deny …The more he got to thinking about it, the more he liked it. He said, "I need a scribe. I need someone to walk around behind me and write down all the amazing things I come up with." *What the heck do you think these Christmas letters have been about??*

Robb can't stand letting anyone sleep in, he has to hold the remote or a knife (yeah, him, too) while watching TV and he can never go to the store alone. But no one wants to go with him. He's like a 95-year-old man with a walker, on a tight budget and total memory loss. Why would you want to shop with this? But one day while Robb was torturing Katie -- his feet on her favorite pillow – and I said I was going to the store, Katie sat up. "Don't let her go shopping alone, Daddy. She can't be trusted with the unit prices. She's an over-spender." I hear this. *"That is low, Katie. I can't believe you threw me under the bus like that."* She says she's sorry but it's about survival. "Daddy, how many times are we going to let her break the bank at the store." *Ooooh, burnage.*

In response: Did you know that Katie, when she was supposed to take a cake from the donut shop to the dumpster, sat down next to the dumpster and ate it? *Oooooooooooooooh, burnage!*

We're the Allreds and we do things the hard way! No reason. We just do. We're idiots.

P.S. Please read Damaged Goods and if you love it ... offer a review on Amazon.com and put us one step closer to the NYTimes Best Seller list. Dare to dream. Also, please note that your purchase will help me buy a new washer ...

Postscript

We're all sitting around the table at Starbucks. Only days earlier, Marshall, Talaya and I had been talking when Marshall told us about the time he "screamed." As Marshall regaled us with the time he and a partner fought their way into a liquor store fire, we were beside ourselves with giggles. As Marshall explained it, bottles of alcohol were exploding and heavy smoke made it impossible to see when he rounded a corner to find a lone person standing in the smoke and fire. It – actually a St. Pauli's girl life size cardboard cut-out, made him scream. As he reenacted the scenario, Talaya and I could hardly breathe we were laughing so hard.

His eyes were wide with excitement as he confided his terror of the St. Pauli girl. The unconquerable Marshall Allen. Oh, if the boys down at the station only knew! But on this day, it is the apple of Marshall's eye who is doing the story telling.

There are about 15 of us, and Talaya is holding court. A few of us had a side bet as to how long it would take before Talaya began talking like a cop – a potty mouth cop. Answer: not long. As she regales us with a hilarious story that ends with language that could make a sailor blush, our laughter finally subsides, and Marshall sighs with pride. "Isn't she precious?" And we all burst out into laughter again. There are days like this one when the world feels perfect, and I can only hope there is another decade to come of our weekly gatherings.

It is the beginning of 2010, and the federal government rolled into town again with the promise they were here to stay until there is a resolution. This time, they brought with them three scientists who were from other parts of the United States, not to be influenced or bullied by Texas politics.

During one meeting, Sue Pope commanded the room. As she entered, accompanied by her own entourage, people took note, and it was fun to watch as she worked the room before taking her seat. She is Midlothian royalty.

At one point when she stood to speak, everyone fell silent. When she was done, the crowd erupted into applause – the only applause of the evening. She was, everyone knew, speaking the gospel truth, and it was both compelling and horrifying. Still, there were those who argued because their own children were fine, there was no problem. Also, I love the ongoing argument, "if we didn't have cement, we'd be driving on dirt." Ah. Thanks for that clarification.

In truth, I do not know one activist, one environmentalist, one business leader or private citizen who wants to see cement go away. Just the dangerous emissions. In fact, in this new era, most of us are trying to find ways for people to save the environment AND jobs. A great confirmation that change is coming came with the announcement that TXI is no longer a member of the Cement Kiln Recycling Coalition, a pro-hazardous waste burning lobbying group that represented TXI and other waste burners in the 1990s! Still, fighting for clean air and industry responsibility is a never ending battle.

My relationship with environmental groups continues as I've been able to meet with senators not just in the United States but in Australia as well. I am repeatedly humbled as I meet people like Sen. Christine Milne and former senator Bob Brown from Tazmania.

There are battles – amazing battles – everywhere you look.

In July 2001, Marshall found Talaya. A decade later, he gave her away at her wedding and the production of *Swingman* was there to record it

When filmmaker Mark Birnbaum called, looking for the great conclusion to Marshall's story, I'd said, "Well, almost a decade after finding her, he's going to be giving Talaya away at her wedding."

Mark was practically drooling but not even he could have envisioned how lovely it would play out. At the reception, I had just leaned over to explain to one of my girls that traditionally, the bride and father have a dance, "but I don't know if …." I stopped and my throat was instantly seized by emotion. There, across the hall, Marshall rolled on to the dance floor, extending a hand to his daughter. There were laughs and tears as she climbed aboard the wheelchair and Marshall whirled them around.

Once upon a time, as impenetrable as he appeared to be, Marshall was uncomfortable in his own skin. Today, he is a role model. And, at long last, he likes himself.

What a joy it has been to see that the documentary film of his life has won multiple international and national humanitarian awards.

What a journey it has been for him, and as he tossed around the idea of retirement, he is making noises about mentoring. When we first discussed the idea of a book Marshall had said all he wanted was to help others, particularly young men, who had the same emotional issues – from depression to mistrust and insecurities, he had had growing up. From there, Marshall had said, "It's about getting on with life."

No one has "gotten on" with life better than Marshall.

Remarkably, ironically, Marshall stands tall—stands for many principles: dignity. Honor. Tolerance. Acceptance. Faith.

Marshall has faith. Even as he's questioned his beliefs, he has always prayed. But he's standing on another kind of faith as well. He believes in us. People. He believes that one day paralysis will be ended, that we can fight city hall and end pollution. And, I promise you, when you sit and talk to a man who appears to have once had it all but now sits paralyzed in a wheelchair, you do not come with pity for a man who is weak; no, you come to reckon with dignity, honor, tolerance, acceptance, and faith.

All of the world's strength, the world's promise, was brought home to me during a conversation with Sal Mier. Sal is, if nothing else, the reluctant environmentalist. He never wanted to make waves. He didn't even want to make a ripple. But his concern for his grandchildren made him ask questions. And before he knew it, Sal tapped into those very qualities that make Marshall the man he is today. When individuals stand up for what they believe in, with the interests of others in their heart, how can their energy and dedication be wrong?

"Our only motivation," Sal said, also speaking on behalf of his wife, Grace, "is that of the children's future – those who are here now and those who are yet to be born. The poem, The *Bridge Builder* clearly portrays all that I believe in and what motivates me when it comes to this issue."

Indeed. Thank you, Sal. In honor of those who have had the courage to stand, the poem is for you:

The Bridge Builder Poem

An old man, going a lone highway,
Came, at the evening, cold and gray,
To a chasm, vast, and deep, and wide,
Through which was flowing a sullen tide.
The old man crossed in the twilight dim;
The sullen stream had no fears for him;
But he turned, when safe on the other side,
And built a bridge to span the tide.

"Old man," said a fellow pilgrim, near,
"You are wasting strength with building here;
Your journey will end with the ending day;
You never again must pass this way;
You have crossed the chasm, deep and wide-
Why build you a bridge at the eventide?"

The builder lifted his old gray head:
"Good friend, in the path I have come," he said,

"There followeth after me today,
A youth, whose feet must pass this way.
This chasm, that has been naught to me,
To that fair-haired youth may a pitfall be.
He, too, must cross in the twilight dim;
Good friend, I am building the bridge for him."

-- Author: Will Allen Dromgoole

To contact Marshall Allen, email him at Marshalleallen@gmail.com

You can find copies of the award-winning documentary, SWINGMAN, through Mark Birnbaum's email at markbirnbaum@gmail.com or check out his site at www.markbirnbaum.com

You can always find Alex's articles with the Waxahachie Daily Light or visit her site at www.alexandratheauthor.com or www.allredbooks.com or through The Writer's Coffee Shop at www.thewriterscoffeeshop.com

Other books of Alexandra Allred:

Damaged Goods, 2012
White Trash, 2013
Roadkill: The Allie Lindell Series, 2013
Sweetbreath: The Allie Lindell Series, 2013
She Cries, 2014
White Tree, 2014

Not the end, but …

To be continued: we are currently working on the disasters to fill our next Christmas letter….

Citations

1. D Magazine, "No Place Like Home," by Tom Boyle, Page 78. May 2005. Volume 32, Number 5.
2. Devine, Robert S., **Bush Vs. the Environment**, Anchor Books, New York, page 33.
3. Devine, Robert S., Bush Vs. The Environment, Anchor Books, New York, page 5.

4. Betty Brink, Fort Worth Weekly, Dec 5, 2002
5. Williams, Lewis A., The Intermountain Indian School. Master's Thesis. Utah State University, 1991.
6. Wilonski, Robert, "The Comeback of Harvey Martin, Dallas Observer News, January 8, 1998, web.
7. USA Today Special Report, "The Smokestack Effect: Toxic Air and America's Schools," December 8, 2008, web.
8. www.downwindersatrisk.org/DownwindersAtRisk-SmogCrisisInDallas.htm.
9. Allred, Alex, "Road to Enlightenment," MansfieldNOW magazine, February, 2008, page 6.
10. Lee, Mike, "Research Finds Link Between Air Pollution, School Absences in Texas," Star Telegram, January 19, 2010; web.
11. Jarvis, Jan, "In D/FW – Sobering Asthma Numbers," Star Telegram, January 14, 2010; web.

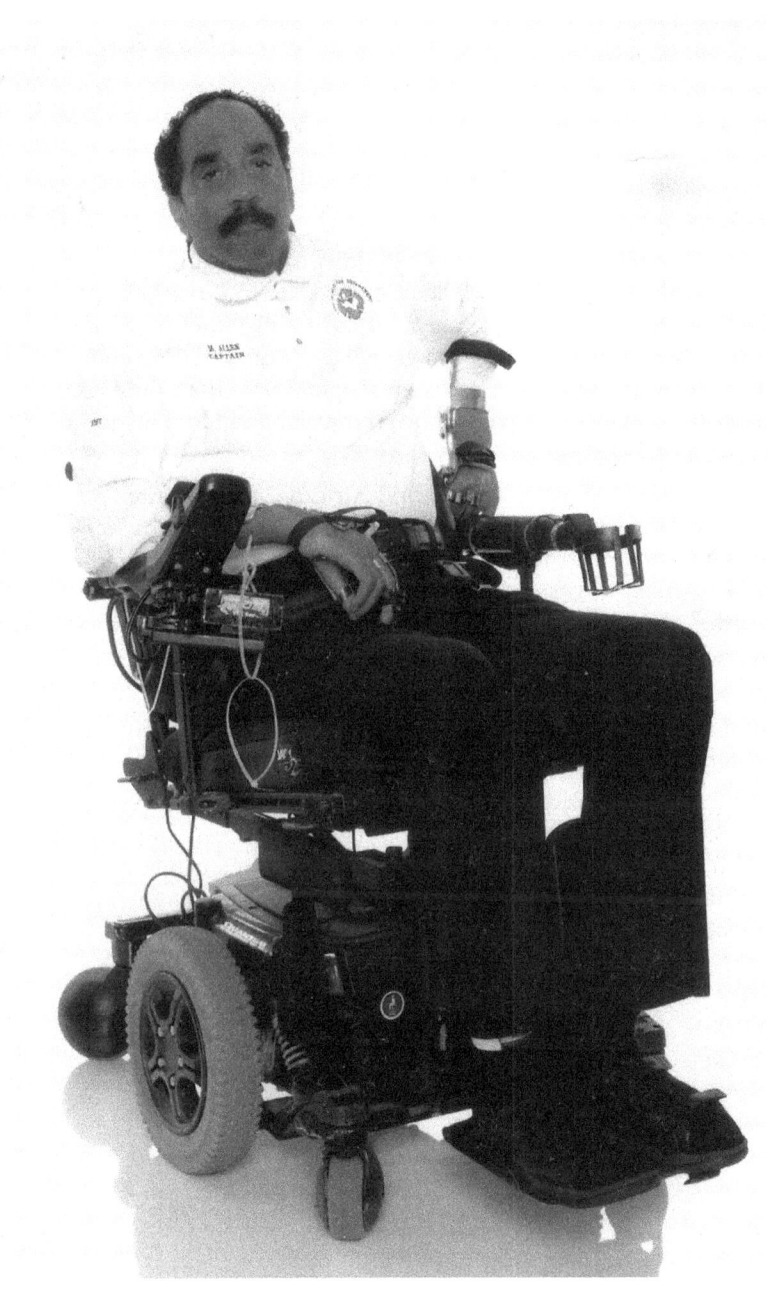

About the Swingman
Captain Marshall Allen

With well over 30 years with the Fort Worth Fire Department in Fort Worth, Texas, Allen has dedicated his life to serving the public. While his retirement date is slated for 2014, this father of six and grandfather of five is currently a captain with the Fire Prevention Bureau. Most recently, Capt. Allen has been assigned over the Commercial Inspection department and can be seen making random inspections throughout Fort Worth.

Since Allen became the first African-American fire fighter in Salt Lake County, Utah in 1978, he has been breaking down barriers and performing good works for the residents of Utah and Texas. From 1996 to 1999, Allen was assigned to "one of the busiest stations in Fort Worth," and served as a Fire Academy instructor for recruits and veterans on his off-days.

While Allen was paralyzed in a freak bicycle accident, the former Golden Gloves boxer still has a powerlifting record that holds among fire fighters today!

An avid reader, Allen rebuilds computers in his spare time and one day hopes to mentor at-risk youth and teach them how to build and design computer software. Allen can be found at any number of Starbucks in Cedar Hill and Fort Worth, Texas with his friends and his new constant companion, Isis, the Mastiff.

About the Author
Alexandra Allred

Alexandra Allred won the U.S. Nationals in September 1994, making sports history as she was named to the first women's bobsled team. When the United States Olympic Committee named her *Athlete of the Year*, it was the beginning of a lucrative sports career as a bobsledder, martial artists and professional football player.

After retiring from professional and national sports, she became an adventure writer for a number of national publications, as well as the international magazine, Volvo, where she tried her hand (and body) at a number of extreme activities, including a citizen fire academy, dog attack training, obstacle course running and the test drive of the Volvo gravity car – the only proto type in the U.S.

Allred is the author of many books, including *Atta Girl! A Celebration of Women in Sport*, works as a personal trainer and fitness instructor and most recently blogged for NBC during the Olympics in "all things bobsledding". She and her family have moved away from Midlothian, Texas.